USING TECHNOLOGY TO SELL

Tactics to Ratchet Up Results

Jonathan London
Martin Lucas

Apress®

Using Technology to Sell: Tactics to Ratchet Up Results

ISBN-13 (pbk): 978-1-4302-3933-8

ISBN-13 (electronic): 978-1-4302-3934-5

Trademarked names may appear in this book. Rather than use a trademark symbol with every occurrence of a trademarked name, we use the names only in an editorial fashion and to the benefit of the trademark owner, with no intention of infringement of the trademark.

President and Publisher: Paul Manning
Lead Editor: Jeff Olson
Editorial Board: Steve Anglin, Mark Beckner, Ewan Buckingham, Gary Cornell, Louise Corrigan, Morgan Ertel, Jonathan Gennick, Jonathan Hassell, Robert Hutchinson, Michelle Lowman, James Markham, Matthew Moodie, Jeff Olson, Jeffrey Pepper, Douglas Pundick, Ben Renow-Clarke, Dominic Shakeshaft, Gwenan Spearing, Matt Wade, Tom Welsh
Coordinating Editor: Rita Fernando
Copy Editor: Terry Kornak
Compositor: Bytheway Publishing Services
Indexer: SPi Global
Cover Designer: Anna Ishchenko

Distributed to the book trade worldwide by Springer-Verlag New York, Inc., 233 Spring Street, 6th Floor, New York, NY 10013. Phone 1-800-SPRINGER, fax 201-348-4505, e-mail orders-ny@springer-sbm.com, or visit www.springeronline.com.

For information on translations, please contact us by e-mail at info@apress.com, or visit www.apress.com.

Apress and friends of ED books may be purchased in bulk for academic, corporate, or promotional use. eBook versions and licenses are also available for most titles. For more information, reference our Special Bulk Sales–eBook Licensing web page at www.apress.com/bulk-sales. To place an order, email your request to support@apress.com

ii

I would like to dedicate this to the people who love, support, and accept me with all my foibles and vulnerabilities.

—Jonathan London

To the girls in my life: Irene, Lola, and my editor in chief for life and fun, Jenny.

—Martin Lucas

Contents

About the Authors v

Acknowledgments vi

Preface viii

Chapter 1: Technology Is Changing Selling 1

Chapter 2: What Hasn't Changed 21

Chapter 3: Foundation: The Sales Process 47

Chapter 4: Technologies Used in Selling 105

Chapter 5: Using Social Media to Sell 149

Chapter 6: Using Technology at Each Stage of the Sale 185

Chapter 7: Using Technology in Managing Your Sales Team 241

Chapter 8: The New Landscape 263

Chapter 9: Selling to X 289

Appendix: Tips and Tactics 305

Index 323

About the Authors

Jonathan London, founder and president of the Improved Performance Group, is known internationally for his expertise in developing, guiding, supporting, and training the sales, channel management, and leadership abilities of this clients in order to drive exceptional results. Based upon his 19 years of executive-level experience and an accomplished track record in both domestic and global sales, London's contemporary practices have served well the interests of IPG's current and former clients, including Cisco, Dell, Rackspace, Lawson Software, Polycom, Mitel, HP, Vidyo, AOL, Millennial Media, Tribal Fusion, SpecificMedia, Cox Digital Media and many other SMB companies. Prior to founding the Improved Performance Group, London was, from 1976 to 1994, in high-tech sales and management with such companies as Olivetti, NBI, ROLM, Wyse Technologies, and PictureTel. In each case, he was the top producer or manager. London is also the author of *The Entrepreneur's Guide to Selling*.

Martin Lucas is president and founder of TSI squared and Phinkit.com. TSI squared is a training and consulting firm specializing in sales improvement, sales messaging, and conferencing consultations. Phinkit.com is a new social media platform that enables people to promote their business and achieve their goals. Unlike other platforms, it puts people, sales, and marketing first. Martin has worked in the technology industry in a number of sales leadership roles and has received numerous awards for sales, management, and inspiration. TSI clients come from a variety of spectrums, industries and markets, giving him a wide breadth of insight.

Acknowledgments

Jonathan London: I would like to acknowledge the following people, who helped create this book:

- Martin Lucas, my co-author (Martin note: Ditto)

- Puja London Hall, my wife and better half

- My entire family, who loves me and is always there

- Karen Ann White, who is a constant hero and inspiration

- Rashida Tewarson, who always helps to the best of her ability

- My close friends, who have made an effort to remain so through thick and thin

- Wendy Walker Cleary, who helps me understand

- All professional sports teams, movie makers, and authors who distract and entertain me

- The makers of anti-cholesterol and other modern medication who keep me healthy

- My customers, who believe in my work, support me, and keep me afloat.

- Jeff Olson, at Apress, for asking me to write and for his patience in getting this book written

- All those who allowed us to reference them or their services

Martin Lucas: I would like to thank all my colleagues past and present (good and bad!) who helped me prove my theories and ideas. I'd especially like to acknowledge my new business guys: Dave, Geeth, Grant, and James. They taught me that you can't improve without learning, listening, debating, or owning a shouty box machine.

Thanks to Clwyd, Simon, Wendy, and Julie for contributing to this book; your wisdom is appreciated. Thanks to Jeff and Rita at Apress for making it an enjoyable experience. Thanks to my lovely wife Jen for giving some semblance to my writing style and editing night after night. It wasn't quite the "have a quick read over it" I sold to you!

And of course, thanks to you for buying the book! It has tons of insight and value, so take what you need and enjoy.

Preface

Technology Is Changing Selling

"While our access to raw information has grown exponentially, our time to process this information has declined rapidly, which has placed an unprecedented premium on the act of meaning-making."

—George Dyson, Futurist

"People are information-rich and theory-poor. If you can give them a way of organizing their experience, then their minds are wide open."

—Malcolm Gladwell, Author

It is a bewildering task to write a book about technology and selling because there are so many technologies available, and they are changing and growing at an unprecedented pace. By the time you have finished reading this, there will be new technologies or iterations of existing ones that didn't exist beforehand. Many will be relevant and interesting.

Technology has always been something that can be used to our advantage or work against us if we don't use it properly. Today, it appears that the opportunity to use or get used by technology is more significant. Sales processes and cycles can be smaller and shorter, so the proper use of technology and information is more and more critical.

Technology hasn't changed the idea of selling, nor its intent and purpose. Wikipedia defines selling as "offering to exchange something of value for something else. The something of value being offered may be tangible or intangible." Selling involves someone being interested in or needing something, and then going about in whatever way they know how to analyze the situation and decide what to buy and how much to spend.

Technology has always played a role in enabling people to respond to the needs of prospects. The wheel allowed people to go further distances to sell their goods. In our era, the radio, TV, billboards, slide and overhead projectors, color printers, word processing, cell phones, software, video, and much more, have all made it easier to reach potential customers.

These technologies seem to pale in comparison to what is happening now. Prior to the advent of the Internet and other recent technological developments, prospects were primarily dependent on the information companies gave them to make a decision, and companies were limited in the ways they could present or deliver it. People might ask for references, or any independent evaluations of your offering, but those tended to be limited and were done by known experts.

The game has changed. The internet, computing power, cloud computing, faster and more available bandwidth, mobile devices, higher-resolution screens and cameras, more sophisticated hardware and software, imagery, software as a service (SaaS), and more all provide more technology and information than ever before. On the one hand, it helps us sell more effectively and makes it easier for prospects to make decisions. It allows companies to market or sell in ways they have never been able to do. On the other hand, it puts a great deal of power in the hands of customers, who can now get as much information as they can handle about your product or service—and you. Paradoxically, all the information and channels of delivery can be overwhelming for salespeople and customers alike.

Yet, as mentioned, the basic sales proposition has not changed—customers have a need, and you need to help them satisfy that need with a product or service. And the basic sales process has not changed, either.

Using Technology to Sell will align the best technologies and the best processes to increase your competitiveness and sales. We will discuss:

- How to differentiate yourself amid the increase in competition because of technology.

- How to deal with different lengths of sales or sales cycles more effectively.

- How customers and prospects are better educated before and during the sales process, such that many feel they don't "need" a salesperson as much or at all.

- Why traditional sales approaches may not be as effective as they once were.

- Why there is now an over reliance on marketing—at the expense of good sales skills.

- How technology can be a great enabler for the salesperson but does not replace a good sales process and selling skills.

- Why salespeople need to be better than ever, because the prospect is more informed and educated. The term "trusted advisor" or subject matter expert is becoming more important.

- Why salespeople and sales organizations need to differentiate themselves by using technology more often and effectively.

- What are the best uses of different technologies at different stages of a sales process.

- How to perform sales-related tasks more easily.

- . . . and much, much more.

Please visit us at www.ipgtraining.com, where we will keep you updated on different technologies and how to use them most effectively. Feel free to let us know about your experiences as well. You can reach Jonathan directly at JLondon@ipgtraining.com and Martin at Martin@phinkit.com. You can also find Martin on www.phinkit.com—connection requests are welcome.

Technology Is Changing Selling

Martin and I both come from sales environments that use technology to sell, so we have a particular interest in how technology enables salespeople and organizations. We also recognized that too many of them were either not using technology to help them improve results or they were using it improperly.

Why We Wrote This Book

While working in the corporate world, Martin and I were fortunate enough to be consistent top performers in our respective sales and management positions. We now have our own sales training and consulting businesses, so we are able to observe what is happening in sales organizations across the globe. Every day, we see that salespeople are:

1. Depending too much on technology to sell at the expense of basic selling skills; or

2. Using technology in sales improperly; or

3. Shying away from using technology in sales altogether; or

4. Using it well, but in a limited fashion throughout the sales process.

Organizationally, it is rare to see a company that uses technology as strategically as it can, or that develops and trains people to take advantage of the strategy they have in place. It is almost unheard of for an organization to apply technology at all stages of the sales process (although most do some) and gain a unique advantage by doing so. We have almost never observed a company making an equal investment in technology *and* sales skills and process to get the best possible results.

In the Beginning

Any piece of technology can change the world. Advancement is the key human behavioral trait. The wheel could be one of the greatest technologies ever created. (Mel Brooks said it was Saran Wrap in his skit the *2000 Year Old Man,* but that is another story.) It changed the world. But how was it commercialized and sold? What were prospects' initial reactions? Did they embrace it immediately because they could see how it would help their lives, or were they afraid of it? Did prospects ask how expensive it was or when the next version would be available? Did they delay buying it? How quickly or slowly did people adapt to it? The point of all this is that even the most incredible technology needs to be, in some form, sold, and the human element cannot be ignored in doing so. That's why throughout the book we emphasize that strong sales skills are paramount to success.

This means that technology, in isolation, is not always the best route to use or the most efficient way to get something done. In this book we look at the most effective practices that enable technology to amplify and strengthen your skills. We'll also provide a holistic view of many technologies and approaches you can use to sell more effectively.

Technology and data are exploding in every facet of our lives—to the point that we can feel overwhelmed or confused with options. Our first challenge is to look at what this explosion means to the world of sales.

Technology and Buying Behavior

The internet, computing power, faster and more available bandwidth, mobile devices, higher-resolution screens and cameras, more sophisticated hardware and software, imagery, apps on mobile devices, voice recognition, GPS, and more provide greater capability than ever before to help people sell, and for a prospect to make a decision. Moore's Law, which says that the number of transistors that can be placed on a chip doubles every 18 to 24 months, doubling performance—was if anything slightly conservative.

Technology advancements also allow companies to expand their markets or sell in numerous ways they have never been able to before. Keeping up with and knowing what technology to use where, how, and when is a challenge for businesses of all types in all industries.

Because information and analytical tools are so widely available, more logical and informed purchasing decisions can be made. More prospects are using data, metrics, and measurements as part of the decision-making process than ever before.

TECHNOLOGY CAN DIMINISH THE VALUE OF AN OFFER

In the advertising community, industry metrics such as comScore that measure the volume of visits to a website, or the conversion rate of a specific action people take online, are standard parts of vendor and budgeting decisions. These are quantitative in nature and diminish the value, and associated pricing, of an offer or the differences between competing offers.

Information comes not only from experts, but also from peers—people who have used the product or service and provide live, current, and (usually) unbiased information about their experience. This information often has more weight than ads, literature, or expert reviews because it is perceived to be "unbiased" and comes from people who have a previous experience without an agenda of selling you something. It's like bumping into your friend and asking about a certain product you are interested in and having him tell you something good or bad about it. But now, you have thousands if not millions of friends/contacts on the Web. And this information can proliferate at a rate that can make or break a company or product. Facebook has made a "thumbs up," which companies will pay for (advertising agencies will pay vendors for each increase in the number of thumbs ups for their clients, in order to improve their exposure via social media) to help sell their product since it connotes favor and acceptance by unbiased sources.

For example, movies are reviewed by professional film critics as they always have, but they are also immediately reviewed by thousands of people on

Rotten Tomatoes and similar sites. Regardless of how much money a studio spends on promoting a certain movie, if the reviews by professionals or people who have seen it are negative, then it is more likely to fail and not generate the projected revenue.

Conversely, a movie or studio (especially with a limited marketing budget) can use the Internet to go viral, to promote or create a buzz about a movie that gets great reviews, and that movie can become a box office hit and Academy Award winner. The *King's Speech* in 2011 is a perfect example. This was a low-budget film, but it created such a buzz, in the media and online, that it got attention it otherwise would not have received. It ultimately won the Oscar for best picture. According to Wikipedia, the movie was made on a budget of £8 million (about $12.5 million) and grossed more than $400 million.

A recent study by Forrester Research[1] established that people who are making business decisions rely on their own research and input from people they know vs. what vendors are telling them. This is having a dramatic impact on people's buying behavior, since they are much better informed. Therefore, the best salesperson needs to emphasize different qualities, like insight into a client's industry and the most productive applications of what they are selling, vs. just spewing generic benefits and or regurgitating reams of data. The terms "subject matter expert" and "trusted advisor" reflect these qualities.

Because prospects are better informed, they have a better filter to decide if what you are saying is valid, valuable, and true. People no longer have to rely on brochures, proposals, or your word.

Perhaps the best example of this phenomenon is buying a car today. You can go online and find out exactly how much a dealer has paid for the model you are interested in and exactly what incentives the manufacturer is providing. You can therefore go into a car dealership knowing exactly how much it costs the dealer. That puts buyers in a much better position to negotiate and choose whom they want to buy from. (One consequence: many dealers now sell more used cars because this information is not as available to buyers and they can charge more.)

What does all this mean for you, the salesperson?

---

[1] http://blogs.forrester.com/khalid_kark

- You need to be ahead of the curve in using technology to your advantage.

- You need to understand people—your target demographic and how they buy using the Web, which methods they prefer (visual, text, PDF, graphics), what they need to know (the content itself), and when (in the sales process) they want information to make a decision in your favor.

The ubiquity of technology and information is a double-edged sword. On one hand, the sheer volume of information can make selling more difficult. It can become unwieldy, confusing, and overwhelming to you and your prospects, thus hurting your sales efforts. However, if you know how to control and use it, know which bits of information are important and which are a distraction, you are in an enviable position to sell more. How you best engage with technology and information and use it to your advantage to get the optimal return is addressed thoroughly in this book. As you'll learn, salespeople need to become master craftsmen, able to do things with the tools they have better than their competitors. This has always been true but more so now because of the impact technology is having.

Used properly, technology allows us to expand our skills and markets, get greater exposure, and allow more people to find us so we have more sales opportunities.

Let's look at some of the issues arising in today's sales world from this onslaught of technology.

Technology and the Web Can Commoditize All Offerings

From the buyer's side, the abundance of products and services to choose from is much greater than ever before. For example, if you enter the words "managed hosting" into a Google search box you will get more than 9 million results. The dilemma of deciphering the differences can be so overwhelming that buyers will often simplify their decisions by making price the deciding factor and lumping all the other variables into a "they're all pretty much the same" category. This makes it easier for them to decide. They might not give you as much time, either, because of the time pressures they are under or the medium you are using. (In general, people give you less time virtually than they do in person.)

Vendors contribute to customers' penchant to commoditize an offer in large part by using the same terms or labels as each other. For example, many vendors in the managed hosting business (companies that host websites for businesses) use the same terms, such as "24/7 support," to compete and differentiate themselves. What this term doesn't tell a buyer is how many people are available at any one time during their 24/7 support, or how well trained or qualified they are. Salespeople therefore need to make sure that their offer is presented in a way that is differentiated from others.

Finally, technology is allowing much greater international competition. Offshore services such as low-cost call centers, for example, are being used more and more often to prospect and sell.

Sales Structures Are Changing

Because of today's technology, companies may no longer need as many salespeople to sell, or they may need them to sell differently. Whether you are a sales individual, entrepreneur, small-to-medium-sized business (SMB), or a large company, how you structure your sales force can be greatly affected by technology. What's happening today is really no different than what happened 100 years ago in automating a manufacturing plant. Computing and technology allow a sales organization to do more in the same amount of time with the same number of or fewer people.

LESS IS MORE?

The confluence of technology and a difficult economy quite often requires salespeople to do more with fewer people to support them. This creates a demand for higher levels of activity that often results in a lower-quality sales effort. That's because there isn't enough time—or it *appears* there isn't enough time—to do things the right way. The situation is often exacerbated by the absence of a sales process, because sales leaders don't believe they have time to train salespeople. A vicious circle indeed. But as this book will show, technology can help salespeople and their managers compress time and reach out to more people with a quality sales effort.

Today you can go to a company's or individual's website, click on videos or product descriptions, and place an order. No people are required up to this point. Or, via an automated process, you might be asked a few questions upon entering a website, and only then will you be handed off to a salesperson who will then chat with you, electronically, and send you a quote with a contract, all within a span of minutes. Or you can have a Web or video conference with someone when you come online, as well many variations of these options.

This isn't necessarily bad; the effectiveness of your solution depends on the technology, how well a salesperson uses good selling techniques and good processes to interact with and sell to the prospect. In other words—and this assumes you have a great product or service—success depends on how well the selling company integrates technology and great selling skills. That's where the changes in sales structure can harm an effort. In our experience, an overdependence on technology at the expense of basic skills hurts the sales effort.

Don't Distract Yourself; Stay Focused

Companies have always needed to define their revenue and profit objectives; what will differentiate them in the marketplace; and how much customers will pay for these differences, whether they are tangible product differences, related to branding and image, or both. Thanks to competition and constant change, it is more difficult to differentiate these days. Windows of advantage—the amount of time you have a truly relevant and unique differentiator—are much shorter (unless you are Apple or Google). Companies and salespeople start chasing the competition and lose their focus on what their real value and advantages are. Salespeople and companies can also get distracted by the constant change and the apparent advantages competitors have and lose confidence in their own offerings. This can lead to lower productivity or salespeople moving to the competition more often, either of which can substantially hurt a company's sales efforts.

This is not to say that salespeople have not always been dependent on what their product or service does and how well it is marketed. However, it is glaringly apparent that more organizations are focusing on the lead generation and marketing aspects (social media, search engine optimization, e-mail, advertising online, etc.) vs. creating a finely honed sales organization that can compete under any circumstances. Both can and should coexist.

What *anyone* can do fantastically well no matter his or her offering is personalize how he or she communicates and empowers the salesforce. The more you use technology correctly in the sales process, the more you can create a more productive sales team and a more personalized customer experience. This should be paramount in any organization, yet it is not always so. If you make some simple adjustments (which we cover) then you will be in a winning position for your initial sale and repeat business.

Instead of staying focused, companies are changing sales methods more frequently than ever, leaving many in a constant react mode. They don't feel they have the time to establish a sales process or they change it constantly. In some cases, they don't have *any* sales process.

Getting to the Right People

Another element of the sales process that has changed is the difficulty in getting to the people you need to sell to. It's more difficult than ever, because:

- The information is freely available to prospects. They don't need to talk to salespeople.

- Prospects are being overwhelmed with all the attempts at reaching them, so they are putting up more technical and procedural defenses

- With staff reductions, people have more work to do. Many are distracted or multitasking, making it difficult to pay attention to your pitch.

- More technology encourages the idea that we live in an "instant" world—everyone needs something "yesterday" and is impatient with your inability to deliver quickly.

- People have found technological methods of keeping you at arm's length. Human gatekeepers are stronger.

Prospects are overwhelmed with the things they have to do, and they are bombarded with salespeople or technology trying to sell to them. The end result is that people are screening incoming efforts with e-mail filters and voicemail. Salespeople have to be more exact in their messaging when they do get to somebody, or more creative in how they message in voicemail and e-mails to get a prospect's attention. Paradoxically, more traditional methods (letters via the postal service) are so rarely used anymore that they can be unique and stand out.

An Overdependence on Marketing

A brand new capability today is how many organizations are now using lead-generation techniques (Google search and keyword advertising, lead-generating software such as Marketo, Genius, HubSpot and many more) to create demand and interest so that prospects reach out to them. Companies also are becoming experts or hiring experts who know how to leverage social media such as Facebook, Twitter, etc. to create awareness of their product or service. GroupOn, Living Social, Fab.com, Gilt, and many other companies now allow companies to reach tens of thousands more people with special incentives. Advertising on the internet is becoming pervasive, intelligent, and effective. According to the October 2010 Interactive Advertising Bureau (IAB) *Internet Advertising Revenue Report*, $12.1 billion was spent for the first 6 months of 2010. In addition:

- Online ad spending for the first half of 2010 was up 11.3% from the same period in 2009.

- Search revenue accounted for 47% of year-to-date revenues.

- Display banner revenue was 36%.

In a report published on January 23, 2011, eMarketer estimates that online advertising in 2011 in the United States will grow beyond offline with an important increase in social media. It estimates, further, that US spending on online advertising will reach $25.8 billion, surpassing for the first time print advertising, estimated at $22.8 billion. This was supported on September 28, 2011, when the IAB reported that Internet ad revenues reached nearly $15 billion in the first-half of 2011. In addition, the IAB stated in a June 11, 2012 press release that a record $8.4 billion was spent for online advertising in Q1 of 2012.

We believe all of these developments are tremendous in increasing brand awareness and opportunities. But such spending has created a distorted emphasis and reliance on creating opportunities that elevate the brand awareness or image of a company. This further comes at the expense of optimizing the sales skills and processes of the sales organization, which could otherwise complement these efforts. People and organizations believe that marketing is now sales. This is a big mistake. You need salespeople to close the sale, to make good on the opportunity marketing has created. Both are important, and both need to be clearly aligned.

Time: A Precious Commodity

As mentioned previously, people from the buyer and seller side are being asked to do more with less time. Technology and a difficult economy have allowed companies to run their businesses efficiently with fewer people using more technology. Needing to do more with less time also means people have more priorities to attend to and cannot necessarily give the amount of time they would like to on important projects. Or, they do allocate more time, but then give less to everything else, which means you as a salesperson will probably be given less time to sell unless your project is deemed top priority.

The proper use of technology can help you work within these shorter time frames, and be more appealing and professional to the prospect.

Something for Nothing, Information for Free

In the eyes of the buyer, if it is on the Web, it is legitimate. If it is presented well, it is even better. If competing companies use the similar words and images to describe their offerings, and it's presented stylishly on the Web, then everything looks the same to the buyer and a company can lose its advantage and become commoditized.

A vivid example is a very successful conferencing company I (Jonathan) worked with over 5 years to train their sales team. It was very well known for its service and training. But the competition realized it could dress up its website and simply use the same terms or nomenclature, and call it the "same" services for a lower price. In reality, they were not nearly the same, but it appeared that way. It was like saying a car is a car if it has an engine and four wheels, so there is no difference between a BMW and a Chevy.

Salespeople at the company I worked with had to learn to define the services they offered more thoroughly, ask questions to understand a prospect's requirements, and present their services more effectively. That way, the competition couldn't compare itself as easily. It also forced them to become better salespeople and a better sales organization because they had to work more diligently for their sales. Once they did these things—combining, technology and basic skills—the company regained its position as a leader.

Images and technology can also make companies appear bigger and better than they are. They offer instant legitimacy. Buyers beware! All is not as it appears on the Internet. It doesn't mean that companies online aren't quality companies. It just means that appearances can be deceiving.

The Internet also allows a prospect or buyer to search for information on blogs, social media, etc., and confirm or deny what you, as a seller or company are saying. Sellers beware! You now have to address any pre-conceived notions a prospect has about your offering (whether they state them or not) and dispel these notions whether they are true or not.

For example, if you look at the samples of websites in Figures 1-1 and 1-2, they both look incredibly impressive (both are), and in this case, both offer excellent products and services. One is a multibillion dollar company, the other about $50 million. Can you tell which is which?

HD Video Conferencing Without Boundaries
Natural. Universal. Affordable.

Figure 1-1. Vidyo.com

Figure 1-2. Polycom.com

By the way, Polycom is the multibillion-dollar company.

How Technology Helps—and Hurts— the Sales Effort

Virtual teams are now standard in sales organizations. People no longer need to be sitting in the same location to work together. If you have a computer and a good Internet connection (cable, DSL, broadband, etc.), then you can communicate effectively internally, and with customers and prospects.

Imagine this scenario. A salesperson in California sits in his living room and he is trying to sell to a prospect in Arizona, some 500 miles away. His technical support team and manager are in the UK, Dallas, and Houston respectively. In turn, the prospect in Arizona wants some other people on this call, and they are located in New York City. It would be next to impossible to bring all of these people together in person without great expense and time spent.

The salesperson could have a conference call, using traditional conferencing services. But he can also use VoIP (Voice over Internet Protocol), which is considerably less expensive or even free. On top of that, any of the people on this sales call who have a camera with their computer can see each other. The salesperson can use many varieties of Web conferencing, (WebEx, Live Meeting, GoToMeeting, and many others) to present.

Using chat, all the people selling can be talking and making recommendations with each other during the call without the prospect knowing—something the prospect's team can do as well. They can also use free video conferencing from companies such as Google, Skype, Apple, and others or dedicated technology from Cisco, Polycom, LifeSize, Vidyo, and many more (see Figure 1-3). Finally, the whole meeting can be recorded so people who were unable to attend can view at their leisure.

Figure 1-3. Author Jonathan London presenting via laptop to a conference room of customers.

There are obvious benefits from a sales perspective in this scenario:

- More people can be involved and available.
- There can be more interactions, if needed since it doesn't take as long or cost as much to meet.

- People can be more productive because they can have multiple meetings of this kind in a day vs. just one.

- More information is available to use and present to prospects in order to sell to them more effectively.

- Salespeople can cover more territory and clients.

- Sales cycles can be better managed and time-to-order improved.

However, there are some negatives as well:

- There is less face-to-face communication and inter-action, which can hurt when making a sale. It is worse when you use only audio conferencing and don't use videoconferencing or any other kind of visual interaction.

- Ironically, there are also fewer face-to-face meetings internally, so people on the same team may not know each other as well.

- There are usually fewer people supporting sales, since technology is supposed to make people more productive.

- People may not have the time to prepare as much as they might otherwise.

- Fewer people are supporting more salespeople, so they don't get to know them as well and presentations or meetings may not flow as smoothly.

- Covering more can create a more shallow approach to more important clients.

- Control of the meeting can also be compromised unless it is well orchestrated and coordinated.

Technology can amplify good sales practices and provide a competitive advantage. A good salesperson will embrace the changes in today's world and use technology to his advantage. Much more is discussed in later chapters, but here is an example of what a person can do in the initial stages of a sales process:

Table 1-1. Example of an Initial Prospecting Step

Step	Use of Technology
Prospecting	Use Google Alerts to discover any current events that might be relevant. Research blogs to get timely and specific data on prospect and company. Use internal databases to see if prospects have expressed interest or what other companies in their industry are using your services. See if you know anybody who can refer you to the person you are contacting via LinkedIn or Facebook.

Technology Helps You Add Value

One of the changes in today's sales environment is the need for a salesperson to become a trusted advisor or subject matter expert. Since people can gather information on their own, salespeople need to know more than the details about their product. They need to know all about the industry they are selling into and the application and value of their offerings in it. They need to be able to quickly and effectively apply their offering and give insights that can't be discovered otherwise. The Internet, through public information or services you pay for, can help a salesperson be more educated about an industry, a company, and a person and his or her responsibilities.

You can add value as an individual or a company by creating a blog, or by publishing white papers or case studies that show the value of your offerings. This gives the salesperson and company a higher level of credibility. A salesperson can read a prospective company's blogs (and vice versa) to see what is happening with that company and be better prepared. Industries and competitors can be researched to get a competitive advantage. Much of this information can be "pushed" to you (sent to you via RSS feeds and other mechanisms), so it is easier. But this can also create an overwhelming amount of data, which can lead to a salesperson becoming counterproductive. To prevent this, you need to have a more focused approach on the industries you want to sell to, which will narrow the amount of data and make it more relevant. This is discussed in greater detail in Chapter 6.

Salespeople can share some of this information with their customers and prospects, which will keep them at the top of their mind and be a constant reminder of the salesperson and his or her company. This can be done as easily as cutting information (legally) and pasting it into an e-mail. Or you can just share a link to the information or website via your browser.

Good salespeople will also be able to interpret knowledge of their products and services into specific solutions that can help a prospect or customer. For example, say a company is expanding. A salesperson who sells moving or relocation services can reach out to a customer about how they might help, or use the information to establish a relationship more deeply by recommending a solution to a prospect.

We often take information that gets pushed to us and send it to our customers or prospects to show them we are aware and on top of their account and industry. People respond to these efforts, which is a solid confirmation and acknowledgment and can help lead to more sales.

Figure 1-4 is an example of Google Alerts that can push information to your e-mail based upon many different criteria.

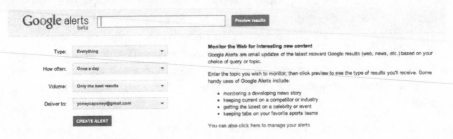

Figure 1-4. Sample of Google Alerts

Figure 1-5 shows what it looks like when it is sent to your e-mail.

From: Google Alerts <googlealerts-noreply@google.com>
Date: Monday, April 18, 2011 5:47 PM
To: Jonathan London 201 788 8922 <JLondon@ipgtraining.com>
Subject: Google Alert – Sales Training Director

News   4 new results for **Sales Training Director**

Sumber Joins Hearst Television as **Director** of Digital **Sales**
Broadcasting & Cable
Sumber is leaving his position as manager of digital accounts & business development for Media Networks, Inc., a division of Time Inc. There, he oversaw **sales training**, sell-through, product and partnership development, as well as managing the Digital ...
See all stories on this topic »

Mavic Promotes Crean, Hires Zimmer
Bicycle Retailer
... managing **director** of Mavic USA. "These guys will be a great resource for our dealers in terms of shop visits, **sales training**, tech clinics, POP installation, and consumer events." Since his promotion last fall to become the first Mavic sales ...
See all stories on this topic »

Business Development Manager
news.careerstructure.com
The Sales and Marketing **Director** is not from this sector and the business would like to recruit someone that have had traditional **sales training**. As well as this the company are looking for an individual that has the ability to solution sell. ...
See all stories on this topic »

Matt Bell appointed Pirelli UK product **training** manager
Tyrepress.com
Bell will design **training** packages for Pirelli **sales** teams, customers and dealers to give them the product and corporate knowledge needed to carry out their roles in the most effective way, a company statement says. Bell says: "This is a very exciting ...
See all stories on this topic »

Figure 1-5. E-mails sent by Google Alerts

So What Hasn't Changed?

In a B2B environment, the sales process is pretty much the same once you meet with a prospect (whether in person or virtually). Although you may have less time in many situations, you still need to:

- Create rapport.

- Ask good questions to discover a prospect's priorities, needs and gain.

- Understand a prospect's decision process, criteria, and budget.

- Differentiate your offer in a way that has meaning and relevance.

- Work well with your team to win business.

- Strategize and negotiate deals wisely.

- And more . . .

Human behavior is also still pretty much the same, although it does seem that there is often less consideration and respect given to salespeople. Respect has always been a scarce commodity. People still:

- Make decisions based on what they want to achieve and what they want to avoid.

- Need to feel comfortable and trust the people or company they are buying from.

- Want to get a good deal or value.

- Rely on others to help them with their decisions.

- Want you to react to them and answer their questions.

- Make decisions based on referrals, quality, convenience, reliability, support, reputation, ease of doing business, safety and security, price, etc.

This book is intended to inform, address, and engage readers around all of these issues. Here's an overview:

1. Technology Is Changing Selling

    - *Covers the many ways technology has changed the marketplace.*

2. What Hasn't Changed: People and the Sales Process

    - *The more things change, the more they stay the same.*

3. Foundation: The Sales Process: In Detail, from Beginning to End

    - *The sales fundamentals that ensure you will prosper today and tomorrow.*

4. Technologies Used in Selling: Conferencing, Multimedia, Screencasting, Social Media, and More

- *This chapter covers the broad range of technology, from hardware to software to methods of interaction underpinning today's best sales methods.*

5. Using Social Media to Sell

   - *It's big and getting bigger; ignore at your peril. Synopsis of how each site was built and the intent of each site.*

6. Using Technology at Each Stage of the Sale: Add Power to Your Sales Skills

   - *How specific practices, programs, and technology improve communication and sales production.*

7. Using Technology in Managing Your Sales Team

   - *Sales managers, as ever, have a huge impact on the success of the team. Note: This chapter will be equally useful for non-managers.*

8. The New Landscape: The Merger of Sales, Marketing, and Customer Service and How Technology Facilitates the Change

   - *While the sales cycle hasn't changed, the context for selling and who does what and when has changed.*

9. Selling to X

   - *Recommendations on variations by market.*

10. Appendix

    - *Miscellaneous information on tips and tactics.*

Most chapters contain:

- Stories, notes, and sidebars

- Exercises you can use

- Examples

- Web addresses to get more information

Summary

To sum up the key points in this chapter:

- Technology and data are overwhelming us at a pace that is impossible to keep up with.

- Technology is impacting buying behavior.

- Technology allows there to be more competition than ever.

- Differences, and/or the value of an offer are often misperceived, or commoditized by the buyer.

- Customers and prospects are better informed before and during the sales process so they don't "need" a salesperson as much, or in some cases at all.

- Because the prospect is more informed and educated, salespeople need to be better than ever. The term "trusted advisor" or subject matter expert is becoming more relevant.

- Traditional sales approaches may not be as effective from a macro (organizational) and micro (individual) perspective.

- There has become an overreliance on marketing, and salespeople are both benefiting (potentially more leads) and being hurt by it (sales skills are not as sharp).

- Salespeople and sales organizations need to differentiate themselves by using technology more often and effectively throughout the sales process vs. just as a stage, or solely as an administrative or forecasting tool.

- The best sales organizations and people use technology as a great differentiator, but do not, we repeat, do not use technology to replace great salespeople, processes, and selling skills.

What Hasn't Changed

People and the Sales Process

As rapidly as technology is changing, and despite the plethora of articles, social "experts," and dogma about the role of social media in selling, the basics of selling in a B2B environment haven't changed much in many areas, especially once the salesperson and the prospect meet. Today, prospects and salespeople may be better informed, but prospects will still have internal decision-making and purchasing processes, and salespeople will have their own approaches and processes (see Figure 2-3) to win as much business as possible.

This chapter covers some of the timeless methods salespeople have used to maximize sales and the value they provide to their customers. Technology is an indispensable tool in each stage, but it cannot replace a deep-rooted knowledge of the best way to satisfy customers and their need for your product or service.

Consultative Selling

Consultative or solution selling has always been the most effective way to sell and avoid being "commoditized" because it positions you and your offer as more valuable and professional than that of your competition and gets you the information you need to win business.

The skills that salespeople need have remained fairly consistent as well. Time management, prospecting, objection handling, closing, and other key skills are just as important now as ever. Human nature hasn't changed much either. According to Inscape Publishing and its DiSC personality profiling system, people behave and make decisions pretty much the same way they did thousands of years ago (more on this later in this chapter).

What is consultative selling and how is it different from any other method of selling? Let's take one of the simplest examples possible, someone buying a pencil:

The Non-Consultative Method:

Customer: I need some pencils.

Seller: How many do you need?

Customer: Four.

Seller: What kind?

Customer: #2.

Seller: Here you go. That's 69 cents each for a total of $2.76.

As you can see, the non-consultative method relies on asking the basic questions and results in a small sale. The consultative method, on the other hand, adds a few more questions.

The Consultative Method:

Customer: I need some pencils.

Seller: Fantastic. Thanks for coming in. We have many pencils. If I can ask a few questions, I can make the proper recommendation. If you don't mind my asking, what will you be using them for?

Customer:	I am taking a drawing class.
Seller:	How nice. I love to draw. What will you be drawing?
Customer:	Not sure. It is an introductory class so I imagine still figures, landscape, things like that.
Seller:	How many classes will you be taking, and will you be traveling far to take them?
Customer:	6 classes over 12 weeks. They are in a local college so I will probably take the bus. Why do you ask?
Seller:	If you are going to travel I want to make sure you protect the pencils so they don't break. You will probably need something to sharpen them as well. Do you have a pencil sharpener?
Customer:	No. Do I need one?
Seller:	If you buy standard pencils, yes. If you buy a mechanical pencil, no. But the mechanical pencils are more expensive to start.
Customer:	Well, I am trying to watch my budget.
Seller:	OK. I would suggest the following: four #2 pencils for the outlining, two #3 pencils for shading, a pencil sharpener, and pencil case. Total is $5.73.

By asking a few questions and showing interest in why the person needed pencils, the seller ensured the customer got more of what he needed to have a good experience and doubled the sale. In addition, the customer will probably go back to the same seller when he needs more pencils or graduates to a more advanced class requiring ink and paints.

It's clear how effective this method can be. Let's look at how and why it works.

All it Takes Is One Question

I (Jonathan London) was training people at a very successful, industry leading computer company, which sold primarily over the phone. When a customer called, the salesperson asked these four questions:

1. What kind of computer(s) do you want?

2. How many?

3. When do you need them?

4. What is your budget?

This model was working for them. They had mastered the art of selling for less, and manufacturing quickly and profitably. The company was so successful that it could hardly keep up with the demand.

The salespeople felt they had no time to probe further or ask additional questions and didn't think it necessary. But I convinced them that if they asked one additional question, they would easily sell more. The question is: "What will you be using these for?"

Here is one example of how things changed when the salesperson added that one question:

Salesperson:	What will you be using these computers for?
Prospect:	We need to do some pretty heavy graphic design.
Salesperson:	Interesting. What kind of design?
Prospect:	Building schematics, architectural drawings, and so forth.
Salesperson:	Anything else?
Prospect:	Normal office stuff, e-mail, Internet, word processing, spreadsheets.
Salesperson:	How will you be sending your designs to people? I ask because if you are doing it electronically, you will need Adobe Acrobat to protect the integrity of the document. It can otherwise get messed up when you send it over e-mail.
Prospect:	I didn't know that.
Salesperson:	It doesn't happen often, but when it does it creates huge problems.
Prospect:	OK.
Salesperson:	Do you have wide document printers?

Prospect:	No, we were going to reduce the size for printout.
Salesperson:	OK, but are you using these to sell your services?
Prospect:	Yes.
Salesperson:	Don't you think it would be more impressive to show them in color on a full scale?
Prospect:	Of course, but those printers are expensive.
Salesperson:	They are more expensive. But may I ask what is the average size of one of your sales?
Prospect:	About $10,000.
Salesperson:	So if you make one more sale with a full-scale, color printout, you will have paid for the printer ten times over.
Prospect:	Let me think about it.
Salesperson:	OK. Is there anything else you need, software, ink for your printers, service contracts for the new computers?
Prospect:	Probably service.
Salesperson:	Smart. I recommend four computers with extra fast processors, a local storage unit you can all share and therefore save money on storage, 21-inch screens for your graphics, Microsoft Office, and Adobe. I assume you have your design software.
Prospect:	Correct.
Salesperson:	OK, the total is $13,750 including a two-year maintenance contract. Do you want to finance these or pay with a credit card?

Asking questions that are intelligent and relevant to the situation demonstrates your expertise, and the questions become part of the customer's internal dialogue and criteria. Your value, and in turn the value of your suggestions and offer, increases. You have opened the person's mind and he is linking your solution to real value. If the customer has to act quickly, or the purchase he is making is critical to his success, then your questions have more impact.

They Don't Want What You're Selling

We often tell salespeople that nobody wants what they are selling on face value. Customers want, or are only interested in products or services that help them get what they want or avoid what they don't want. For example, you probably bought this book to be a better salesperson, not just to read a book. Think about what is it that you are selling and how it helps people get what they want and avoid what they don't want in achieving their professional goals and concomitant personal satisfaction?

What were the many things the person buying the pencils wanted or didn't want? He obviously wanted pencils, but he also wanted to watch his budget, he wanted to do well and have the right pencils for the class, and he didn't want the pencils to break. How about the people buying the computers? They wanted to make more sales and increased profits, they wanted their presentations to reflect the quality of their company and offer, and they wanted to be more competitive. The more you can touch into the buyer's needs, and the more you connect with the benefits of your offer, the more you and the prospect will both get what you want.

In today's digital, information-driven world, customers are better able than ever to "commoditize" your offer. They can get every piece of information they need about specs, pricing, and general product details online. They can also find out about the size and scope of your company, professional and peer opinions and experiences about the offering, incentives available, and more. When you engage them, whether in person, over the phone, or on the Internet, they will often already have much of the information they need, or think they need.

For example, before I (Jonathan) buy a car, I am able to find out exactly what a dealer paid for the car and what incentives, if any, he or she is getting. I also get expert and user feedback on the quality of a car. What I don't have is the salesperson's expertise—his or her ability and knowledge of how the offer or product works in relation to what I want to do. Salespeople need to understand their product inside and out so they can apply its benefits to more customer situations. By asking me questions and understanding why I am looking for a car, what I will be using it for, what my buying criteria are (budget, utilization, length of ownership, etc.), a professional salesperson can better relate the offer and the value and benefits to me and make a much more compelling argument to buy a particular car model—or another one better suited to my needs.

I bought my first Honda Civic when I was a little stretched for money. I wasn't sure which model to buy, and the salesperson sensed my confusion. She asked me questions I hadn't thought about, like how long I hold onto a car, how old my children were, how many miles I was going to drive per year, and so on. She then presented the pros and cons of the two models I was considering. She compared the immediate price difference—my main focus—to the price over the number of years I was going to use the car. She also put the figures in terms of monthly payments vs. purchase price, which made it easy for me to decide to go with the more expensive model. Looking back, this seems so logical, but I was so emotionally wrought about how little money I had that I lost perspective. The salesperson helped me find it. I have been driving Hondas for the last 25 years.

You and Your Offering Must Add Value

If you are a professional salesperson with extensive knowledge of your product/service, and similar knowledge and experience in the industry you are selling to, you have a tremendous advantage that will help you sell more and avoid becoming commoditized.

This is not to say that your offer shouldn't have real differentiators. But as a salesperson, you still need to know who would need your differentiators the most and how they would benefit. Do you know the unique qualities of your solutions, the benefits they provide, and what type of customer needs them the most? If you are selling a true commodity, do you know how to convey the benefits you and your company bring to the table so what you have appears to be better and different?

Are all shoe stores the same because they sell shoes? Are all suits the same because they clothe you? Are all watches the same because they tell time? Are all cars the same because they have four wheels, an engine, and seats? Are all airlines the same because they can fly you from Chicago to New York in two hours? Are all restaurants the same because they serve food? Are all hospitals the same because they care for sick people? What about schools? Are they the same because they teach people? How about appliances? Are all toasters the same because they toast bread, or washing machines the same because they clean clothing?

Of course they aren't. What makes the difference? Among other things are the following:

- Quality
- Features
- Service
- Availability
- Cost
- Image
- Reliability
- Value to the buyer
- Reputation
- Ease of doing business
- Policies
- Competence of the salesperson in relating her product to the prospect's priorities, needs, and personal gain

Because of the tendency for prospects to commoditize you, the limited amount of time they might give you to sell to them, and many other potential variables, the quality of good selling, of understanding a person's priorities and how you can uniquely address them, is more important now than ever.

Skiing is a good analogy. Let's say that in the past, the sales process and time you had to sell was like skiing a big wide bowl with extra wide paths and nice, soft snow. Skiing was easier, and if you made a mistake, you were less likely to get hurt, or, metaphorically, lose the sale. Today, the sales process is a steep, double-diamond ski slope that is icy. You can't afford to make mistakes because you can get seriously hurt and you will lose the sale. You must be more prepared and proficient because you might have less time and be in a more difficult selling situation.

The Old Selling Adages: As True as Ever

People are still people, regardless of the preponderance of data now available on your product and company. In fact, in some cases there is too much data and people need help understanding and making sense of all the information. What's more, age-old selling-related aphorisms have more relevance today than ever, including these:

- People make decisions based on emotion and then rationalize them.

- People buy you first and then your solution.

What does it mean that people make decisions based on emotion? Fear, desire, frustration, greed, hope, ambition, trust, confusion, safety, and anxiety are all unspoken feelings we need to be sensitive to when selling to people. For example, the business decision a person makes might have a direct impact on how much money he makes, which in turn will or won't allow him to send his child to college or to buy the car of his dreams.

■ **Note** Never forget that people make buying decisions based on emotions and impulses like fear, desire, hope, trust, convenience, first impressions and so forth.

Further, if prospects like, trust, and are comfortable with you, and see you as competent and honest, they will be more likely to buy from you. This is a critical element of being a great salesperson, regardless of whether you are selling face-to-face or virtually via phone, web, or video conferencing.

Another popular adage is that people buy in the following order (although they are probably not conscious of this):

- You

- Your company

- Your solution

Let's break down each element.

You includes pacing (how fast or slow you talk or behave—not too fast or slow depending on the person), commonality (past experiences, jobs, interests, education, etc.), knowledge, experience, listening skills, empathy, responsiveness, honesty, or how present and attentive you are when speaking with someone.

Company includes background/history, image, financial stability, customer support, and references.

Solution includes the functional fit to a prospect's needs, time on market, stability, support, experience, and financial fit.

Pacing

Let's look at one of the "You" items in greater depth: pacing. Have you ever been with someone you like or care about who, at times, moves too fast or too slow, offers too much or little information, or is either too cold and removed or too familiar? Any one of these behavior styles is uncomfortable to be around. If all three are occurring at the same time, it is exasperating.

Imagine this kind of situation when you are trying to sell to someone you don't know. Maybe you're a warm, friendly person, and your prospect is aloof. Or maybe your prospect is a "give me the short version fast" kind of person and you are a dramatic storyteller. Whatever the disconnect, your chances of selling to that person are diminished.

Pacing—or mirroring as it is often called—is all about adjusting your own pace, words, and tone to those of the person to whom you are selling. It can also be physical, and quite often on an unconscious level. For example, if your arms are crossed, your prospect might also cross her arms (or vice versa). Or if one is leaning back in their chair or speaking in a certain way, the other might as well. Doing this consciously—being aware of it without being obvious—is another way of making people feel more comfortable with you.

The more comfortable a prospect is with you, the better. When people are comfortable with you, they are less guarded, will tell you more, and are more receptive to what you are saying. Are you prepared and relaxed enough to pick up and mirror the signals the person is projecting, or are you too wound up to do so? Do you go in with a receptive, open, empathetic listening manner or a telling, forceful, fixed, unreceptive manner? When meeting a prospect, is your agenda more to sell to them or to sell to them by understanding what is important to them? If you are focused simply on the sale, you will be less able to pick up on and respond to the subtle messages and signals people send you, making it harder to mirror them.

1. We created an implementation plan that we took to every first meeting with prospects. It covered, step-by-step, exactly what would happen if they moved to our solution. Prospects understood there would be no surprises.

2. A representative from each division of the sales unit called all the users who moved to us from a competitor to reinforce the understanding that they had bought a solid, safe solution. This simple act dramatically increased usage, revenue, and customer satisfaction.

That was all we had to do for an unheard of 87% close rate. We had identified that everyone else was just pitching services with no value or thought to the buyers' preferences based on DiSC style. By thinking differently, we were able to see that our main prospects would just want us to take responsibility for their conferencing requirements. We did, and sales zoomed.

Here is another way of thinking about this. Total the number of months it takes to sell to someone and the number of months he stays with you as a customer. For example, if it takes an average of 3 months to sell to someone and he remains a customer for 4 years, then the total lifetime of your relationship is 51 months. By focusing on showing what the first 48 months of service, support, etc., would look like, the "High S," for example, can get a much better picture of how well he will be taken care of, and will feel much safer choosing you and your company.

After the initial success—pitching the offer in terms the Steadfast personality type would respond to—we then took it further by adapting our message to each of the other personality types. We explained the benefits in terms each would appreciate.

This was a key differentiator that distinguished us in the market—important in a field that was quickly becoming commoditized. Instead of just describing what a product or service could do, we extended the messaging to include the benefits sought by each DiSC style. Table 2-3 illustrates the benefit of one feature, tailored to each DISC style.

Table 2-3. Tailoring a Benefit to Personality Style

Feature	Dominant	Influential	Steadfast	Conscientious
Support	You can tell us what you want us to do and when.	Our support will make you look better in front of your customers.	Our support will make your environment safer and more predictable.	Our support will give you the highest possible quality at all times.

Essential Skills

If you understand people and what motivates their buying habits, then you're much of the way toward a long and lucrative sales career. But there are other elements that turn sales pros into superstars. First and foremost is a solid command of the sales process. Then there's the desire to constantly learn, manage time, set goals, and expand your network of people and prospects. In the chapters that follow you'll learn how technology can assist you every step of the way. But technology isn't a shortcut to mastering the key skills deeply ingrained in expert salespeople.

Let's look at each of these key skills in turn.

Master the Sales Process

You should think of a sales process the way professional sports teams think of plays. They outline and define the best plays and how to execute them to win the game. A sales process does the same thing. Figure 2-3 is a sample sales process for a B2B environment.

	1. Identify Territory	2. Gain Access to Power: Prospecting	3. Discover, Qualify, and Influence	4. Confirm, Fit, and Decide to Engage	5. Propose, Present, and/or Demonstrate	6. Work Strategy	7. Negotiate	8. Close
Objective of Sales Step	Research territory and generate leads based on target profiles.	Prepare for and contact prospect. Qualify and obtain first meeting.	Establish mutual interest and understand business problems, decision criteria, process, and compelling event.	Evaluate if you should engage and can win.	Provide formal proposal or demonstrate present your solution. TCO/ROI	Execute agreed-upon tactics to win deal.	Formalize verbal and written commitments.	Complete deal contract.
Metrics	• Research territory. • Research companies. • Leverage channels. • Create target account list. • Enter into CRM/SFA.	• Analyze selection criteria. • Establish call objectives. • Identify value of your offer. • Identify key contacts. • Create prospecting message and delivery mechanism. • Prequalify once appointment is confirmed.	• Define priorities (key business drivers and pain points) • Identify a compelling event • Qualify time frame, decision process, decision criteria, budget • Plant seeds and create traps for competition • Get commitment for a next step that favors you • Identify key contacts • Understand customer's buying process	• Match information from initial meeting to determine if it is a real opportunity and your chances of winning are good. • If you decide to engage, start building team and strategy to win the deal. • Being able to identify and develop coach.	• Provide formal proposal or presentation with your unique solution. • Demonstrate solution, showing off capabilities and ROI. • Align above with information from S.PRI.N.G. dialogues and other sources. • Address priorities, needs, decision process, decision criteria. • Set traps for competition. • Provide initial pricing. • Align with your strategy. • Gain next step to put you in position to win.	• Using S.C.O.O.P., meet more often with team as the decision comes nearer. • Person in charge holds team accountable to execute on plan. • Continue to develop coach. • If there is a dramatic change in circumstances (either good or bad), evaluate a strategy change and supporting tactics.	• If not done already, deliver T's & C's. • Put team together to negotiate. • Meet with prospect's negotiating team if not done so already. • Establish negotiation strategy.	• Receive legal, finance, network approval. • Receive signed contract. • Complete Best Practice Form. • Update CRM/SFA.
Skills	• Territory management. • Access to power/prospect. • Channel management.	• Access to power. • S.PRI.N.G. dialogue. • DISC. • Objection handling.	• Selling strategically • Team selling • S.PRI.N.G. dialogue • Closing	• R.E.A.L. presentations. • Team selling. • Executive-level selling.	• R.E.A.L. presentations. • Negotiations.	• Negotiations. • Objection handling. • Closing.	• Negotiations. • Objection handling. • Closing.	• Team selling. • Implementation.
Probability to Close	0%	20%	50%	60%	80%	90%	100%	

Figure 2-3. A sample B2B sales process.

You have been introduced to a sales process that has worked in the past, works now, and will continue to work for decades hence. Each stage, if executed properly, improves your chances of winning business. For example, by getting to the right people at the right time in Stage 2 with a reference, they are already more open to you. If you do an excellent job in Stage 3, then your presentation in Stage 5 should go even better. Even though advances in technology have deeply affected the sales process and profession, salespeople must still execute a sales process, and customers must still go through a buying process. Any good sales process must understand a prospect's buying process as early as possible and adjust accordingly. The objective for salespersons or organizations is to shorten the time for a decision to be made in their favor. This can be done by mastering their own sales process.

Chapter 3 covers the sales process and the special terms in the chart in much greater depth, and beginning with Chapter 4, we'll show you how technology will help you speed the sales process and extend your reach, among many other benefits.

Don't Neglect Training

Training is as important as ever. To use the analogy of a sports team, even the greatest teams and athletes constantly practice their skills, plays, and strategies. This allows everyone to share best practices and bring together the best of you and your people. What you train for needs to align with your sales process and cover keys skills, knowledge, and roles. Quantum leaps in productivity come from big and small improvements and insights. Consider the impact of even the simplest changes (like our DiSC examples).

An easy way to analyze where you or your sales team might need training is to define what needs improvement in three key areas:

1. Skills: Include all the sales skills we define in the sales process chart and more. It can also include more esoteric skills such as problem solving or creative thinking.

2. Knowledge: Knowledge can be broken into three major categories: internal (processes, company/product history), products, and external (market, competition).

3. Attributes: These are perhaps the hardest to develop. They include teamwork, assertiveness, honesty, and many more.

Time Management for Salespeople

Time management is as important in the sales profession as it is in any other career—maybe even more so. Reaching your sales goals absolutely demands that you budget and prioritize your time carefully and on a daily basis. Disorganized salespeople usually have poor time management skills, and they rarely last long in the profession.

Time hasn't changed. Ever. There are still 60 seconds in a minute and 60 minutes in an hour. Time, more than ever, is money. If you can give yourself 1 more hour a day to sell, it can equal up to nearly 5 extra weeks of selling time. Here's how:

- Let's say, taking into account vacation and holidays, you work 48 weeks a year

- 5 days a week x 48 = 240 days

- 1 more hour a day to sell = 240 hours

- 240 hours divided by a 10-hour day = 24 more days

- 24 more days divided by 5 (days a week) = One day short of 5 weeks

Do you know where you waste time? For a day or a week, keep a time log that tracks, to the minute, how you spent your time. This simple act will show you how much better you can use your time.

Here are some areas you might want to look at and ask yourself:

1. Do I check my e-mails at predesignated times or do I react to each one as it arrives?

2. Do I "batch" certain administrative functions (paperwork, quotes, proposals) and do them all at once, or individually as they are requested?

3. Do I qualify requests from customers, prospects, and internal departments based on when they need something vs. jumping immediately at the request?

4. Do I set voice/e-mail messages letting people know when I am not available?

5. Do I delegate and follow up on my tasks, or do I perform them all myself?

6. Do my customers know the right people to contact for different service, support, billing needs, etc. or do they come to me for everything?

7. Do I have one system in which I keep notes, to do lists, etc.?

8. Am I good at multitasking (e.g., checking e-mails while talking on the phone)? If I multitask, do I save time or waste time by starting and stopping?

9. Do I type well or do I hunt and peck?

10. Do I know how to operate the software packages and internal systems well or am I constantly searching manuals or the Internet for instructions?

11. Do I procrastinate and push off the lengthy or difficult tasks (even though they may be the most important)?

12. Am I good at handling all the different paperwork that comes my way?

13. In working my territory, do I try to make multiple appointments in the same area at the same time so I don't waste time traveling back and forth?

14. Do I often browse the web on non-work-related items?

15. Do I gossip too much?

16. Do I qualify appointments and consider whether I can handle them on the phone vs. in person?

17. Do I qualify internal appointments as to whether who should or should not attend?

18. Do I use my selling hours to sell and complete non-sales tasks at the appropriate time?

19. Do I plan and prioritize the events for each day or week ahead of time and try to keep to it as much as possible?

20. Do I set proper expectations with all as to when I will respond to them or do I just do whatever they ask whenever they ask?

21. Am I still smoking, which is wasting time and killing me?

22. Do I multitask too often, which makes me less productive?

23. Do I use automation for my mundane, difficult, or high-volume tasks?

Goal Setting

It's not only how much time you have but what you do with that time. The best way to get the most out of your time is to create S.M.A.R.T. goals and priorities for you and your team.

S.M.A.R.T. stands for:

- Specific (usually a number or %)

- Measurable (the end result and the steps to get the result you want)

- Aligned and Agreed Upon (with your boss and those who help and support you inside and outside of your business environment)

- Realistic (you have the resources, time, etc., needed)

- Timed (when you will accomplish the goal and priorities)

When written out, a S.M.A.R.T. goal might look like this:

"I will meet 110% of my annual quota this year," or "I will be the #1 salesperson in my division this fiscal year," or "I will make X amount of money the next 12 months."

A S.M.A.R.T. goal gets done by your deciding on the most important things to do, how much time needs to be allocated, defining the resources you need, and getting the support and alignment you need in your organization and then executing them. Let's take the preceding example: "I will meet 110% of my annual quota this year" and outline it in Figure 2-4.

Steps/Priorities	What I'll Do	How Much/Often # Hours	By When	Resources Needed	What Will Others Do/$ Required
Prospecting	Define my territory.	10 hours	30 days	Add database	Maybe $500
Qualify Deals Better	See if they are in the market or just being educated.	Always	Now	None	None
Learn S.PRI.N.G. (A great sales interview process.)	Create a S.PRI.N.G. form to use for all meetings. Use it to discuss deals with manager.	All meetings	Now	Create form	Support my effort
Stay on top of competition	Evaluate top competitors and new entries.	3 hours/month	ASAP	Product Marketing	Need person to help me with this

Figure 2-4. S.M.A.R.T. goals worksheet.

The final step is to time activate your priorities into your calendar by making appointments with yourself. Figure 2-5 shows an example of a weekly calendar that has the priorities (learn Facebook, prospect to largest new business, work on book) built in.

Figure 2-5. Making appointments with yourself to reach goals

Expand Your Network

As the saying goes, it's not what you know but who you know. Maintaining and expanding a network takes skill, just like setting goals or managing time. Keep your Rolodex (your what?) or electronic contact database up to date. Stay in touch with everyone you have ever done business with or met. Because people are so busy, and the number of people wanting to sell to them has increased, the most effective way to get to the people you don't already know and want to sell to is via a referral. (A recent webinar done by the Executive Conversation Group stated you have a 70% chance to get to a C-Level executive with a good referral.) We imagine a real Rolodex still exists, but keeping track of contacts is an area where technology can really help salespeople. We will go into greater depth with this in later chapters, but consider this:

- More than 900,000,000 people are currently using Facebook.

- LinkedIn now has 150,000,000 profiles.

Personal contacts can lead you to, or become, professional contacts. All of these can be dissected to an exact demographic, title, industry, location, or whatever other variable you like, allowing you to find and reach out to more people than ever before.

Whether you work alone or with a company, your network should also include your own advisory board—people you will meet with formally or informally whom you can bounce ideas off of and get advice.

Competition

Though there has always been competition, it seems as if there is more than ever before. The Internet is allowing people to create things, emulate others, and come to market faster than ever before. Market windows (the time you, your company, or product have a unique offer) have decreased dramatically. Individuals and companies need to dedicate more time to this than they have in the past. Customers and prospects also want to have more choice and fewer restrictions from a contractual perspective. For both, you need to be able to justify the value of your solution on a long-term contract and the downside of changing or moving away from your offer. SaaS (software as a service), the ability to buy only what you need when you need it, is accelerating these contractual issues. Remember, quality services and products that once cost thousands of dollars are now free. Also consider that you can get good quality services free. For example, videoconferencing via Skype or Gmail is free. It certainly isn't as good, consistent, or reliable as services from dedicated vendors, but it is free. There is also a growing tendency among salespeople and companies that you have to constantly change to keep up with the competition. It is our opinion that you have to stay focused on your core values, continually evaluate the market, and make adjustments to your offer without completely changing or reversing what you are doing. This creates too much confusion and complexity for everyone, internally and your customers.

Additional items and issues to be considered are:

- People and companies are inclined to want to change as quickly and often as the market does or when they hear about new competitors. This is a recipe for disaster. Stay focused and evaluate as needed.

- The grass is not always greener. There is a human tendency to focus on what you don't have vs. mastering what you do have. Focus on the latter.

- Being a quality salesperson is always relevant. It will help you flourish in good times and be more competitive in bad times.

- Lead-generation technology and social networks are becoming more important, but they should not come at the price of neglecting great sales processes, skills, methodologies, and your own prospecting.

- Time, skills, and knowledge are all we have and can control. Be the best at each and you will be a great salesperson.

- If you have a good product in a good territory then you can be extremely successful by being a great salesperson and focusing on your goals and on your sweet spot.

We have here laid the foundational elements of great salespeople that need to be mastered to achieve success as a salesperson. This mastery allows you to take advantage of technology vs. being dependent on it; it will make you even more effective. We now begin a deeper discussion regarding the value, best uses of, and things to avoid when using technology to sell.

Foundation: The Sales Process

In Detail, from Beginning to End

As mentioned in the previous chapter, the sales process is like a sports team's playbook. It is a description of how things will be done, or the best plays to run to win the game or, in sales, to win more business. It is coveted and closely held by the sales team because of its importance.

A typical sales process for selling B2B (business to business) might look something like this:

1. Profile territory and assignment.

2. Prospect and gain access to key contacts.

3. Meet with prospects to discover, qualify, and influence in order to understand the customer's decision making and buying process.

4. Confirm fit and decide to engage or not; begin to develop team and sales strategy.

5. Propose, present, or demonstrate solution.

6. Work sales strategy.

7. Negotiate and close.

B2C: DIFFERENT PROCEDURE

If you are in B2C (business to consumer) business, the sales process is a bit different than with B2B. Rather, it might look something like this:

1. Receive incoming calls or leads.

2. Discover, qualify, and influence.

3. Confirm fit and decide to engage or not.

4. Propose, present, or demonstrate solution.

5. Handle objections.

6. Gain commitment and close.

There are many steps in a sales process, each of which can positively or negatively affect one or more of the others. I (Jonathan) do a great deal of sales training. Recently, I was with a client to help the client's team prospect more effectively and strategize over the largest deals they want to win. We went back and forth between the two to keep each fresh.

While prospecting, their sales leader was having a contest with the team together in a room (and virtually as well, since two people were participating via video). All of them were sitting in front of their PCs or Macs, with access to an online database of names and addresses, and sending e-mails to targeted accounts. This was a great session to watch, but it became even more interesting when we started strategizing about how to win the biggest deals. We could do so because we were able to see that their largest deals had several things in common, and it all started with prospecting.

Specifically, the biggest deals—where the salespeople were in a strong position—were at a VP level, and the salesperson was involved in the deal very early on. In all the deals where they were in a weak position, they were selling to people at a very low level and had come to the deal late. I helped bring these points to the forefront, and the salespeople were able to resume their prospecting with a very specific intention to meet with decision-makers at the higher levels.

Each step of the process also has many elements. If they are exploited properly, they will help you win more business. Elements in each step include:

- Information needed before and during the sale

- Internal tools or materials that you can use to win

- Technology (to be discussed in great detail in Chapters 4 through 9)

- SMEs (subject matter experts), or people who can help you during the sale

- Knowledge of partners or channels to work with

- Team composition, including executives

- And more

This chapter breaks down each element of the sales process. It describes the skills and actions to be applied, and it begins to show how technology can be applied to give you a competitive advantage. A more detailed description of how technology can be applied is in Chapter 6.

Stage 1. Profile Territory and Assignment

Table 3-1 provides an overview of Stage 1.

Table 3-1. Overview of Stage 1: Profile Territory and Assignment

Stage 1 Goals:

- **Research territory and generate leads based on target profiles.**
- **Identify sweet spot.**

Actions	Technology	Resources
• Research territory. • Research companies. • Leverage channels. • Create target account list. • Enter into customer relationship management (CRM)/sales force automation (SFA).	• D+B/Hoovers • OneSource • LinkedIn • Salesforce.com • Vertical databases • Lexis/Nexis	• Other salespeople • Marketing and product management • Internal database • Library • Competitive Analyst

Skills
• Territory management • Channel management

Having a territory, or assigned accounts, is like having your own business or franchise. You need to understand what you are selling and analyze your assignment to see where the business opportunities are most abundant. If you work with partners, then you need to decide on which partners you want to work with and where you might have to recruit additional partners (see Table 3-2).

Table 3-2. Analyzing Your Assignment

1	2	3	4	5
Your Company's Unique Strengths (products and services)	Industries (consider past successes, ties to strengths, and the economy)	Applications/ Departments to Contact (that can benefit from your offer, potentially regardless of industry)	Current Customers (as references or to see trends)	Potential Partners (to help get you in)
Click to call (customers can call you immediately from website)	Service (florists, restaurants, hair salons)	Customer service contact centers	Paul's Florists BND Contact Center	Supply companies Telecom- munications

In this stage of the sale, you are profiling your territory or assignment, which could be geographical, by vertical/industry, by application (HR, sales, etc.), or assigned accounts.

▨ **Note** If you have an "open territory" be very careful about chasing and selling to everyone and everything. This is like being a baseball player and swinging for the fences on every pitch if you have a short distance to hit a home run. You will strike out a lot. You should follow the same principles outlined in this section.

This is done via the technology and resources identified, your own knowledge and experience, your company's track record, and more.

A chart like Table 3-2 can be extremely helpful with profiling your territory. You will need to customize the second (and additional) rows based on your unique situation, as we've done. To make the best use of it, take the following five actions based on each of the columns:

1. In column 1, define your company's greatest strengths and most unique capabilities.

2. In columns 2 and 3, write down which industries (verticals) or departments (horizontal applications) where these strengths and capabilities would be most compelling, relevant, and well received.

3. In column 4, write down current customers and analyze them both to validate the first three columns, and also to see if you can use any as references to secure more business. You can also start with column 4 to see if there is a trend or abundance of industries or applications your company sells to.

4. In column 5, determine if there are any partners you think you could work with to get into the industries or departments in the preceding columns.

5. Choose three or four of the items in columns 2 and 3 that you feel are the best opportunities to pursue given your strengths. Then, to start, see if your current customers or potential partners (columns 4 and 5) can introduce you to potential new customers. You should also add additional criteria or filters such as your own experience, expertise, and the financial condition of an industry and whether being geographically close to the prospect is important.

Using this table as described will put you in a better position to sell since you are aligning your strengths with those who need it most and will see your value more easily. In essence, it describes your "sweet spot"—the area in which you'll find your greatest success. To use a football analogy, by doing this properly you will start with the ball on your own 45-yard line every time you have an opportunity, which obviously puts you in a better position to score, or win deals.

When Martin started his own business a few years ago, he used this strategy to define his sweet spot. Coming from BT Conferencing, he knew an obvious vertical to approach for sales training was other conferencing companies because of his knowledge and experience in that industry. He also chose BT itself because he knew a lot of people. In a very short time, he landed two deals with other conferencing companies. This year, Martin and Jonathan trained approximately 300 people in a division of BT.

Jonathan has used this strategy in his entire sales career and it has never failed. One of his favorite examples is how he has used it in the two last recessions. Jonathan looked at the industries that can use his services and would be least affected, or actually prosper, in a weak economy. By doing so, he ended up selling services to the largest video conferencing companies, managed hosting and online advertising networks in the world.

Similarly, one of Jonathan's clients sold remote surveillance via the Internet. While he was consulting with them, the news was full of stories about horrible things happening in schools and churches. It was a perfect situation for that company to sell their services—it fit right into their sweet spot. Another client of Jonathan's is the only vendor on a contract through which schools and nonprofit organizations can buy their product and bypass the laborious and tedious RFP (Request for Proposal) process. They are unstoppable in this space.

Keep your eyes open for these kinds of situations in your territory or assignment and you will always have a sales advantage.

Pay Attention to the Channel

Channel management is important if your company has formal agreements to sell through distribution points or resellers. In this case, you should understand their strengths as well and factor them into where you will spend your time. This knowledge can also help you drive your partners and channels into the best places to sell your products or services. Quite often, partners will have dedicated teams that sell into a specific vertical, like health care or GEM (government/education/medical). If your solution targets one of those verticals, that is where you should spend more of your time. If they don't have anything that specific, then you would want to align with the partner's best sales team or people so that you get the most from that partner.

▓ **Note** You can also have informal partners that can be as good as or better than your formal partners. Jonathan and Martin work with executive recruiters because they can tell them when a company is hiring or looking for training. In turn Jonathan and Martin can tell them about companies looking to hire VPs of sales.

Stage 2. Prospect and Gain Access to Key Contacts

This is the stage at which you reach out to your prospects and get more appointments, with the right people so you can sell more of your services more consistently. Table 3-3 provides an overview.

Table 3-3. Overview of Stage 2: Prospecting and Gaining Access to Key Contacts

Stage 2 Goals:		
• **Prepare for and contact prospect.**		
• **Prequalify and obtain first meeting.**		
Actions	**Technology**	**Resources**
• Analyze selection criteria.	• LinkedIn	• Other salespeople
• Establish call objectives.	• Salesforce.com	• Marketing and product management
• Identify value of your offer.	• Vertical databases	
• Identify key contacts.	• E-mail	• Internal database
• Create prospecting message and delivery mechanism.	• Desktop video	
• Prequalify once appointment is confirmed.	• Streaming	
	• Social media	
Skills		
• Gaining access to power (aka, prospecting)		
• Objection handling		

If salespeople think of prospecting as their own form of marketing, it will expand their vision and improve the effectiveness of their efforts. It is getting harder and harder to reach people because there are more ways to "gatekeep" you—bar access to people who make buying decisions. But prospecting must be done all the time for the same reasons companies advertise all the time: to build awareness and stimulate people when they are thinking about buying something you are selling, or even better, are ready to buy.

Regardless of the media you use to reach out to people (phone, social media, e-mail, invitations to events, etc.), prospects will be in 1 of 4 stages of receptivity:

1. Not interested and never will be. They are legitimately not good prospects (e.g., trying to sell a feminine hygiene product to a man).

2. Just started to consider what you are selling.

3. Will be buying something and are deciding from whom.

4. Just bought something and therefore are not really interested.

 Note People often ask us how to shorten a sales cycle. One of the best ways we know is to get to the right person with the right authority level when they are in stages 2 or early- to mid-stages of 3.

Good companies know that they have to constantly market. Good salespeople know they have to constantly prospect in order to reach people in receptivity stages 2 or 3 as often as possible. I (Jonathan) learned this very early in my career when I was selling Olivetti typewriters and competing with IBM. Where I would have city blocks to cover, they would have five salespeople in the same building. They were always in front of the prospects. So I had to increase my territory coverage via mailings (snail mail) and decide where I wanted to focus these efforts, which was directly at my sweet spot. In this instance, I had unique advantages in the legal, financial, printing, and architectural and engineering industries, so this where I focused my efforts.

There is nothing more important in the world of sales than prospecting! Why is it so important? It will help you:

- Win as much as business as possible.

- Be as confident as possible.

- Avoid the emotional roller coaster of sales.

- Build a strong pipeline so there is a continuous flow of business.

- Sell more to companies that appear to be best suited for the product or service you are selling.

Unfortunately, most salespeople do not like prospecting. Here's why:

- It is the hardest part of selling.

- There is a lot of rejection.

- They are doing OK without it.

- There are more fun things to do.

- They fear change.

- They feel like they are infringing or bothering people.

This last point in particular needs to be addressed. If you are selling something of value, you are not bothering somebody. In fact, you might be calling him at precisely the key moment and influence him to do the most important thing he can do at the moment. For example, we sell sales training. When I call a VP of sales, I am calling because I believe that if my program is used properly, then her sales team will perform the best it possibly can and sell the most. What could be more important than that? So I call with a sense of purpose and confidence, which helps my prospecting.

Do you understand the potential value of your offering? If not, use Table 3-4 to consider the impact of your offering on the companies you are calling. It will help you immensely.

Table 3-4. Understanding the Value of Your Offering

Product or Service	Industry	Department or Function	Impact
Sales Training	Online Advertising	Sales	Increase revenue by millions of dollars, increase market share, differentiate offer, help private companies go public

If prospecting is done as described, you will learn:

1. To focus on products by vertical or application that gives you a better return on your effort.

2. To make every call a warm-to-hot call vs. a cold call.

3. To use current events in a company or an industry as legitimate reasons to call someone.

4. The importance of building a network of people to help you gain access to other people.

5. To leverage the Internet, Web, and all the wonderful technological things available to you to make your prospecting more effective.

6. The best time to prospect.

7. To use e-mail as an effective way of getting to people.

8. To structure your communications so that people will listen to you.

No matter how successful you are, how big your company is, or how "hot" you are, "gaining access to power"—a phrase synonymous with prospecting—is not optional. If you want to make as much money as possible for yourself and your company, you must make prospecting a priority and constant activity.

IPG's Gaining Access to Power System

We will now take you through our Gaining Access to Power System that we have built our own business on, and which has helped thousands of salespeople get more quality appointments.

1. Build a Strategic Territory Plan

This step helps you identify your sweet spot. If you owned your own business (which you do in a way even if you work for somebody else), you would want to identify the people or companies you want to target, or those that would be most attracted to your offer. This is your sweet spot. It is where your unique and/or strongest offerings meet the needs of an industry, functional department (legal, HR, finance, manufacturing, etc.), or application (billing, call recording, writing long documents, spreadsheets, etc.). If you have a unique offering for protecting online data, for example, you would want to sell to the finance or legal industries (or verticals as they are also known) since this is an important concern for them. You might also want to sell to the functional departments (legal and finance) in these or any industry since your offer has such significance.

Note This is particularly effective when you want to sell to a company that has already standardized on your competitor. When Jonathan sold word processing, he would often sell to the legal department because his system had such a great fit *and* because they had enough authority and independence to do whatever they wanted.

The more data you can access via public or private databases, the better. If your company has a history of sales you can look at, this will also lead you in the right direction. For example, if your company's previous sales can be broken down in your territory by product, size, industry, application/department, etc., you can use that information to help you decide on what strategy to use.

In addition, you might factor in your experience and knowledge, whether an industry is growing or declining (this is significant when the overall economy is weak because you want to focus on industries that are doing well and have money to spend) and if there are any geographical or demographic trends from other parts of the country or world can put you ahead of the competition. This happens in the online/digital or new media advertising industry, where things often happen sooner in the United States than in Europe, or when they happen in New York City before they do in Dallas. The most important part of this stage is *always go where you have unique advantage, knowledge, or track record of success—it puts you in an advantageous position from the very beginning.*

MEET WITH YOUR PROSPECTS

Having prospects actually meet with you or see you can make the difference in whether you win or lose a deal. It is not happening as much as it should because salespeople are becoming overly dependent on technology—one of its improper uses. It is also easier to manage your business if your territory is close by and easy to travel to. Quite often, we see people chasing business in the most remote, time-consuming, and expensive (to travel to) parts of their territory because they feel it is their responsibility to do so. This is counterproductive because you may not be able to visit them in person as much as you must to win business.

2. Initiate a Multipronged Attack

There is always one best person (or person with a certain title like CTO if you are selling technology) you want to meet with. Therefore many people make the mistake of going after only that one person. But many can benefit from your services and help you get into the organization and begin the sales process. For example, if you are selling something that can help a company get more leads for less money, the VP of sales is the primary target. But the VP of marketing or CFO might also be interested, since the purchase affects them, and can help them, as well. It is also effective to reach out to peer levels simultaneously to trigger their interest.

For example, Jonathan noticed that a telecommunications company was doing a lot of advertising on TV and print. He got about 10 of these printed ads, stapled them together, and wrote a letter to both the VP of sales and VP of marketing praising the advertising but asking if the money they were spending was converting into the number of sales they desired. He got a call from the VP of sales to discuss how to increase sales.

Some people feel it is a bit risky, and at times it might be, but it works when used properly.

3. Never Cold Call Again

Creating or discovering legitimate reasons to call someone (referencing people you both know, mentioning references customers have provided, or relating current events to their business) are key to gaining access.

Think about how you react when you get a cold call from somebody when you are at home or work. Most people are very annoyed because it is uninvited, intrusive, and bothersome (so much so that in the United States, a law was passed preventing certain types of cold calling or telemarketing). Now contrast that with a call from somebody who was referred to you whom you both know ("Annie Tompkins suggested I call you"). Or maybe someone is calling you about a matter that is relevant to you at the time of the call ("I know you're struggling right now integrating a new database"). Most people are less bothered and more welcoming and receptive in these situations.

▨ **Note** If you are a telemarketer, this comparison may not be relevant (although still valid), since you are strictly playing a numbers game. Yet you should still do your best to have a message that will resonate.

However, if you have defined territories or accounts, this is the best and only way to prospect. You should call prospects about something that is going on in their world—personally, or involving their company or their industry, or something that is happening in the world as a whole that affects them, i.e. government regulations they have to respond to.

EVENTS DRIVE BUSINESS

In the years 2000 and 2001, people had frozen budgets and stopped much of their traveling because of the economy and 9/11. But they still needed to run their businesses. IPG realized that audio and video conferencing would benefit from this set of circumstances so they called the VP of sales in the companies, offering these services with a compelling value statement. IPG sold to every major vendor in the United States, Canada, and the United Kingdom.

The best way to get through to someone is through a good reference, since it instantly breaks down barriers. In the next chapter we delineate the many ways technology can help you keep track of and find referrals and legitimate reasons to call.

4. Use Different Methods to Contact People

Companies that market do so over many media including TV, radio, Internet, print, direct mail, e-mail, fliers in newspapers, etc. They do so to reach people in as many ways as possible, and/or in the way prospects prefer. The same is true of prospecting. Your prospect may prefer an e-mail vs. a call to the office. She may respond to a handwritten off-sized envelope or a FedEx package. You should certainly have a foundation or primary way of prospecting (e.g., phone with e-mail, references, or invitations to webinars). But you need to try different ways in case you are having difficulty reaching people, or to test if there are better ways than your current approach.

THINK "CRAZY"

The advertising and new media industries do the strangest things to get appointments. They will send pizzas asking people if they can get a slice of their time. Or they'll send cupcakes with funny prospecting messages. One woman sent a bag of oranges asking if the prospect could squeeze her in. Another had her best prospects shag balls during batting practice at Fenway Park (her company paid, of course).

There are many different techniques a salesperson can use. An oldie but goodie is sending someone a shoe or sneaker with the message "now that I have one foot in the door, can we meet?" Martin once sent a piggy bank with a little note coming out where you deposit money. When the prospect slipped the note out, it had a prospecting message asking for a meeting. A client told me he sent a mini-garbage can with a note attached asking the person not to put his message in the garbage.

As you can see, only the imagination limits what you can do to get your message in front of someone. But whatever you do, make sure your message reflects you and your company well, and is not inappropriate for the target.

5. Craft Effective Messages for Voicemail

Many people don't like to leave voicemails. We are not sure why because it is an opportunity to say something that might whet the appetite of the person you are calling. Our rule is to leave enough to do just this, such as "My name is [name], and Joe Jones suggested I call. I will call back but if you have a moment please call me at [number]" or "My name is [name]. I am calling regarding your recent product announcement. Please call me at [number]." You can drop names as well: "My name is [name] and I was calling to discuss some recent installations at company X, Y, and Z."

■ **Note** After leaving a voice message, you can also "0" out to a receptionist and ask to be transferred to the same person for whom you just left a voicemail. If the person was screening her calls, she might pick up because it is now an internal transfer vs. an outside call.

What if you can't get the number of the person you want? Call the main number, ask for any department or office (the president, investor relations, customer service, etc.), and then when someone picks up, ask if the person can transfer you to the person you really want to speak with.

It is not uncommon to have to leave more than one message, so it helps to have a series of voicemails planned in such a way that each one builds on the other. There are many technologies that do this, but with a little effort, you can create your own voicemail campaigns.

Table 3-5 might help you in developing your campaign.

Table 3-5. Leaving Voicemail Messages

Day	Call No.	Voice Message
Day 1	1st voice-mail	"Sally Smith suggested I call."
Day 4	2nd voice-mail	"Since I haven't heard back, I sent you an e-mail."
Day 7	3rd voice-mail	"The program I wanted to discuss with you will be expiring in 30 days."
Day 10	4th voice-mail	"I wouldn't be so persistent if I didn't think it would help. I will reach out to your assistant."

6. Get Past Gatekeepers

Although much less frequent than in the past, many executives have, or share executive assistants. One of the main responsibilities of their jobs is to keep salespeople away from their boss, and they take that responsibility very seriously. There are some ways to get past gatekeepers, however. These include:

- Send e-mail directly to the executive, especially at off hours or on the weekend when his e-mail inbox is less crowded.

- Call early or late, when the gatekeeper might not be in.

- Ask gatekeepers for their help. Their behavioral style is often high i or S DiSC, so they like to help. For example, "I was hoping you can help me. I am calling about [give the person the three benefits]. Is that Ms. Crane or somebody else?"

- Have a referral—that makes it much harder, if not impossible, for the gatekeeper to keep you from your prospect.

7. The Moment of Truth: Three Musts When the Prospect Picks Up the Phone, Opens Your E-mail, or Views Your Response

Unless you have a referral, and the referral has told your prospect that you will be calling, you are at best disturbing somebody when you call them.

The person you are calling is not hanging around the phone waiting for you to call. It's not as if he would refuse a lunch date to take your call. And he didn't say to his wife that morning, "Honey, I really hope somebody from company X calls me today."

REFERENCE ETIQUETTE

Here are four things you should do if a person is generous enough to refer you:

1. Ask if you can use her name.

2. Ask if she knows the issues the person is dealing with so you can use her in your initial benefit statement.

3. Ask if she can call the person you want to speak with and say he should make an appointment with you.

4. Keep her aware of how things are going, good or bad.

People are overwhelmingly busy these days and most of the time they pick up the phone because they ARE hoping it is somebody they want to speak with. When they hear your voice, well, let's just say they are at best mildly disappointed.

So how do you get past this upset and turn the call into a win for both of you?

When you are prospecting, three things must happen quickly once a person answers the phone or opens an e-mail message. You must:

- Create immediate credibility.

- Generate interest as early in the call as possible with two or three reasons or benefits of speaking with you.

- Close for an action.

To that end, always:

- Keep your comments short and sweet.

- Be yourself and use a conversational tone.

- Prepare before you make a call.

- Be respectful of people's time.

- Again, offer two to three benefits—it can increase your odds up to 65%.

Never (no matter how many times you have called):

- Sound canned.

- Be confrontational.

- Be arrogant.

Here is a sample call to a business owner:

> *Good morning, Ms. Jones. My name is Sam Smith with XYZ Marketing Solutions. Andrew Blanish suggested I call.* **(Credibility).**
>
> *Andrew suggested I call because of our recent success at his company and how our solutions might help you in the same way by:*
>
> - *Finding you more high-paying customers* **(Benefit 1)**
>
> - *Attracting more quality leads* **(Benefit 2)**
>
> - *Promoting you in more places and to more people* **(Benefit 3)**
>
> *Do you have some next Tuesday or Friday to talk?"*

Here is the same message sent via e-mail and following the same rules:

Subject: Andrew Blanish Asked Me to Reach Out

Dear Ms. Jones,

Andrew Blanish [Credibility] asked me to reach out because of the tremendous success we had with his company in:

- Finding him **high paying** customers [Benefit 1]

- Attracting **more quality** leads [Benefit 2]

- **Promoting him** in more places and to more people [Benefit 3]

I want to see if we can do the same for you. Are you free next Tuesday or Friday? If I don't hear from you, I will reach out again.

Sincerely,

Jonathan London / President / www.ipgtraining.com

Notice several important elements of how this e-mail is formatted:

- The subject line is what you would have said to her if you had called, giving immediate credibility.

- The referral is put first since many people check their e-mails on smartphones and don't see the whole message line.

- The reader can see your whole message in her preview screen (which is represented by the box).

- Good white space balance makes the message pleasing to the eye.

- Benefits fit on one line and key words are in **bold** to highlight them.

- The signature line is flat, vs. vertical, to shorten the entire message.

- There are no logos or images since that increases the chance your e-mail will go into spam.

I used the formatting capabilities of Outlook so that it maintains its form. Otherwise it could get distorted and look bad on the receiving end.

8. Anticipate and Handle Objections to Your Offer

No matter how good a prospector you are, you will get many objections. If you use the system we have described so far, you will get fewer because you are no longer cold calling, but rather calling about something the person cares about. Regardless, you will still get many objections, such as, "We're not interested," "We are busy," "This isn't a priority for us right now," "We don't have budget," and others.

The best way to handle an objection is to say something before the prospect does. For example, if you know the person you are calling is busy because you have tried seven times before to get through, you might say, "I know you are busy, so I will be brief." Or if you are prospecting at the end of a fiscal year and you expect people won't have budget to spend, you might say "I am calling even though you probably have no more money in the budget." Doing this takes the objection away from them or "takes the wind out of their sails." You still need to give the person the two or three benefits, but this should make him a bit more receptive.

If you can't anticipate the objection (which will be most of the time), the rule is to acknowledge the objection, and then say or ask something to start a conversation and then find an opening to get an appointment. Using the same objections just mentioned, you might say "I appreciate how busy you are, which is why I am calling now to set something up in three to four weeks." Or if the objection is no budget you might say, "I appreciate that money is tight at this time of the year, but that is why I think we should meet now."

Three great responses are:

- That is why I am calling.

- That is why we should meet.

- That is why our customers have done or do business with us.

Use Table 3-6 to help build your responses.

Table 3-6. Anticipating and Handling Objections

Objection	How To Anticipate	If You Can't Anticipate
Too Busy	"I know you are busy so I will be brief."	"That is why I am calling." "I can appreciate that, and that is exactly why we should meet."
Using a Competitor	"Hi. My name is Nancy Highmark and the reason I am calling is that I know you are using Product X. We find our best customers complement their investment in Product X and get . . ."	
No Budget	"Hi. My name is Jonathan London. I know at this time of the year you might not have any budget, but . . ."	
We have other priorities	"Mr. Krane, I am sure you are very busy with other priorities, and that is why I am reaching out . . ."	

9. Always Follow Up Appropriately

It is unimaginable to prospect today without some form of automation. Whether it is a simple list management function, Excel, or sophisticated software like Salesforce.com, you must automate your prospecting to manage all your activity, especially your follow up (on average it takes 10 attempts to reach somebody, less if you use our system).

When I started my career and prospecting consisted of sending letters and then following up by knocking on an office door, I used to keep track of what I was wearing the last time I went into their building. I would also keep track of:

- What kind of voicemail message I left so I didn't repeat it.

- Which competitor the prospect using.

- If the equipment was rented or leased, I would note when the agreement expired.

This is so basic compared to what can be done today, and we will discuss this topic in the following chapters.

In the meantime, here are some guidelines on follow up. Follow up as often as you like, but you should leave no more than two to three messages in the first several weeks. You don't want to seem desperate. These can be voice messages or e-mail. After that, you should still leave messages, but taper off to once a week. At this point, if you haven't already, you should consider who else you might want to meet with. Remember, there is usually more than one person in an organization who can benefit from your offer.

You should also vary the time of day at which you follow up, and the method.

Remember, when you are prospecting, you are just trying to get a meeting (which is hard enough). Don't make it more difficult by trying to sell the prospect on the phone. Look for any opening or question by the prospect that would allow you to say, "That is why I want to meet." For example, if a customer starts to ask questions about your offering you would say, "Ms. Blinker, these are great questions but it will take much too long to answer on the phone, which is why I was hoping we could meet."

Using the steps in this process will get you more appointments and put you in a better position to win deals. So start using it right away. To summarize:

1. Choose the accounts and applications you think are the best.

2. Create a list of accounts; rank them A/B/C.

3. Look for referrals or legitimate reasons to call. Use LinkedIn, iSell, Google Alerts, blogs, etc.

4. Choose the best times to prospect (usually early and late). That leaves you open to do everything else. Considering doing group exercises (webinars, breakfasts, golf outings, etc.) to get to many people at the same time.

5. Remember three things, regardless of the form the message takes: Credibility – Benefit – Close.

6. Make appointments with yourself to prospect and put them into your calendar. Treat them with the same importance as a meeting with a client or your boss.

7. Always prospect.

Stage 3. Meet with Prospects to Discover, Qualify, and Influence

This stage of the sales process is important for many reasons since it is the first time you are meeting with the prospect and, if done properly, will give you the information you need to move forward and win the business (see Table 3-7).

This stage of the sales process is essential for many reasons. You need to:

1. Get enough information to decide if there is a real sales opportunity, including a compelling event with a specific date associated.

2. Decide if you want to engage based upon objective or subjective criteria if you can win the opportunity.

3. Influence the prospect's thinking and feeling about your offer so he is more favorably inclined toward you than he was before the meeting.

4. Identify or develop a "coach," somebody who wants you to win and will help you do so.

Table 3-7. Overview of Stage 3: Meeting with Prospects to Discover, Qualify, and Influence

Stage 3 Goals: • **Discover, qualify, and influence.**		
Actions	**Technology**	**Resources**
• Understand the current situation. • Build rapport and show expertise. • Define priorities including a compelling event. • Qualify time frame, decision process, decision criteria, budget. • Plant seeds and create traps for competition. • Get commitment for a next step that favors you. • Analyze selection criteria. • Establish call objectives. • Identify value of your offer. • Identify key contacts. • Identify key business drivers. and pain points. • Address business problem you can solve.	• LinkedIn • Salesforce.com • Vertical data bases • E-mail • Desktop video or web conferencing • Streaming • Social media • Laptop • iPad or tablet • Wireless	• Manager • Pre/post technical support • SMEs (subject matter experts) • Brochures • Case studies • References
Skills		
• DiSC • S.PRI.NG dialogue • Presenting • Objection handling		

It is our belief that the sale is made, or lost, at this stage, and that too many salespeople rely on the presentation, demonstration, or proposal to win. If this stage is handled properly, those events will happen with the prospect being more open and receptive to your offer. If not handled well, you may not even get to present, and if you do, it will be to a less receptive, indifferent, or even hostile environment.

The best salespeople will know exactly what questions they want to ask and how they will influence the prospect's thinking. They do so by having a strong set of standard questions relating to the prospect, knowing the unique and compelling differences of their offer, and making sure they ask questions or make statements directed toward these differences. For example, if one of your company's strengths is the ability to customize an offer quickly and deeply, you might ask, "To what level would you want your program to be as specific and unique to you as possible?" Or, "If you could have us customize your solution in any way, what would that look like?" If your strength is financing options, you can ask "We have financing options that range from month-to-month to five-year leases, all at low rates. Which is your preference?"

Remember in the first chapter we mentioned that prospects have access to so much information that they need you less for information and more as a subject-matter expert and advisor. The qualities of a salesperson need to evolve from information provider to providing insight and being more empathetic. These elements, as well as developing rapport and credibility, begin to be established in this stage. Doing this requires excellent preparation, listening skills, expertise, and mirroring the prospect's behavior style. By being aware of and adjusting to prospects' DiSC style, and establishing areas of commonality, you will be going a long way to making a sale.

S.PRI.NG. Dialogue

IPG's S.PRI.N.G. dialogue can you give you the structure to consistently get more and better information from your initial meetings. We like to think of it as a map or GPS that guides you to your destination as efficiently as possible, even if there are detours on the way.

Think of it this way: The first time you meet somebody is like going on a trip or destination you have never been before. You usually use a map or GPS to make sure you get there as easily and safely as possibly. Like a GPS or map, you will never get lost because S.PRI.N.G. tells you exactly where you are and want to go, detours or not.

S.PRI.N.G. stands for:

SITUATION: The first part of this process is to try and get a picture of the prospects' current situation from their perspective and job responsibilities. This is also the beginning of your interaction, so the S also means getting off to a good *start* by making a good impression on the prospect. You can also begin to identify her DiSC style. Here are some ideas:

- Thank her for the appointment.

- Confirm the amount of time.

- State your objectives, which is to tell her about your company but also to ask questions to understand her priorities as well.

- Start with something interesting, topical, in common that you are aware of.

- Confirm or ask relevant things about her current environment.

Here are a few examples of how you might begin:

- "Thank you for agreeing to spend time with me today to discuss your priorities and needs. Today, I would like to find out a little more about your organization and priorities. From there, I can be specific as possible in describing our approach and how we can help."

- "Ultimately, we need to get to specific pricing and configurations, but in order to do that, I need to ask some higher level business questions. Would that be OK?"

- "I am excited to discuss your technical requirements and our new solution. I would like to understand the business initiatives behind this project, if that is OK with you."

- "To prepare for this meeting, I did some research about your current situation. I see that you have 23 locations with approximately 4,500 people. Is that correct?"

PRIORITIES: These are the reasons a person or committee has agreed to speak with you—to see if there is a way that you can help her with her priorities and resolve her problems. You should use this part of the interaction to understand her priorities, why they are priorities, and what the impact of success or failure around these priorities will have for her. This is also a time you can begin to start planting seeds or criteria for your solution that will help influence the deal and set landmines for the competition.

A *priority* is a catch-all word that, depending on who you are speaking with, can also mean goals, challenges, projects, problems, issues, etc. It is meant to determine the most important things the prospect needs to address.

Some ways to ask include:

- "Can you share with your top three priorities and their order of importance"

- "In relation to your project, what are your top three priorities and in what order"

A more sophisticated way (because it implies knowledge and experience) is:

- "It has been my experience in working with people in your position that four of the top priorities are:

  - Controlling the proliferation of mobile devices

  - Enhancing security and backup

  - Cost reduction

  - Leveraging IT investments already made

"Are these your priorities or do you have others?"

There is an array of questions that you can ask in relation to almost any priority, including:

- "Tell me more. Why is that the most important? Why now?"

- "What are the business drivers? Who is the executive sponsor?"

- "What is the link between these priorities and business priorities?"

- "What have you done to address this priority?"

- "What is working well?"

- "What isn't working well?"

- "What are the greatest pressures you have to deal with?"

- "What are the consequences of success or failure for you, your department, and the company from a financial and business perspective?"

- "What are the key measurements being used for you and your organization?"

- "How well are they being met?"

- "What would you like to be able to do that you can't today?"

- "What would you like to stop from happening that is interfering with your success?"

- "How are you using XYZ to address these priorities?"

- "Who else benefits or is impacted by these priorities?"

NEEDS: This part of the dialogue has two purposes. The first is to suggest ideas (which is like planting seeds for you and your company) on what the prospect needs to do to address her priorities and resolve her business problems. The second part is to discover what you need to know to win the deal: you ask questions about the timing, decision criteria competition, decision process, politics, budget, obstacles (in that order), and more if necessary to develop effective strategies and win the business. In other words, you will ask questions that you earlier hadn't earned the right to ask, and therefore probably would have diminished or ended your chances. Seeds and criteria should continue to be planted here that establish the value of your capabilities.

You should practice different ways to ask the more difficult questions. For example, questions about a decision process can be asked in many ways, including:

- "In the past, how have you made these types of decisions?" After the person answers, you can ask, "What if anything will be different this time?"

- "Can you share with me the steps from now to issuing a purchase order, and who is involved and the role he or she plays?

- "Can you share with me your decision process so I can align my approach and resources accordingly?"

GAIN: This is the most sensitive, personal, and perhaps the most important question, so we save it for last. Here you uncover how the prospect gains personally if these priorities are met, and what potential consequences there are if they aren't. This is crucial when presenting solutions, building strategies, and tactics, or handling objections. This question internalizes and associates what the prospects wants with you. You have to be careful and sensitive how you ask. Don't ever ask the question in front of others if possible.

Some examples are:

- "What would it mean to you as IT director, and to your department, if you are successful? What would it mean to you personally?"

- "If it didn't happen, what would that look like?"

- "Independent of whether you choose us, what does success look like and what would your personal and professional gain be?"

- "Twelve months from now, what would things look like if you have the success you want?"

Next Steps

You can begin to control the sales process by suggesting follow-up steps and actions that are relevant to the prospect, favor you, and help you win the deal. Do you know what they are? Can you delineate the actions a prospect takes with you when you win? Examples of good next steps include bringing prospects to your main office, visiting prospects at their place of business, having them meet with your technical team, reading or viewing certain materials you send, and so forth.

Another important next step for you is to identify and develop a coach. A *coach* is defined as someone who wants you to win and champions your cause, and who gives you insights and guidance into what is happening in the account and decision process. This is more than someone merely giving you information. The coach is your inside "mole" and will answer questions you don't have answers for. It is important that nobody at the prospect's account knows who your coach is because people may not be as open with him or her.

Some indicators of suitable coaches are:

- You have good chemistry with them.

- They are the ones who called you in to meet.

- They are active and verbal about your solution.

- They respond to e-mails and requests quickly.

Ways of developing coaches include:

- Entertaining them and getting to know them personally.

- Being extra responsive to them.

- Making them look good in front of their boss.

- Giving them information that nobody else has so they look good.

- Involving them in your team and your strategy.

Now that you have the information you need, you can go to stage 4 and decide if you want to engage, and if so, how you will win.

Stage 4: Confirm Fit and Decide to Engage or Not; Begin to Develop Team and Sales Strategy

This stage is important because you need to determine if you want to move forward and commit your time and company's limited resources (see Table 3-8).

Table 3-8. Overview of Stage 4: Confirming Fit and Deciding Whether to Engage or Not; Begin to Develop Team and Sales Strategy

Stage 4 Goals:
- **Decide to engage, confirm fit.**
- **Begin team building and strategy.**

Actions	Technology	Resources
• Match information from initial meeting to determine if it is a real opportunity and your chances of winning are good enough. • If you decide to engage, start building team and strategy to win the deal.	• LinkedIn • Salesforce.com • E-mail • Desktop video or web conferencing • Streaming • Social media • Laptop • iPad or tablet • Wireless	• Manager • Pre/post technical support • SMEs (subject matter experts) • Brochures • Case studies • References • S.C.O.O.P. strategy sheets • Previous Sales • Sweet spot profile

Skills

- Resource management
- Team selling
- Selling strategically using S.C.O.O.P.

You should have a set of criteria that you can compare any opportunity with to evaluate your chances of winning. Use items such as the following, but add your own unique criteria:

- Access to decision makers

- Realistic budget

- Useful relationships

- Technical fit

- Ability to service and support

- References in their industry

- Other

Taking the information you gained in the S.PRI.N.G. dialogue (as well as other relevant experience you and your company have), compare it to these variables. That will enable you to do a logical and analytical initial evaluation of the opportunity and your chances of winning it. Your goal is to arrive at a thumbs up/thumbs down decision.

BE HONEST ABOUT YOUR CHANCES

Great salespeople tend to think they can win anything and very rarely walk away from an opportunity. This is exacerbated when a salesperson doesn't have enough opportunity and becomes a bit desperate. (You can avoid this fate by prospecting often and well.) Use this stage to be as honest as possible with yourself about your chances of winning. You might be better off spending time finding and closing deals you have a better chance of winning.

Once this is done, you can begin to start building a team to win the sale.

Teams can include people from all parts of your company including service, support, training, finance, product management, executives, and more. It should also include a partner if your go-to-market strategy is through partners. It can also include the person who referred you if you if that is how you found out about the opportunity, or your coach. Some of the variables that might affect who is on your team are age and gender of the prospect, level of expertise in a certain area, size of the deal, specific characteristics of the deal (very technical or in a certain vertical), and more.

Sales is a team effort, and the best salespeople know which resources to use in what situations. Too many salespeople use too few resources, and/or they use them too late.

Bringing in a system engineer or SME (subject matter expert) to understand the technical aspects of a deal and to ask questions that have been unasked or not answered by the prospect can be invaluable.

With your team delineated, it's time to choose a strategy. You can choose from six strategies (Table 3-9).

Table 3-9. Prospecting Strategies

Strategy	When to Use
Head On	When you are in a position of clear strength because of product fit, relations, installed customer, or any other compelling reason.
Change the View	When you need to change the criteria because you are competitive, but not in a position of total strength.
End Around, or Divide and Conquer	When you need to get into the account but it is not through the current decision- makers.
Slow Down	When you have found out about the deal too late, or you are losing the business and need to delay the decision to give you time.
Win–Win	A philosophical approach that will differentiate you from the competition and engages the customer as a part of the strategy. Strategy of choice for when you have happy customers or when you have influenced the criteria early.
Walk	You can't win, so you will politely and professionally tell the prospect that you will not engage.

A great way to capture all of the information in this chapter is to use IPG's S.C.O.O.P. (strategic – comprehensive – online – optimized – process) form and methodology. As the acronym denotes, this is an automated form and process, integrated into Salesforce.com (and others if needed). It can also be used as a standalone Word document. It captures all the critical elements and information required to help you decide what strategy you should use, including (but not limited to):

- Fit to your sweet spot
- Decision process, players and their roles
- Tactics to win a deal

- Team
- Which strategy to use based upon strengths and weaknesses
- Traps set for the competition

There are vivid examples of this form and capability in Chapter 6.

Stage 5: Present, Propose, or Demonstrate a Solution

At this stage, you might have to do one or all three things: present, propose, or demonstrate (Table 3-10).

The presentation/proposal/demo stage gives you the opportunity to move your strategy forward; set traps for your competition; and address a prospect's priorities, needs, and criteria. It also lets you validate the seeds and traps you established in your S.PRI.N.G. dialogue.

Many people make the mistake of thinking this is where you make the sale. This is especially true in the advertising, digital or new media industry. A good demo, proposal, presentation, or mix of these is certainly essential (especially if the prospect's buying process makes this your only contact with them). In most cases, however, this is your opportunity to *prove* the capabilities you discussed and really showcase them. However, if prospects aren't receptive to you because you didn't do some of the work we have already discussed, it will be hard to move the sale forward.

Table 3-10. Overview of Stage 5: Presenting, Proposing, or Demonstrating a Solution

Stage 5 Goal:		
• **Present, propose, or demonstrate solution**		
Actions	**Technology**	**Resources**
• Provide a formal proposal or presentation with your unique solution. • Demonstrate the solution, showing off capabilities and return on investment (ROI). • Align above with information from S.PRI.N.G. dialogues and other sources. • Address priorities, needs, decision. process, decision criteria • Set traps for competition • Provide initial pricing • Align with your strategy • Trial close and/or gain next step to put you in position to win	• Desktop video or Web conferencing • Streaming • Social media • Laptop • iPad or tablet • Wireless • PowerPoint or other like offering • Screen capture • YouTube or other video • Online images or photos	• Management • Pre/post technical support • SMEs (subject matter experts) • Brochures • Case studies • References • Presentation planners • Channels • S.C.O.O.P. strategy sheets
Skills		
• Presentations and demonstration • Team selling • DiSC • Objection handling		

Use of Technology in This Stage

If you are selling technology, then demonstrating your technology obviously plays a significant role. Regardless, other technologies that help you sell take on a paramount role at this stage. Collaboration technologies (Web, video, audio conferencing, chat), PowerPoint (and similar technologies), the Internet/Web, and more, can make your presentation really stand out against the competition.

Since you often have to offer a proposal and provide pricing at this stage, having tools that automatically configure and price, as well as build a professional proposal, can really help you win business. There are also many pieces of technology (Dropbox, SharePoint, and others) that can enable team members to co-create your proposal or presentation. And you can be just about anywhere—in the client's office or at opposite ends of the world. These technologies are discussed in Chapter 6.

Presentation Skills

A good presentation achieves many things, including a positive emotional response from your prospects, setting traps for your competition, confirmation of what you have established in your previous interactions (including your S.PRI.N.G. dialogue), highlighting your unique value technically and financially, and more. You want people to be reacting like

this

and not this

A good flow for any presentation or proposal (over the phone, in person, via Web) is:

- Get feedback from the coach or account in shaping the presentation.

- Introduce people as if you were introducing guest speakers; have the prospect or customer introduce his own people.

- Give an overview of the agenda.

- Review and confirm understanding from S.PRI.N.G. dialogue and ask if anything has changed.

- Present your corporate pitch with benefits.

- Present your solution and the capabilities that are most unique to you—give benefits.

- Show your return on investment (ROI) and time to value (TTV).

- Provide references.

- Summarize the key points.

- Define the next steps.

The more time you and your team give to preparing for your presentation, the better it will be. It is like the cast of a Broadway show rehearsing before it performs—practice makes all the difference.

Figure 3-1 is a good planner to help you with your presentations. It ensures you take into consideration the room dynamics, attendees, materials, etc. It also helps the team member in charge of each aspect of the presentation.

What	Who	Notes
What is the objective of this presentation or demonstration?		
What is your game plan and strategy? How are you going to "wow" the prospect?		
Who is attending from the customer and your company? Do you need to bring people with you or can they attend virtually?		
Create agenda for meeting.		
Confirm attendees and avoid no-shows.		
Any materials that need to be sent to the customer.		
Communicate plan and roles with other attendees.		
Confirm the setting.		
Request special AV or other equipment for the demo.		
Other.		

Figure 3-1. Presentations logistics planner

The presentation organizer (Figure 3-2) delineates the details of the actual presentation. Use it in conjunction with the logistics planner above. Both are important. If you have a great presentation but are presenting in a bad environment, it won't go as well as you would like.

What	Who	Notes
How will you start? What will you do at the beginning to make a statement or impact? Will you use an "ice breaker"?		
Introduce your people in an illustrative way (like they were guest speakers).		
Give an overview of the agenda and ask prospects for confirmation, input, and if there are any changes they'd like.		
Ask what they want to have accomplished in the time together so they would feel comfortable buying you.		
Have the prospects introduce their people and their roles.		
Review and confirm your understanding of their current situation and their desires, priorities, and needs.		
Present your corporate pitch with modifications and benefits to their world.		
Present your solution with the top capabilities that are most relevant to the prospect and most unique to you.		
Potentially, demonstrate the top capabilities that are most relevant to the prospect and most unique to you.		
Show your ROI and TTV (time to value).		
Provide references.		
Q&A and summary. Make sure that all subjects they were interested in were covered.		
Define the next steps.		
Other.		

Figure 3-2. Presentation organizer.

THE VALUE OF THE DEMO

A great demonstration can win the deal. It should be customized as much as possible so the prospect can see their actual environment. (Jonathan's own experience, as well as those of several clients, suggests you will have an 80% close ratio when doing this.) Your demo, like your presentations, should start at a macro level explaining what your offer does and why it is better and then go into the details of how it works. Depending on the simplicity or complexity of your offer, you might want the person to try working with the system himself, but make sure it is simple because people can become confused and turned off if it is not.

One of Jonathan's favorite experiences was having the CEO of a well-known retailer come to a demonstration of his system and—15 minutes into the demo—telling his IT people, "I want it. Make it happen." Thirty days later he had a million-dollar deal at standard discount rates.

This is the stage at which you will have to deal with a prospect's initial objections, concerns, and issues. Fortunately, these can all be handled the same way via the following process (which will also be helpful during the negotiation stage):

1. Don't overreact.

2. Acknowledge the objection or issue.

3. Clarify. Ask questions to understand the issue and to lead the prospect to your response.

4. Respond. There are four main types of responses: Direct, Analogy, Forest from the Trees, U-Turn.

5. Verify/trial close. Confirm with the prospect he is satisfied with your answer and will move forward.

Note Many salespeople, and almost all technical support people, make the mistake of responding to an objection, or a seemingly benign question, without asking any questions. Quite often they can get away with this, but when they don't, it can really hurt. Why? Objections or questions can be meant to set you up and make you look bad.

Here is an example of handling an objection poorly:

Prospect: I am concerned about your timeframes to deliver.

Salesperson: We can deliver within 30 days without a problem.

Prospect: Your competition says they can do it within 2 weeks.

Even worse, the prospect says nothing about delivery dates, but uses it against you in the decision process.

Here's an example of handling an objection well:

Prospect: I am concerned about your timeframes to deliver.

Salesperson: I appreciate your candor. Can you tell me why it concerns you?

Prospect: Your competition says they can do it within 2 weeks.

Salesperson: We have delivered it sooner but the reason we usually quote 30 days is because of all the things that have to happen once you place an order, including ordering the network, preparing your site, training, and several other items for the installation to go properly. Can you see why we suggest 30 days?

Prospect: I do but if we take care of these things can you deliver in 2 weeks?

Salesperson: Yes, we can. Are you comfortable with that?

Prospect: Yes, I am.

It is also essential that you test the waters on how well your presentation is going by simply asking trial questions. This is especially true when you are presenting without any visual input because people can be distracted and/or doing other things while you are talking. Some examples of questions that validate whether your presentation is going well, or poorly, are:

- "What do you think?"
- "How do you feel about . . .?"
- "Can you share with me how you would use the capability I just described?"
- "Are there any questions before I move on?"

All of these, except the last, are open ended so people have to verbalize their thoughts and feelings. The last question is close ended, which requires a yes-or-no answer. Please use open-ended questions for the points in your presentation that are most important.

If your presentation goes well, you had the prospect involved and confirming that your solution would work for him, then you should have next steps that the prospect will take with you. Whatever the outcome, favorable or not, this needs to be factored into your strategy and tactics you will use to win the business.

Stage 6: Work Strategy

This stage is particularly important because you need to keep the prospect engaged and focused on your offering instead of focusing on other offers or even other initiatives (see table 3-11).

Table 3-11. Overview of Stage 6: Work Strategy

Stage 6 Goal: • **Work the sales strategy.**		
Actions	**Technology**	**Resources**
• Using S.C.O.O.P., meet more often with team as the decision comes nearer. • Person in charge holds team accountable to execute on actions, including executives. • If using a "Change the View" strategy, begin ideation of the "Change the View" tactic. • Continue to develop the coach. • If there is a dramatic change in circumstances (either good or bad) evaluate a strategy change and supporting tactic(s).	• Desktop video or Web conferencing • Streaming • Social media • Laptop • iPad or tablet • Wireless	• Management • Pre/post technical support • SMEs (subject matter experts) • Brochures • Case studies • References • Presentation planners • Channels • S.C.O.O.P. strategy sheets
Skills		
• Selling Strategically/S.C.O.O.P. • Team selling • Objection handling • Time management		

This stage can make or break the sale and all the efforts you have made up to this point. There are many reasons a deal can go astray. Depending upon the complexity of your product, the size of the company you are selling to, your relationships, the strength/timing of the compelling event—and many other variables out of anyone's control (weather, bad earnings, a recession, somebody leaving the company, etc.)—this stage could be very short or very long. It is easy for the prospect to put you off in this stage, get distracted, or for you to go into a "black hole" where nothing seems to get done. It is during this stage that you must have a coach so you can be informed about what is happening with the opportunity.

Regardless, you should have a list of actions or tactics that keep you top of mind, differentiate you, and get the prospect more involved with you. What you want is more TE³M (Time – Energy – Emotion – Ego – Money) from the prospect than the competition is getting. This is important because the more TE³M somebody gives you during the sales process, the more they want to get a return on their investment. It also allows you to build a stronger relationship and hopefully keep the prospect away from your competition.

TE³M is made up of a series of small to big or minor to significant events and actions that are relevant to the prospect, and favor you. These should be well defined and chosen based on the strategy. Here is a good example. Let's say you have identified that you win business more often when a prospect visits your corporate headquarters, meets with your support team, and talks to references. You also know the decision-maker is a High-i on the DiSC grid, so you want to do some entertaining. Each of these steps addresses some or all aspects of TE³M, all of which makes it harder for them to say "no" at the end. As a result, you make it a high priority to get the prospect to agree to a visit to the main office.

TE³M is even more important if a prospect is remote from you, and/or when the sales cycle is long. It is easy to lose sight of the opportunity if you are working other deals, and it is even easier for them to lose sight of you. You can lose the deal simply because your competition is paying more attention, or visits more often. You should punctuate larger events such as site visits or lunches with smaller actions like sending relevant e-mails, setting up agreed upon check-in meetings, asking for some information from them or anything else that keeps the prospect engaged.

Technology should play an important role in this stage because you can use collaboration to stay in touch remotely. You can use the Web to stay on top of events occurring in the client's business and use them to stay in touch or show the value of your offer. You could also record or send a recording of something relative to the client and helpful to you. If they are close by, you should visit or socialize with them if they are so inclined.

How important is this stage? Here's a story. When I (Jonathan) was a director of sales for PictureTel, a videoconferencing company, I and my salesperson had sold and installed two systems in the City University of

New York (CUNY) administrative offices. And they loved them—so much so that our contacts introduced us to the top people of the CUNY campuses. We wined and dined them at one of the oldest restaurants in New York City and it went extremely well. CUNY is a city government institute, so it took a very long time to decide and process an order. We were very busy, felt confident about our position, and we forgot to stay in touch and stay active. We found out the ramifications of doing so when we read an article in one of the industry journals that our competitor had just won a $1,000,000 deal at CUNY. Needless to say, we never lost sight of another big deal.

Stage 7. Negotiate and Close

If you have done everything correctly up to this point, then a negotiation and close should be a fait accompli. The prospect has fairly certainly decided he will be going with you (or wouldn't be negotiating) but he wants to negotiate the best terms for himself and his company (see Table 3-12).

Table 3-12. Overview of Stage 7: Negotiating and Closing

Stage 7 Goal:		
• **Negotiate successfully and close.**		
Actions	**Technology**	**Resources**
• If not done already, deliver terms and conditions. • Put team together to negotiate. • Meet with the prospect's negotiating team if not done so already. • Establish negotiation strategy.	• Desktop video or Web conferencing • Laptop • iPad or tablet • Wireless	• Management • Legal • Channels • Finance • Sales ops if special deal required • S.C.O.O.P. strategy sheets
Skills		
• Selling Strategically/S.C.O.O.P. • Negotiations • Objection handling		

There are certainly exceptions to this. Companies can change their minds if a negotiation becomes problematic. Nor are we suggesting that negotiations are easy. However, like other parts of the selling process, negotiations don't happen in a void. The negotiation is the end result of a selling process that should help both parties feel satisfied with what they have achieved and negotiated for. But negotiations can be complicated and stressful. Some of the variables that come to play in a negotiation are:

- The level of trust between the negotiating parties

- The different personalities of the people involved: DiSC

- How well you qualified the deal and established the *unique value* of your solution. If this has not been done, then you are a commodity to them and vulnerable to becoming very disadvantaged on price.

- The business and monetary issues that are involved, or how much value your offer brings to them in dollars and cents. Will your offer make or save them a lot of money in comparison to what they will pay? If so, you can negotiate to your value, which is a good thing.

- How well the salesperson has anticipated issues and answered them. Most of the issues that come up in a negotiation should have been addressed during the sales cycles. By addressing them earlier, you should probably have an easier time handling them. For example, if you have made it clear that discounts are tied to volumes, people will know they can't press too hard on a better price for a lower volume of business.

- The paradigm from which the companies are negotiating. Most companies are respectful of a vendor's priorities and need to negotiate something that works for both parties. However, there are some companies that couldn't care less and will do everything and anything to get the most from you.

- Time pressures and tactics. Whoever has the most pressure to close a deal in a certain amount of time is in a weaker position while negotiating because that date has more importance than the negotiation itself.

- Your ability to handle objections as part of a negotiation. All issues that come up in a negotiation can be handled as objections.

- The ability to avoid being commoditized by addressing the business, political, and personal values of your solution. Your value can have many levels. The more it is related to business and personal issues, the more value you have and the better position you are in, if you are aware of it.

Based on these variables, and others seen in the Negotiation Planner, you can then decide what strategy you want to use. There are four common types of negotiation strategies. You use these depending on the circumstances involved.

1. **Hard:** Both positions take firm stances on issues and won't budge. This can create acrimony and bad relationships.

2. **Soft:** One party (usually the **vendor**) caves in and gives everything. Only one party wins.

3. **Conditional** (most common): **Each** party gives in on certain points to get something in return. Also known as Give/Get.

4. **Mutual Benefit:** As much a **philosophy** as it is approach, each party endeavors to create something unique that favors both parties and is more than just a conditional buy–sell agreement.

Once you decide on one strategy, the other strategies revert to tactics to support your chosen strategy. For example, you can decide on a hard strategy but decide to play it soft on a particular issue.

Can you describe different situations in which each of these is used most often in your company?

Figure 3-3 is a very helpful exercise that will help you choose and prepare the best negotiation strategies to use to win more business. The words in the boxes are examples—fill in your own responses based on your unique situation.

Hard: Both positions take firm stances on issues and won't budge.

> For example, happy customer, competition has been eliminated, you have what they need, or there is nothing left to give.

Soft: One party (usually the vendor) caves in and gives everything.

> For example, you made some mistakes and want to make amends, or it is a way to gain a large account, or you will make up the lost revenue or margin in the future, or you need to close as much business as possible by the end of your quarter or fiscal year.

Give/Get: Each party gives in to certain points to get something in return. Most commonly used. The hard and soft strategies become tactics.

> For example, you might stay firm on your price, but soft on extra training. Or you might give them additional services but you will want to get a bigger order or have the order filled sooner.

Mutual Benefit: As much a philosophy as it is approach, each party endeavors to create something unique that favors both parties and is more than just a Give/Get agreement. Used most often with satisfied customers or because you are in such a good position with a prospect that you can pursue something even more than just their buying your services.

> For example, you might co-create a new capability and give them a 1-year exclusive on it. Or if they give you a larger order, you might reciprocate by giving them business from your company.

Figure 3-3. Choosing and preparing negotiation strategies.

Give/Get Tactics

As mentioned, the most common strategy used is the conditional or Give/Get. This strategy involves a series of back and forth, giving and getting, and providing alternative offers on the different issues that a prospect has. For example, if a prospect says she wants a 10% discount, you might respond with an alternative offer of 4% and filling the order faster than it might otherwise take. Or you might ask for a larger order if you were to give 10%. You could even give somebody something she wants (10% discount) in return for something you want (e.g., payment up front).

Table 3-13 can help you prepare for your Give/Get negotiation.

Table 3-13. Give/Get Tactics

The Customer Wants	Your Alternative Offer	Get from the Customer
Better price	Services that cost you less and are beneficial to the customer	The order right away
Faster delivery	A date in between your offer and their request	Some money up front
Pilot or trial	Install in stages	Higher price if they only go with smaller deal

DiSC Analysis

Another important variable is a prospect's DiSC style. You should be as sensitive to DiSC in this stage as in all others, particularly when the prospect introduces a person into the negotiation you have never met before. For example, if a deal becomes particularly technical or financial, a High-C behavior style might get involved. If you are not very High-C, it would be wise to get a High-C with a technical or financial background involved.

Figure 3-4 is a quick reference/reminder of DiSC styles and how they express themselves.

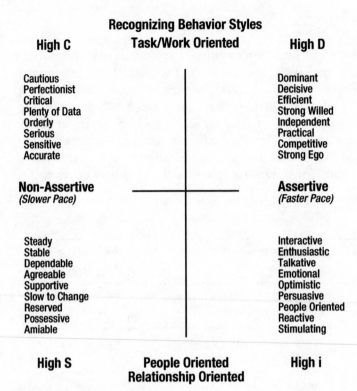

Recognizing Behavior Styles

High C	Task/Work Oriented	High D
Cautious		Dominant
Perfectionist		Decisive
Critical		Efficient
Plenty of Data		Strong Willed
Orderly		Independent
Serious		Practical
Sensitive		Competitive
Accurate		Strong Ego
Non-Assertive		**Assertive**
(Slower Pace)		*(Faster Pace)*
Steady		Interactive
Stable		Enthusiastic
Dependable		Talkative
Agreeable		Emotional
Supportive		Optimistic
Slow to Change		Persuasive
Reserved		People Oriented
Possessive		Reactive
Amiable		Stimulating
High S	People Oriented	High i
	Relationship Oriented	

Figure 3-4. DiSC styles.

Here's a story that illustrates how important DiSC is in a negotiation. We were negotiating with a purchasing agent who was a High-S (Steadfast). We were under much of pressure to close this large and profitable deal, and being High-Ds (Dominant), we were pushing hard. Jonathan and his manager went to meet with the prospect. We asked him when he was going to make a decision and he said, "I have to put it in the oven and let it bake." We both responded at the same time by saying, "Do you think you could put it in the microwave?" and we all started laughing. This broke the ice for all of us, and we were able to slow down and explain, step by step, how we would install our solution with very little risk. We walked out with the order.

Resistance in Negotiations

People always ask how to handle a particular issue, problem, or resistance during a negotiation. Our first suggestion is that there is no such thing as a negotiation issue, that they are all objections in a different form. Whether it is a simple "issue" like wanting to have a longer payment term (45 days vs. 30) to a very complex issue (rights to your intellectual property), they can all be handled as objections. You should prepare for a negotiation by anticipating the issues, concerns, objections, and tactics (more on this later).

The best way to handle any objection or issue is via this four-step process we discussed earlier in this chapter:

1. Acknowledge the objection or issue.

2. Clarify. Ask questions to understand the issue and to lead the prospect to your response.

3. Respond. As mentioned previously, there are four main types of responses: Direct, Analogy, Forest from the Trees, U-Turn.

4. Verify/trial close. Confirm with the prospect she is satisfied with your answer and will move forward.

Here's how it might go:

Customer: Your price is too high.

You: **(Acknowledge)** I appreciate your candor.

You: **(Clarify)** May I ask you some questions to understand this better? [Ask in the following order until you get to the heart of the matter.]

   1. "Can you tell me more?"

   2. "Are you speaking about a specific item in our costs?"

   3. "Are you comparing us to another alternative or is it more than your budget allows?"

   4. "Have you compared the cost to what you will get for that?"

5. "How much more are we in dollars and cents?"

6. "Are there any other concerns you have?"

Once you have an idea of what the objection is about, you can use a number of strategies to regain the sale.

You: **(Respond)**

1. [Direct] "The reason our offer is more expensive is because of all the capability it has and the support that is included to make sure your business requirements will be addressed."

2. [Analogy] "Your company is known as one of the best in your industry, and justifiably, because of all you bring to the table. You are able to charge a higher price because of what your products do for your customers. Similarly, our company . . ."

3. [Forest from the Trees] "You are right—we are more expensive. But I think it is important to look at what you get for that additional expense: . . ."

[U-Turn] "Based upon what I know about your requirements and goals, I would be suspicious of any offer that was the cheapest, because it's likely that something is missing that is important to you. Let's go over your requirements again . . ."

You: **(Verify/trial close)** "I hope I have done a better job of explaining why we are more expensive. What would you say if we . . ." [perhaps offer a Give/Get but only if you think it's necessary]

Issues, resistances, and problems can be different from tactics. A tactic is something someone does to put themselves in a better position to get what he or she wants. Professional negotiators are taught tactics to put you on the defensive and give them an advantage. Some examples are:

1. Time pressures (yours, not theirs) so they delay: They tell you they are in no rush but know you are so that you will make concessions to get the order sooner.

2. Very low offer: They offer to pay 50% of your proposal.

3. Playing you between two people in their company: They say they have to talk to others to get their opinion to make you feel insecure when they may not have to do so at all.

4. Strong demands: They become belligerent and inflexible. For example, they say you have to reduce your price "just because" they ask.

5. Technical change: They change the specs on a deal that costs you more but they want it for the same price.

6. Financial change: They want to rent it or pay over a longer time frame vs. the net 30 terms you have offered.

7. Lack of authority: They tell you it is not their decision and you have to talk to others.

8. Tough guy approach: Similar to strong demands.

9. Change of negotiators: The prospect changes negotiators to throw you off and have you start all over again.

10. Buyer becomes unresponsive: The buyer intentionally doesn't respond to make you feel insecure so you will make more concessions.

11. Ask for concession at end of process: The prospect waits intentionally to wear you down because he knows you want the deal.

12. Reduce size of order at end of process: But they want the same discount percentage or services.

You should not go into a negotiation without being prepared for these tactics and how you will handle them. Nor should you negotiate without being mindful of the prospect's priorities, needs, and the value you bring.

Please use Figure 3-5 to help you prepare for your future negotiations. It is also available at our website www.ipgtraining.com/usingtechnologytosell.

Key Contact	Contact #2	Contact #3
Title	Title	Title
Role in Decision	Role in Decision	Role in Decision
Personality Profile (DiSC)	Personality Profile (DiSC)	Personality Profile (DiSC)

Describe current customer environment:

_____

Describe competition:

_____

Opportunity Size	Length of Commitment You Are Looking For	Product(s) and Services Being Used/Proposed	Revenue Running Through Your Product(s)

Describe your strategy (Hard, Soft, Give/Get, Mutual Benefit):

_____

How will you begin the negotiation? (What is the key person's DiSC style; how strong is your relationship; do you want to position a Mutual Benefit approach; do you need to ask their priorities, needs, gain, other)

What is the compelling event and timing? (Business, Financial, Political/Personal, DiSC)	Benefits of Your Offer? What is unique that the competition can't offer?	What Happens if They Don't Go with You? (Business, financial, political/personal, DiSC)

Objections/Issues/ Concerns/Tactics	How Will You Respond? (What questions will you ask before you respond)	Who Will Handle

Willing to Give for a Get Alternative Offers	Not Willing to Give (What is your bottom line?)

When do you need to close by and what will be the next steps you recommend if you can't close the deal on this call?

Figure 3-5. IPG's negotiation planner.

Since this is the last step in the process, it is imperative for you to bring all the skills we have discussed to bear so the negotiation goes as well as possible in the shortest appropriate time. Using this form will help that happen. Also having someone with you while you negotiate can help as well.

Technologies Used in Selling

Conferencing, Multimedia, Screencasting, Social Media, and More

This chapter covers a broad range of technology and our recommended approaches underpinning today's best sales methods. Technology has enabled increasingly rich sales content delivery for creative and engaging interactions with your customers and prospects. Ignoring this wealth of opportunity to drive interesting discussions and new leads is now a risk. Even if you are not getting up to speed with these technologies, we can guarantee your competitors will be, so don't get left behind. The technologies we discuss in this chapter also provide more flexibility than ever before and are brilliantly suited for working in an increasingly globalized business world. Imagine being able to instantly call in the help of an expert based in China while you work from your home in Boston and your client is in her office in New York. We explore a number of tools you can use to enhance your sales process, cover more ground than ever before, and ultimately win more business.

A Confused Mind Always Says No

When faced with the variety of sales-assisting technology now available, salespeople usually respond in one of two ways:

- "Aaarrrggghhh!"

- "Wow! Now, how do I pick which one to use from these 20 options?"

These are normal reactions to the boundless choices that the age of technology has created. Whereas ten years ago we would have had a few options on types of technology, we now have an incredible array that only the truly devoted techie can keep up with. As a result, many of us specialize in what we enjoy the most or where we are most familiar—sometimes to our own detriment.

As you'll see in this chapter, the use of technology in selling can help you:

- Improve how you sell, resulting in shorter sales cycles, larger deals, or closing more opportunities.

- Find opportunities more easily.

- Reach more people to sell to.

- Keep up to speed with customers and key contacts.

- Avoid wasting time and give you more time to sell or enjoy life.

- Provide better customer service.

- Qualify and nurture leads.

- Keep customers and prospects abreast of your product and service offerings.

- Differentiate you as a better salesperson than others.

- Give you an advantage of faster and better quality responses.

Think of Your Customer Base

It's human nature to be consumed by your own life and its activities and challenges. That means you need to have some prompts to remind yourself that sales is about the customer and his or her priorities, needs, goals, and time, not yours. Although that may be a blindingly obvious statement, we constantly find it to be an issue with salespeople, sales units, and businesses in general. Unless you are Apple and had Steve Jobs' vision, if you do things that matter to you instead of the customer, then you will be worse off. Later in this chapter we cover some standard approaches you should adopt, but for now take a moment to consider your reaction after you read the next two paragraphs.

Look at Things from Your Customer's Point of View

Paramount to evaluating which technology you decide to employ is to see things from your prospect's or customer's point of view. When using a certain technology, ask yourself if you find it comfortable and appealing to use. For example, if you are using a video call, how simple is it to set up and carry out the call? Is the quality of the video and audio acceptable? If you were being sold to, would you want to use the same technology because it is clean and simple, or do you find it cumbersome and slow?

Always consider whether the technology works for all parties. Otherwise, you may be causing needless frustration and may start your interaction in a negative way. For the same reason, you should feel comfortable with what you use on a technical level, given that if anything goes wrong, you may need to take on the role of technical support in fixing it. Naturally, you'll want to do some pilot runs to make sure everything works just as you expect it to. Also, you may want to check what support is offered from the technology provider beforehand and how to access it. To continue with the video call example, if you are using Ten Hands to carry out a video call with a customer, make sure you understand how to access his or her support quickly and easily in case any problems arise at the time of use.

Our selling process, described in Chapter 2, discussed what to use and when. Now align that with what you know about *your* customers. Choose what they will respond to, match up to their DiSC style (see Chapter 2), and above all choose personal content and products that can help you make the customer feel unique.

Example: Never Assume

Here is a great example of why you should never make assumptions about your decision maker's motivations for buying. An acquaintance who sells conferencing services was trying to close a large opportunity for Cisco's TelePresence video conferencing. This is the highest-end, latest tech in HD video conferencing.

The challenge was that he didn't fully understand the main decision-maker's needs or buying criteria. He assumed that the decision-maker had his own incentives to buy this cutting-edge video service. At the next meeting, my acquaintance simply asked, "What technology do you like to use for communication?"

The buyer's response: "I don't see the value in HD video. I much prefer Web-based. I've been given this project and it's all about the executive team reducing their first-class travel, so this HD video solution is being geared more toward meeting their preferences than mine." This was completely different from what my contact had assumed and asking this simple question revealed the valuable understanding that the decision-maker's needs were not those driving the buying criteria.

To tailor his approach to the decision-maker's needs during the sales process, he managed all the non–face-to-face meetings using Cisco WebEx, including the meeting in which he won their business! The lesson is, never assume that the reason a business wants something matches what the decision-maker personally wants or prefers. In this case, the salesperson, with the right questioning, was able to uncover the needs of all of the stakeholders and match the sales process and proposal to these to successfully win the business.

Technologies

Let's now look at a number of relevant technologies and the details of some providers. Also included is our advice on when to use or indeed when not to use each of them.

- Internet

- E-mail

- Databases and customer relationship management (CRM)

- Conferencing and collaboration

- Video and unified communications (UC)—alternatives to conferencing

- Video streaming online

- Visual media

- Self-generated multimedia content

- Screencasting

- Social media

- Search engine optimization (SEO)

- Tablets and smartphones

- Networking groups

- Presentation technologies

- E-mail and marketing campaigns

- Cloud technology

Internet

As a sales tool the Internet is unrivaled; for salespeople it is all about using it in the most time-efficient and productive way. You already know the power of the internet, so let's look at five key ways it can help you increase your sales.

1. Get the Internet Working for You

Google Alerts (www.google.com/alerts) is a fantastic tool that every single salesperson should be using, no question. The basic premise is that Google will go to work for you by finding content across the entire Internet based on keywords you provide; the replies come back in e-mails for which you can set the frequency. It does take a little trial and error to find a solid middle ground, as you can end up with too much or too little information.

Our tip is to set it for your target industry, the job function you are selling to, the events you want to follow, and the region or location you are working in.

Example: Sales Training

We sell sales training globally but we want to work mainly in the UK and the USA.

- Jonathan sets his Google Alerts to "Sales VP, US."
- Martin sets his to "Head of Sales, UK."

Every time we get a notification of a new appointment to a senior sales position, we send that person an e-mail. All we do is congratulate them on the new position and tell them we will contact them in a month to discuss how we can help. We get just over a 20% hit rate on this. It takes almost no time, and our best buyers are those new to the role because they want to make an immediate impact.

2. Know Your Competition

It never ceases to amaze us that so few salespeople spend any time on competitors' websites. A little research here provides a continuous source of advantage if you look for the right things. Most people will look at the competitors' product or service offerings and move on. For me, that's just getting started. Being the best at what you do is all about finding the small differences and turning them into big advantages.

Note We have larger competitors who spend a lot of time and money doing in-depth research on sales or sales training, which they offer free online in return for your name and e-mail. That gives us access to, and the benefit of, the same information they give their own salespeople. Thank you!

Example—Technology Wins with No Technology

I (Martin) was working for a dominant player in the UK when we lost a big chunk of business to more aggressive, smaller companies that had recently set up in the UK. We sold conferencing, a technology services sale, but we were now getting beaten on price in what had become a commoditized space. To counter this, I analyzed our competitors' websites, brochures, blogs, customer service, and just about everything else. What became apparent was their complete lack of understanding of users being people with discrete requirements and responsibilities.

Treating potential buyers as human beings is something I have always cared deeply about and I put it at the forefront of our sales strategy. We went to market with a proposition about enabling people in their roles instead of just "push the button" training, which is what the competition was doing.

That year, our closure rate with this approach was 87% against 23% the previous year. This was outstanding, but actually we were selling exactly the same product as the year before with a higher price point. The difference was that we were selling the value of the technology to individual users.

3. Find the Small Wins

We discuss social media in more depth in the next chapter, but for now, a very simple tip is to check LinkedIn for your prospect's profile. The insight you gain can be very powerful. People's biographies are a good indicator of their DiSC style; how open they are is a good indicator of how straight a talker they are or what their work persona is. The same is true for their voice-mail message and e-mail auto-signatures. Observational skills are key—look for all the small indicators that will allow you to understand how to adjust your own behavior, presentations, and proposals to a particular person.

4. Understand Your Target Market

The more you know about the industry you're selling into, the more you can offer. This is another good one for Google Alerts. Set it for the industry, company name, or the city the prospect lives in. The more relevant information in your arsenal, the stronger your position will be. Nothing that we mention in this book is designed to make things take longer; it's all about doing the right things to be more efficient. Are you registered for all the industry newsletters, blogs, events, and websites? Are you in the same mindset as your target market? If not, then make the changes to get there. If you can find out where your target audience goes online, then you can join them there and create a strong awareness of your services. The Internet can help you do that in numerous ways, so there's no excuse for not having at least a general knowledge of your field.

5. Find Legitimate Reasons to Call

When prospecting, it is essential to be concise. The main thing you want to establish is immediate credibility. That helps you gain the person's interest. There are lots of ways to do this, but the important thing is not to overthink this. Consider how you like to be sold to, or think about a good call you received. What you'll discover is that the more salespeople relate to the prospect instead of themselves and their products, the better.

You can find legitimate, prospect-centered reasons to call by scouring the Internet for these items:

- Google Alerts that provide news
- Industry announcements gained by subscribing to industry news
- Changes in content on the prospect's website
- Competitor changes that may be of interest to the prospect
- New innovation in the prospect's field
- Changes to the prospect's own business
- Referrals

The small details are often the main reasons you can win business; to find them get the Internet working for you and find your edge.

E-mail

We discuss this more in the Appendix, but we believe as a communication tool, e-mail has become too guided by our own agendas. We would argue it has always been that way; when e-mail arrived did anyone tell you which standards to adopt? In most cases, that probably didn't happen. We were left to figure "e-mail" out for ourselves, and we all too often view it as a personal, not a customer, tool. Human nature being what it is, we often do things on our time, in our own way. For salespeople, that is not acceptable; we need to avoid the common issues we create for ourselves. Following are three things to keep in mind, always, as you use e-mail to prospect, sell, and close.

1. Always Keep in Mind: "Speed of response, quality of response"

In sales, your work e-mail—like your work self—needs to be proactive, put customer service first, and be ultra-responsive. Many non–customer-facing people use e-mail as an "as and when" tool, that is, a tool they use at their discretion but not necessarily in the best interests of the customer. In sales, we need to treat it as something to impress people with. To accomplish this, adopt a simple approach: Respond as quickly as you can and with the appropriate quality. Recognize that not everyone is the same; for some people, not receiving a reply for a day or even a few hours can feel like they're being ignored.

These are the guidelines I follow:

- If I see a prospect or customer in the morning, I send her the meeting summary, appropriate content, and follow-up date and time as soon as I'm back in the office. That's *before* I do anything else.

- If I see a prospect or customer in the afternoon, I use the same approach, but I try to send the response in the early evening or by 10:00 a.m. the next morning if it's a late meeting or if I have to travel.

- If a customer e-mails me but I don't have an immediate answer, I always, *always* send a bridging e-mail. For example, "'I will get back to you by Thursday."

"Speed of response, quality of response." It is a simple mantra that has won me a great deal of business, but cost me early in my career before I followed it. It is also a fantastic management tool for teams.

2. Don't Take the Risk

Do you know what your competitor is doing?

Of course you don't, so why take the risk? If you wait 2 days after a meeting to send the outcome but your competitor does it within 2 hours, then who looks better?

This takes point no. 1—speed of response, quality of response—and flips it on its head. It's another way to think about it: consider the risks of not responding promptly and with care. If you are not attending to your customers' needs, you can guarantee that at some point, someone else will.

Eliminate the potential. It may be the thing that makes the difference or it may not, but it's within your control so why take the risk?

3. Use the Out-of-Office Message

If you do not use your out-of-office message when you are out for a half-day, few hours, or on holiday, then you should start right now. It is not just a functional activity; when used correctly it can be highly effective. My usual approach is to tell people to call my mobile when I am out and about visiting people. It generally means I will pick up any urgent calls and respond to everything else immediately on my return. Obviously, mobile e-mail means we need to use the out-of-office message less. You should also let people know who to reach out to if you are not available. Service and accounts billable/payable are two important areas for which people should have contact information.

When you do go for longer breaks, make sure you detail to the person covering for you what your expectations are. If the person is not up to the mark, then choose someone else; your standards should not alter because you are away.

4. Employ the "No Scroll" Rule in E-mails

There is a very simple winning formula for structuring your e-mails for prospecting (this work for both calls and e-mails): Your e-mail should be no longer than the preview window you get on your inbox. This is also called "above the fold," which refers to the location of the top news article or picture on the upper half of the front page of a newspaper. In the case of webpages, it's the part of a page that's visible on your screen without scrolling. We apply the same principle to e-mail—the key information should appear on the recipient's screen without having to scroll down.

Why has this approach proven effective?

If the message is longer, reading it puts people. Plus, prospects don't know you yet. So even if you have a great message, you don't need to throw everything at them; all you want is for them to agree to meet you or talk to you.

Refining your message will make you better at what you do. Here's how.

Establish Credibility

This links back to the legitimate reasons to call that we discussed earlier in this chapter. Finding legitimate, prospect-centered reasons to contact your customers or prospects is crucial in establishing your credibility and gaining their trust. If you understand your customers and monitor their changing needs, it will become second-nature to contact them whenever you have an idea they will be interested in discussing.

You can establish credibility using e-mail by following this approach combined with those described later. You need to begin your e-mail messages with something that makes the people receiving them pay attention. Ideally, this should be about them, their business, their industry, or something you know they will be interested in.

Offer Three Benefits

Offer three benefits in three lines only. The benefits can all be about your offering; this can work very well. But if you want to really knock it out of the park then split the benefits accordingly:

- **Them**. Show prospects how they would gain from meeting with you. This could be based on information and knowledge you have.

- **You**. Describe past work you or your company has done, or something about your experience.

- **Product**. Say something you have that should interest them. You do not need to make this about any product or service by name; it should be about the upside.

Close for an Action

Suggest you meet.

It is as simple as that. Do not oversell; do not overwrite. Everyone is time-conscious, so until you earn the right to take up more of their time, don't expect people to read or care about lots of content.

Example One: IPG Training

Jonathan's core business at IPG is sales training. Here's a typical e-mail message he might send to prospects:

Subject Line: Your Recent Blog

Dear Martin,

I noticed your blog entry about sales challenges, so I thought you would be interested in what I do:

- *Having worked with companies ABC and XYZ, we can offer you some additional insights to selling to the client without alienating the agency.*
- *At IPG, we have trained more than 17,000 employees and worked in 23 countries. This expertise brings you a broader, unique, and much more compelling way of selling.*
- *Everyone at IPG is an award-winning salesperson. We've all been the best in our respective fields; we come with ideas that drive sales.*

Can we set up a 15-minute introductory chat? I am free next Thursday if that works for you. If not, please let me know what would work better.

Kind regards,

Jonathan London

President, IPG Training

P.S. Check out what three industry leaders say about us at ...

Example Two: TSI Squared

Martin's business, TSI, offers a conferencing savings solution.

Dear Jonathan,

We have just finished a project for X, which I thought you may be interested in.

- We have identified some similarities with your company, and I want to share the findings of our research.

- On average, we save companies more than 54% on their costs, both direct and hidden.

- We create as well as consult. You can read more here: http://www.tsisquared.com/client_testimonials.html

I am keen to involve Ben from company X. Could you offer me some times you are free on Thursday and Friday, when Ben is available?

Kind regards,

Martin Lucas

Owner, TSI Squared

In both examples, we have a solution we want to sell, but we're positioning based on intrigue. As with any messaging, it is important not to let people make assumptions. Assumptions are created as soon as we say what we do. Human nature is such that we refer to our last good or bad experience—in this case, the prospect's last sales experience, so until you earn the right to get to pitch them what you do and build more of an emotional connection, sell the benefits, not the bore!

Databases and CRM

A professional contact database is essential for keeping track of contacts and employing customer relationship management (CRM). Although the database(s) you use and your CRM system or plan can be separate things, they work together to form your sales contact strategy. In some businesses, your CRM system and contact database are integrated and the terms are then used interchangeably. For smaller companies, you may have a simple offline database in Outlook or Excel and a CRM plan that you apply to this database.

Either way, your contact database is vital in keeping the dialogue moving. If you have a following on social media—your website, blog, or newsletter—then keep it fresh, educational, insightful, and fun. You can divide your customers and prospects into meaningful groups (say, by industry or job role—or both!) and target them with messaging tailored to their specific needs and profile.

A note using social media for CRM. There is almost no such thing as too much communication on social media, as people can pick and choose what they are interested in. That said, your messaging *must* be interesting and relevant to break through all the other information your audience receives.

CRM

CRM (customer relationship management) is key; contact with new and existing clients will keep them mindful of you and your solution and help show how much care and attention you put into it. Two of the worst habits salespeople can fall into are having poor response times and not delivering when they say they will. CRM is a vital tool to make sure you deliver and do it well.

CRM is also a flow for prospecting, and you may be lucky enough to have an internal CRM system in your company. These vary widely and can often be customized for your business, and because of this we can't comment on the use of company-specific CRM systems. However, the principles of using databases for CRM are widely applicable, so you will be able to apply the following guidance regardless of which database you use.

If you don't have a company-specific contact database, your mothership for this is generally Salesforce.com. Salesforce.com is an all-encompassing CRM online system. It covers everything from your database to pipeline reporting, contact management, group messaging, and many other components. Not only is it good for database management, but it also integrates with more than 1,700 partners, which makes your flow from database to research to prospecting to contact an integrated and efficient approach.

Although a mountain of online CRM tools is available, ranging from tools for small business such as Goldmine to customized, feature-rich, integrated CRM systems such as Oracle, we here focus on Salesforce.com and some of its most popular partners. Remember, you can apply the same principles regardless of which tool you use.

Here are some ways Salesforce.com and a few of its partners can help you.

Salesforce.com—Your Personal Contact Database

Using Salesforce.com as your database platform for contact management, closed orders, and pipeline reporting is paramount to the success of a good sales organization and person. You can upload everything into Salesforce.com and schedule callbacks and activities. As a management tool, the upsides are similar, not least if someone is out sick or leaves the company because you can readily pick up what needs to be done. E-mail calendars and Excel files may work for some but using them as a preferred method is not a not a productive or controlled way to be a leading salesperson.

Hoover's Business Database

Easily integrated into Salesforce.com, Hoover's offers an endless array of database content, company information, and financial and industry data. It is excellent for creating mailing lists, sourcing opportunities, and adding to your CRM.

LexisNexis

The Nexis service goes a step beyond Hoover's in that it aggregates a huge range of business and news information sources and databases into a single, searchable repository. That means you get the widest range of information in one place. It allows you to deeply research individual businesses, build targeted lists of companies and individuals to prospect from, and set up keyword and industry alerts to inform you when something of interest happens. This is a great way to track your key clients and prospects and any developments in their business or industry, which can create new opportunities and points of discussion. People are always impressed if you are informed and know something about their business; failing to be informed can be fatal.

OneSource

OneSource offers a product called iSell that delivers an automated feed of prospecting personalized to each salesperson's needs—by target industry, company size, geography, and more—and provides a depth of contact details and other information about each contact and company. iSell includes relevant sales triggers such as new funding, changes to the executive team, and other key events in real-time so you can identify new opportunities and initiate discussions at the right time.

As previously mentioned, Salesforce.com is not the only product out there. However, it is the one we have used for most of our careers and it works incredibly well, especially in conjunction with some of the great services listed previously. Whatever combination of CRM and databases you use, it should be viewed as your central hub in driving, controlling, and generating contact with prospects and clients and revenue.

You may also want to consider leveraging your contact database to send out newsletters to your customer base or targeted groups within this. Let's have a quick look at tools and best practice for creating newsletters.

Publishing Software

Adobe Acrobat and Adobe Publishing are our preferred software for the creation of newsletter and sales materials. Both are fantastic at generating something beyond a plain Word document, and they allow you to customize to each and every client. These tools are simple to use. They are very much like using Word, with which you are most likely already very familiar. Don't worry too much about the design of your newsletter—it can simply be text-based with your company logo appearing at the top, and your marketing department will be able to provide you with scalable images if needed. You can use these tools whether you are creating a newsletter to send online or in print.

A PDF file looks polished and has a final edge to it; if you combine this with customization, then you can add to your sales value.

Newsletters

From a sales perspective, newsletters can be a great way to keep your contacts up to date with new products or services, industry developments, special offers, testimonials, and more. This is perfect for reaching a wide audience, and you can also target specific customer groups with information tailored to them. An e-newsletter arriving in someone's e-mail inbox, or one that arrives in hard copy, gives a more personal impression than social media updates or a blog, for example, because it is delivered directly to your contacts. If you follow our tips that follow, you will have the best chance of successfully using newsletters to unearth new sales opportunities and revenues.

We recommend that newsletters are issued no more frequently than monthly, and only about 20% of the content should be about your products. The rest should be customer outcomes, testimonials, and commentary and educational material.

When considering a newsletter, our top tips are as follows:

- Content should be about the industry in general, not just your business.

- Interviews and quotes are highly valued, and you win by showing other companies you are quoting.

- Calls to action, such as links to your website or videos, add a multimedia feel. For example, "Learn more at www.ipgtraining.com."

- Don't overthink or overwrite. Being concise is key. Everyone buys differently, so start with a more content-light approach and have links for further detail.

- You can offer countless examples of case studies, which are simply related stories.

- Take a blog approach. In other words, write about the value and benefits you can offer and include opinion and personality, rather than simply saying "here is my product." That's what sales collateral is for. To help your work and business come alive, include content about everything you do, big or small, including customer service examples, testimonials, or going the extra mile. These are all valid things to include in your newsletter; *everything* you do can make the difference in winning business.

Conferencing and Collaboration

Conferencing and collaboration is a huge industry that has gone through a massive amount of commoditization, and it has come out the other side with a variety of value-based solutions. Sample companies in this field include Arkadin, AT&T, BT, Intercall, Verizon, and PGI (Premier), among others.

Conferencing and collaboration covers:

- Audio conferencing

- Video conferencing (more on this later)

- Web conferencing (i.e., collaboration tools)

- Streaming (more on this later)

- Unified communications via Cisco and Microsoft (more on this later, too)

In this section, we look at the benefits of using conferencing in general, as well as take a closer look at using Web conferencing technologies in your sales role. We will focus on video conferencing, streaming, and unified communications (UC) in later sections.

Using Conferencing

Conferencing technologies include audio, video, and Web conferencing services, all of which offer a range of benefits as a sales tools:

- Reducing the time to close deals
- Improving management of the sales cycle
- Reducing travel time and costs
- Eliminating wasted time
- Enabling quick responses to customers and prospects
- Facilitating engaging virtual meetings
- Increasing the number of touch points during the sales process
- Enabling real-time collaboration, reducing delays

For these reasons and more, conference calls—whether audio, video, or Web—are a fantastic way to manage your sales cycle. You should always end one meeting with a commitment for another meeting or action. You can better control the cycle if your contacts have committed to a meeting—face to face or virtual—in their diary. This is much more powerful a commitment than saying you'll be in contact at an undetermined time or even agreeing to call them at a certain time. Ensuring a time and call details are agreed on and placed into everyone's calendar, especially if multiple people will be in attendance, is a commitment equivalent to that for a face-to-face meeting. Audio, Web, and video conferencing are excellent ways to do this.

Jonathan and I have each worked in this market for more than 25 years. We've found that people turn up for conference calls more often than simply putting in a diary reminder that you will call them (which they often miss). We believe it is the psychological difference between having to take an action (dial into a conference call) and not (receiving a call).

Selling with Conferencing

Conferencing is a highly effective and flexible sales tool, particularly because you can bring in experts and colleagues—whether local or on the opposite side of the world—all at a moment's notice. Your prospect can do the same. This is a great way to bring in your prospect's boss or other people involved in the buying process. It's a call; it's quicker and easier to commit to than a face-to-face meeting. Conferencing helps time-conscious people avoid having to make commitments that may needlessly elongate your sales cycle. While we do want our key contacts to maintain a level of ongoing commitment throughout the sales process, other people involved in the sale more intermittently may find it easier to participate via this type of technology, especially if they aren't able to travel easily to join the meeting in person. You may also want to involve other experts on the call from within your business who may be too busy to take 2 hours to attend an off-site meeting but who could easily give you 20 minutes of their time on a conference call. Using conferencing can also make it easier to sell and close, which we discuss next.

Failsafe Selling

This simple technique is great for managers to silently coach their salespeople or when you have something to sell that you need an expert's help with. All "failsafe selling" means is that if you sell using virtual meeting technologies, you can have others on your conference calls who can provide feedback to you as you go. You can have side conversations online so you are all getting a read on the prospect and advising each other and modifying the approach as you go.

While experts and sales managers can of course also attend and provide support at face-to-face meetings, failsafe selling is about having that added channel of communication from which the client is excluded. The ability to have side conversations online or get visual cues from each other if you are in the same room as your colleagues on the call means you can share a separate layer of information just among your colleagues or partners to adapt the conversation, your style or tactics on the fly. Let's look at an example of why this can be so powerful.

Example

I had a new team member who had joined us from a competitor. I had just taken over the sales unit, so I hadn't recruited him myself. I was concerned because his previous organization was a price-led environment. He was pursuing a sale and said his prospect was interested only in price.

We set up a joint call with his prospect. During the call, we were negotiating price and the potential implementation. The prospect said, "The training was poor last time we changed." My salesperson just ignored this and jumped on the price comments. I messaged him to just take a break and ask the prospect what was wrong with the training. It turned out that the prospect had a lot of issues because the implementation was weak and not people-focused. I sent my salesperson a few questions and then dropped in a few benefits; we came back to the subject of price only about 30 minutes later. The prospect concluded, "If you come close to the price you can have the business."

Here, the clever use of the online chat feature of the Web conferencing service allowed me to coach the salesperson during the call, without the client knowing. Because listening skills are always an issue, in a face-to-face meeting, I could not have told my salesperson what he was doing wrong or how to change tack and could have missed out on an opportunity.

Collaboration

Collaboration technology allows you to meet, share documents, and collaborate from multiple locations in real-time using Web conferencing.

This combines audio and Web conferencing, document-based collaboration, and sharing of desktops and applications. Video-enabled Web conferencing adds the element of video streaming so you can also get visual cues from other participants in the meeting.

Collaboration tools also provide additional features such as white boarding, text chat, and polling or voting with instant results calculation. As with audio and video conferencing, you have the ability to record and capture voice, Web, and video collaboration so you can share and replay the call later.

Similar to audio and video conferencing, the price for collaboration (i.e., Web conferencing) has come down significantly. It is now readily affordable and highly effective no matter what your business.

There are countless products out there; most conferencing providers have their own versions of these, which in the main are simply not as good as the key market players in terms of focus, investment, and resources. Our favorites:

Cisco WebEx. This is the most popular in the world, which means a large proportion of people have already used, downloaded, and understand how to use it. WebEx is great for delivering webinars and e-learning (through the Training Center feature), giving online product demonstrations, and providing remote support (through the Support Center feature). The video element is good as well, although for sales, we focus on it mainly as a presentation tool.

Microsoft Live Meeting. Live Meeting is a long-time favorite. We still use it, but that tends to be based on a client's preference rather than our own, because stylistically it is an old interface. (And who wants to present using something that can give that impression?) What Live Meeting is really good for is its self-recording function (see Self-Generated Content later on in this chapter).

Go To Meeting. Provides core Web conferencing features and executes these very well, but other services offer more advanced features for about the same price. Renowned for its ease of use, it also supports iPad 1 and 2. Video support is still being developed and use cases such as delivery of webinars and e-learning need specialized products. You get a free 30-day trial. It is a good contender for smaller businesses because the cost is low and the functionality is solid.

Adobe Connect. This tends to be the go-to service for webinars, mainly because the customer journey to join is easy, you can control the look and feel, and it offers simple tools for management. In fact, Adobe Connect is simple to use all-around, making it a very good option to consider. It is the best-of-breed tool for e-Learning and great for webinar delivery. One drawback is that it is not designed for remote technical support, so bear this in mind if you will be running a technically complex call.

If you are selling to a low-tech company or person, then choose the service with the simplest joining journey (Adobe) or match up to their in-house solution. Web conferencing has a high first-time fail rate because you need to be able to walk your attendees through it. It's not difficult; just don't try to do too much simply because you can! Consider your prospect's point of view.

Pros and Cons of Collaborative Tools

- Pro: Fantastic for closing business, managing sales cycles, and failsafe selling.

- Con: Web-based, so make sure your connection speed and location are going to work well. It is less of a mobile solution and better if you're office-based, although this is rapidly changing as mobile Internet access improves.

- Pro: Its entire basis is visual, which makes for great presentations.

- Con: The presentation is only as good as your content so mix it up and get creative. Infographics (graphic visual representations of information) are hot right now; can you create and present one? More on this later.

- Pro: You can record and send out the meeting for review. This also means you have captured any commitment that the customer has made to proceed with next steps in the sales journey.

- Con: Some people fear technology, so use it only if you are comfortable with troubleshooting the basics. Do some dry runs to gain some confidence.

We've used all of these to present to our customers (when not face-to-face), because Web conferencing is a professional tool that allows you to control the content and the audience. These services tend to make up the backbone of most webinars.

Video and Unified Communications: Alternatives to Conferencing

Earlier, we discussed the benefits of using conferencing in general. In this section, we will take a closer look at video conference and call services and unified communications (UC). Let's start with video.

The benefit of video (i.e., "being there" without being there) is that it puts you as close to being in the meeting room as possible. Like being in the room, video calls give you a read on body language, varying whom you direct questions to (and how you ask them) and getting a better understanding on how things are going.

The following is a rundown of several non-conferencing video communications services.

Freemium

Freemium means it's a free service, but you pay for extra usage or features. Recommended choices:

Skype. Skype is a fantastic medium for doing audio and video calls combined with screen-sharing (i.e., you can see each other's screen—a great feature when a picture is worth a thousand words). One-to-one calls work really well. We do not use it for groups, because the quality tends to be a bit unreliable. Also, because Skype is a free service, you don't have much recourse when things go poorly. You can pay for group video but whether you prefer Skype to another service is a personal preference—Jonathan will use it, but Martin would not—and who you are selling to.

Ten Hands. As Jack Blaeser, cofounder of Ten Hands[1], has said, "With the advancement of personal computing environments and workforce globalization, video is becoming expected as a standard tool for running a successful business." Unlike Skype, Ten Hands is not a peer-to-peer solution, so the service is steadier and it provides HD-quality video with security. It is also a freemium service, so you pay only if use it a lot. It is also predictable and affordable, which makes it a great value for business users. Ten Hands is also browser-based, so while using the service is very simple, it ensures a business-class experience every time. Try it out; it's free.

Paid Options

Earlier, we mentioned a number of conferencing service providers, all of whom provide reliable paid-for video conference call services and hardware

---

[1] www.tenhands.com

and are relatively equal in price and service. In terms of hardware, the biggest players are Cisco, Polycom, and Tandberg—all providing reliable equipment with a range of features and prices.

A couple of independent video conferencing service providers worth noting:

iMeet offers unlimited online video meetings on your computer, tablet, or smart phone with up to 15 people at a time for a low, flat-rate monthly fee. This service facilitates easy video meetings online without the need for any downloads or software.

Vidyo is also an excellent service offering secure online video conference calls on your computer, mobile device, or on an in-room video conference system. Generally sold on a per-license basis, Vidyo aims to attract business users who want peace of mind and a more feature-rich service.

Unified Communications

UC is the integration of real-time communication services (e.g., instant messaging, presence tracking, audio and video calling, collaborative tools) with non–real-time communication services (e.g., voice-mail, e-mail, text messaging, and fax). UC is a suite of products providing a unified user experience across multiple devices and media types.

UC allows you to send a message using one medium and receive it on another medium. For example, you can get a voice-mail message and choose to access it through e-mail or your cell phone. If the person who left you the voice-mail is online according to her presence information, you can send your response immediately using text chat or a video call. If the person is not currently available, your response may be sent as a non–real-time message instead that can be accessed through a variety of media.

I (Martin) think we are yet to see the full evolution of UC, as there are many players (just about every major communication provider you can think of) going after the same thing but with vastly different approaches. As a businesswide solution (with its genesis in Microsoft Communicator and other similar applications), the industry is targeting its sales toward medium to large corporations.

My impression is that it is sold on productivity gains that don't flow through to people's behavior. Until someone comes to market with something that does everything in a true cloud environment instead of on each company's network, UC offers less value for money. For instance, Avaya is selling bolt-on after bolt-on to someone else's network. What's needed is something like Microsoft Lync but with a lot less licensing complexity and a lot more open access so that if I am using it, I can connect with Lync users globally that are not in my company. Everything is converging together at such a rapid pace that patience will be rewarded, in my opinion.

You could easily envision a product that combines cloud, security, voice, video, e-mail, videomail, database, and chat in one place. Add social media, blogging, and other functions and that, to me, is then truly UC. Cisco may be getting close with Jabber, which combines access to presence information, instant messaging, voice, video, desktop sharing, and conferencing and is platform-agnostic. It looks really impressive.

Video Streaming Online

Video streaming on the Web is the delivery of media, including audio or video of live or recorded events, demonstrations, and presentations. These share some similarities to video and Web conference calls in that they allow you to share live audio and video, but whereas video and Web conferencing are often considered a more collaborative tool, streaming tends to be more for unidirectional delivery of content. Depending on the tool you use to do it, streaming can also include interactive elements as well. Streaming content is an excellent way to drive sales opportunities forward, make announcements, and hold virtual events. As streaming is more one-way, you can set your event up so that the presenter is delivering the content one-way (i.e., none of the other participants can contribute out loud), and have a queue of questions that come in to you privately via the online tools. This allows you to control which questions you publicly respond to on the call much more than if you were running a dial-in Web conference call where questions can be asked publicly. It's about matching the right technology to the purpose.

For example, you might want to run a virtual event to stream a live presentation on a newly launched product you are selling, inviting a range of existing customers of all different profiles as well as any prospects. By using streaming to maintain a unidirectional presentation, you can have a variety of clients and prospects in attendance without worrying about what might be asked. You might have an existing customer who raises a question about a technical issue he has experienced due to incompatibility with one of his company's customized internal systems. You may have solved this previously, but it is a concern for this client and the question is legitimate— *for this client*—but this is not the ideal environment to ask about it. You do not want to scare away prospects with a problem that may be unique to one person. Equally, you do not want one person dominating the Q&A session. By managing the questions via a queue that is visible only to you, you can answer the most appropriate and useful questions for everyone and ensure you keep things relevant to the event at hand.

Mixing video content with slides means you can provide a rich multimedia experience. We recommend a 20-minute maximum plus the Q & A session for streaming events. Twenty minutes is plenty of time for you to cover what you need to and is short enough to keep people engaged. Ideally, your hook for such events will be to have a client or industry person presenting. The sell is not necessarily your product—that's generally the byproduct of attending—so look for an angle based around what your target market will be interested in, such as examples of how your customers have saved time or costs by using your product or service and how they might benefit from the same. Some of this may sound similar to creating webinar content, and in essence, they are both web-based seminars. The main differences are that webinars are typically longer presentations or e-learning sessions and will have open Q&A throughout or at the end of the call (so there is an element of two-way interaction), whereas streaming is totally one-directional either with no Q&A or with a controlled, private stream of questions visible only to the presenter or moderator, which they can choose to answer or not.

Example: Video Streaming Using Web Conferencing Tools

We used to hold online events focusing on topical areas that targeted different groups. A few examples:

- Corporate Social Responsibility
- Personal Assistants
- Sales
- Marketing
- IT

The incentive to get people to join was that someone in their field would be talking about how her organization benefits from the product either directly or indirectly. Attendance was strong and, because we had set the streaming service to capture names, e-mail addresses, and phone numbers, we had a list of people to contact afterwards. Using speed and quality of response, we called everyone within a day of their attendance. A secondary activity was contacting those who had registered but not joined the event. Following up with the event's participants gives you a legitimate reason to call and you know they are warm leads as they have already registered their interest in your product or service by attending the event in the first place. This is a simple but highly effective approach for finding and developing sales opportunities.

Visual Media

Videos are going to be the hot search results in the next 12 to 18 months. You may have already noticed when you search the Web for something you will occasionally see a thumbnail of a video instead of the text for a site. Video is growing fast; video blogging (vlogging) and creating YouTube channels is incredibly popular with the current generation.

Creating a video can be of benefit in so many areas:

- On your website

- In front of customers

- On your social media pages

- Posting on forums

- Posting in networking groups

Sites such as Xtranormal make creating animated videos straightforward, and self-recorded content is simple to do. What you need to consider is the type of message you want to deliver. Humor is good for social media and finding customers. A value and benefit message is good for existing clients and your target market.

Top tip: Video testimonials are very powerful. They're all within your control to create and it's very simple to do (see Create Your Own Content later in this chapter). The first and only rule of testimonials: If you do something well, just ask your clients if they are willing to give you some feedback on video or e-mail.

Creating a YouTube channel with multiple videos will help with your website ranking and SEO, discussed later in this chapter.

You can also use video testimonials in your resume. Martin did this when interviewing for a job at BT.

Self-generated Multimedia Content

We have touched on a number of types of media and alluded to the ration of content you can use to drive sales and revenue. But where does it all come from? The real question is: Where *should* it all come from? In short, it depends.

You may be able to share existing multimedia content created by your company; perhaps your marketing department has been asked to create some videos for sales, which you can use to share with customers on live Web or video calls or send out to be watched at your customer's discretion. The reality is, even if you are lucky enough to have some multimedia content available to share as a starting point, you will be most successful in increasing your sales by using engaging, relevant, and timely content, not just the standard corporate marketing stock. To do this effectively, you may need to take matters into your own hands to create this content yourself, but it is worth giving it a try. Here is the big secret: you don't need a studio! Generating your own recorded content and videos is actually very simple and it is getting easier all the time.

Here are some examples of tools to consider and what you can use them for:

Microsoft Live Meeting. We have used this to present and record sales pitches and presentations that can be shared and replayed later. You can use Live Meeting for a group recording or one-to-one. It works as voiceover to your content. You can also use this to go the extra mile for a client and create custom bite-sized training or educational content.

Kwiksta. A great example of a start-up doing things really well, Kwiksta is an e-learning platform where you can mix all types of media as well as questions and assignments. What makes it stand out is the personal support they offer; you get assigned a support person and it feels very high-touch and consultative.

HD video phones. Videomessaging and mail is and will become easier to use and more of a standard in a short space of time. It is easy to do and can help you stand out from the crowd; making someone laugh, smile, and remember you can make all the difference. People buy from people, so do something different to impress!

Screencasting

Screencasts—computer desktop recordings—are more engaging and accessible than any other type of communication. Screencasts allow you to convey step-by-step instructions with dynamic examples that can include video, images, narration, audio, captions, and visual or audio cues to guide your viewers' experience. This is an efficient and cost-effective way to produce and deliver content via the Web to inform, inspire, and motivate your customers and prospects.

You can use screencasting software to show people what you see on your computer screen, record presentations, and share your knowledge and insights. Here are two of our favorite screencasting tools:

Camtasia. A great screen recording technology that also allows you to re-record the audio separately, which is handy. A wide range of features allow you to highlight areas of your screen, add effects, show keystrokes, and combine existing media into your screencasts. Unlike ScreenFlow, Camtasia provides versions for both Mac and Windows users.

ScreenFlow. Another great tool that is easy to learn and use to record the contents of your entire desktop while simultaneously capturing video and audio in real-time. ScreenFlow has the added advantage of separating out the audio from the video portions of the recording, making it easy to add another voiceover (perhaps in an English voiceover for your US customer base and a German voiceover for your contacts in Germany). ScreenFlow offers a decent range of professional effects and easy-to-use editing using a timeline.

By using screencasting technologies to turn your computer screen into a recording device, it is easy to create step-by-step tutorials that demonstrate products to customers and build engaging multimedia content for use in selling or presenting insights to customers, prospects, and suppliers.

Consider the possibilities of what you could offer:

- Demos
- Immediate solutions—"Let me do it and send it right over"
- Presentations
- Meeting summaries
- Project updates
- Feedback and insight programs

About now, you might also be asking yourself where you should store all this content and how to make it easily accessible to your audience. You could certainly use YouTube, which we discussed earlier in this chapter; a great alternate is Screencast.com.

Screencast.com. This is an online hosting service providing you with 2 GB of free space to start with. You can upload your screencasts to this site so you can easily share your sales and promotional videos with prospects or colleagues. It also allows you to control who views your content and you're not restricted to hosting your screencasts there; you can also store videos, image, documents or anything else on Screencast.com. Upgrades are reasonable too, so if you don't have your own hosting, you may seriously want to consider it.

Using screencasts, like any of the media we've already discussed, is all about focusing on the product or service you sell, and this could be as simple as retailers doing 360-degree shots of their products and sending them out to their audience online. You could do the same with design models or blueprints. Add a webcam and you have a very simple but very creative way to sell.

Summary of Multimedia Content

We have now covered a number of different types of media you can use in your sales role to engage with customers and prospects, uncover opportunities for new business, and drive revenue. To recap, multimedia content is the best way to showcase content relating to the product or service you sell because appeals to multiple senses, so it is the best way to get and keep people's attention. Studies about cognitive learning show that if you have a balance of image, narration, and text, then people retain information better. (Run a Web search on "multimedia learning" or "cognitive learning" for more information.)

Social Media

Chapter 5 is all about social media so, for now, we will get you warmed up with a general overview of social media and a list of some of the best and hottest sites along with their core purpose. If you have yet to try out social media or the word alone sends shivers of fear down your spine, don't worry. Social media is incredibly simple to use and if you are in sales (We suspect you are if you're reading this book), now is the time to dip your toes in the water. You may find out what you're missing and want to jump in with both feet!

Let's start by looking at that list of top social media sites and their main purpose:

- Facebook – for interacting with friends

- LinkedIn – for professional profiles and jobs

- Twitter – for marketing and following celebrities

- Pinterest – for visual representation of personal interests

- Phinkit – for selling and business promotion

- MySpace – for friends and music

- Google+ – for friends and work (this lacks clarity, but hey, it's Google and they are using it to optimize search!)

- Bebo – for interacting with friends

- Tumblr – for blogging

- Reddit – for bookmarking

There are countless sites: a recent poll showed more than 2,000 social media sites in its responses. There are also many niche sites out there of interest to a specific gender and specific ethnicities, needs and industries.

Knowing which (if any) to use is the real trick. The people who use social media the most successfully concentrate on one site and use it as their hub to draw in people from others. For example, they write in their Facebook business page and post the link in Twitter.

Getting these sites working together is the key to a successful strategy. Using dashboard tools such as Hoot Suite and Sprout Social can make the management and workload much simpler to administer.

If you have not yet taken the leap into the world of social media for business, a good place to start is by setting up a LinkedIn profile and following a few people on Twitter. Chapter 5 covers all this and more in greater detail.

SEO

What is SEO? Search engine optimization is a technique that helps search engines find and rank your site, picking it out from the millions of other sites in response to a search query that someone types into Google or Bing. So SEO helps you get traffic from search engines, which can turn into customers and profit. Because of the large amounts of money that are spent online, this market has become highly competitive, with the best SEO practitioners able to charge large fees for their services.

White Hat vs. Black Hat

SEO techniques are broadly categorized in two ways: techniques that search engines recommend as part of good design (white hat) and techniques of which search engines disapprove (black hat). White hats conform to the search engines' guidelines and their methods involve no deception, so they generally produce results that last a long time and are focused on creating content for users, not search engines. Black hats are primarily seeking short-term gains and anticipate that their sites may at some point be banned temporarily or permanently once the search engines discover they are using methods that are frowned upon to improve rankings by attempting to trick the algorithm from its intended purpose. It goes without saying which approach we recommend if you're looking for long-term and reliable SEO results and profits.

THE CURRENT STATE OF THE SEO LANDSCAPE

If you read the news about recent changes to the Google algorithm you would think the SEO landscape is changing and changing fast. Techniques that have worked in the past, no longer work and clients are losing faith in the ability of SEO 'gurus' to deliver on their promise of great SEO rankings. Take a small step back and you will begin to understand that this change is a constant; the major search providers are always doing something different and the best SEO professionals work within this state of constant flux. The problem has always been for the business user—how to identify the true professional White Hat wizards who can build long term value from the Black Hats who are just out to make a quick profit and move on?

Clwyd Probert

Director, White Hat SEO Ltd.

www.whitehat-seo.co.uk

Tablets and Smartphones

The point of mobility is to increase your productivity and decrease the amount of time you need to spend on things you'd have otherwise missed once you get back to the office. Being productive on the road is obviously about making more calls, managing your sales cycle, and responding to e-mails, but it has become so much more.

Top tips:

- Use the knowledge that mobile-to-mobile calls get answered more than landline-to-mobile calls.

- Your phone is now a mobile GPS, so use it as such to avoid getting lost or to find more direct routes to where you want to go.

- Salesforce.com is one example of a great app for managing and creating activity out of your database wherever you are.

- Research on the move is now simple to do. For example, you may want to know if the company you are en route to meet with has recently been in the news; accessing the Web on your smartphone can quickly provide you this information to fuel great points of discussion that may unearth new sales opportunities.

- Dictation phone apps are a fantastic solution for capturing your ideas instead of notes you can lose. If you leave a meeting full of ideas, it can be quicker and easier to record your notes and thoughts on the move rather than writing them out.

- Let's face it, tablets are very cool! A presentation on an iPad or tablet device has a great impact and wow factor.

- The same goes for live searches or demo-ing your product (if applicable) in a meeting; it's undeniably engaging.

Networking Groups

Should you start an online group? Online groups can be of great value in reaching your target audience. It is great to join existing groups, but as a subject-matter expert in your product or service, you can raise your profile by creating your own networking group online, assembling like-minded people in one place and leading interesting and engaging dialogue. This is a great way to develop contacts, establish yourself as an expert in your field, and build up referrals and sales opportunities.

To succeed you will need to:

- Invest a lot of time at the outset.

- Have a winning concept and reason for people to join.

- Commit 2 to 3 hours per week to keep driving it.

Let's take LinkedIn as an obvious example: people enjoy being in groups that are about their industry or job role. These groups are a place to get your questions answered and pose problems. Not many people have joined LinkedIn for the purpose of being sold to; therefore, you need to either have a solutions orientation or to simply run such a good group that you are valued and are driving business based on being well-respected in your field.

Example: You Sell Smartphones

Your business is Smartphone Metropolis, a business-to-business smartphone vendor.

You do not want to give your LinkedIn group the name of your business. People might make assumptions and think, "Oh, that group is just about that business."

You need to get creative and think about the *value* you could bring to others. You know smart phones inside out and you probably know the apps really well, because they're your big upsell.

Possible group names:

- Apps for business
- Understanding Smart (phone) Business

Whatever you do, if you are driving value, you will drive traffic. Start by inviting all your friends, colleagues, and LinkedIn connections.

Example: R.E.A.L. Selling

Jonathan runs his own group on LinkedIn[2], which works really well because he offers a service. His group is valued because its members are people who have been recommended or who have taken his courses. He is known as one of the best in the business, his contributions to the group are always insightful, and he shares lots of knowledge from other sources.

Networking Groups: Face-to-Face

Networking groups, such as BNI (Business Networking International—the largest business networking organization in the world), can offer

---

[2] www.linkedin.com/groups?gid=67190

tremendous value, provide leads, and generate new connections. You just need to be aware of the commitment you are undertaking and view it as the sum of all its parts, rather just lead generation. What we mean by this is that there are a number of benefits of being a member of networking groups beyond developing leads; this includes improving your networking skills, sales approach, and presentation skills, and learning about what works best from other members.

Example: BNI Westfield

I (Martin) attend the BNI chapter in West London. The group itself is mainly small businesses and start-ups, which on the face of it isn't my target market. However, of a group of 22, over half come from large corporations, and I have had numerous leads and business from them. I've accomplished a lot of this by offering my services for free: sales messaging, marketing advice, using social media effectively, advice on buying conferencing and collaboration services, and of course sales training insight.

And I get a lot out of the group—it's a two-way street. As I was building Phinkit.com (social media for business), I also used the group for a lot of research into the needs of SMEs (Small to Medium Enterprises).

The social aspect tends to be strong, and every week I drive home the messages about my business by telling related stories and following up with videos, e-mails, and spending time on Skype with different group members.

As I am one of the few in the group with sales experience, over time, my views have become increasingly valued. To use the BNI motto, "Givers gain." The more you put in, the more you get back.

Presentation Technologies

Like anything, when done well a presentation can make the sale; when done badly it can undo all your good work. There is a reason that "death by PowerPoint" is a common phrase; presentation overkill is common and it makes me, for one, want to walk out of the room when people are pitching to me.

Why?

The most common reasons are:

- Irrelevant content that matters to the salesperson and not to the buyer.

- Lots of irrelevant company information that the salesperson thinks they should show.

- Salespeople not truly listening to the customer, and so arriving with the wrong pitch.

- Obviously substandard presentations.

- No customization or content about the *buyer's* needs.

- No summary of the reason for the meeting and its objective.

- No call to action.

- Plain, boring, text-only slides (or, equally, slides using too many pointless animations).

Avoid all of these pitfalls! No one ever said a presentation should be 50 slides or that you have to talk through each one, so why do we do it? Standard presentations are annoying; you are your own person with your own skill set. That should not go out the window just because you need to deliver some slideware. We live in a multimedia, fasting moving, Internet-savvy world; your presentations should reflect that.

Let's look at some technologies:

PowerPoint. The granddaddy both in age and in usage. A solid platform built with some aging features (such as clip art and animations). It does the job; just avoid too many text-only slides (and go easy on the text in the first place). You need variety, including images, diagrams, quotes, and videos. A presentation is only as good as its content and how it is delivered. Present using PowerPoint as a reference, not as the main vehicle. The main vehicle is you—everything flows through you.

Slide Rocket. This is much more of a cutting-edge piece of technology. Highly visual and creative, Slide Rocket makes for a more appealing approach. Everything is stored in the cloud (more on cloud technology shortly), which means you can collaborate with colleagues and share content without sending multiple editions back and forth on e-mail. You can embed real-time data from Google and other sources so your content stays up to date and relevant. It also offers analytics on your presentations so you can track trends, responses, and behaviors to improve what you create. All of this can be presented easily on PCs, tablets, and mobile phones.

SlideShare. This is a very different slant on selling. You can post your presentations on SlideShare.com for others to see, and viewers can comment on them—and every comment should be seen as an opportunity to have a conversation. The can also tweet them and post to Facebook, Google+, and LinkedIn. SlideShare is a useful tool for any salesperson. If you have a good presentation, why waste it? Get it out there and working for you!

While creating your presentations, you may want to consider including some interesting charts or graphics; imagery can be a great way of demonstrating a point and for breaking up text-only slides. One of the more creative and increasingly popular ways to do this is by creating infographics.

While infographics tend to be more of a marketing tool—because of their complexity and design—they are trending very highly as a presentation tool. An infographic is effectively a compact and creative approach to data visualization— a very cool way to show results, growth, and statistical information.

Here is a great example of a range of infographics showing the growth of social media: www.searchenginejournal.com/the-growth-of-social-media-an-infographic/32788/

There are many great examples of infographics on the Web; run a Web search and you'll see the variety of what can be created—you are limited only by your imagination! Several great free tools for creating infographics are available online and some offer the ability to create images based on your own data or vast arrays of publicly available data. Though we won't go into detail on each of these here, some of the free tools you might want to check out include: Visual.ly, Wordle, Hohli, ManyEyes, Google Public Data Explorer, Stat Planet, and Creately.

The Golden Rules of Presentations

To avoid some of the common pitfalls of creating ineffectual sales presentations, we recommend following these golden rules:

- The better the content, the better your chances of making the sale.

- Get creative. The people you sell to will not complain about seeing something different.

- Know your competition and focus on what they don't do well, or simply what they can't do.

- Know your position of power as a salesperson. Everyone has the capacity to offer something more. We explore this further in Chapter 8.

Here's an example. We know someone who sells Business Development coaching and services; he's an incredibly smart guy who started his own business. He bought some marketing software and programs and was doing OK for the first 18 months. He wanted to be the hub that businesses work with in order to fuel their growth; instead of having a distributed team with a Web person here, a marketing person there, and a telesales person somewhere else, his business made available all of these services in one place for growing companies. He was creating presentations to business owners that covered his business aim: to integrate SEO, social media, sales, and many other business functions. Again, he was doing OK but not great, and his business wasn't growing.

Then he made a single change. He made his presentation revolve around the question: "What is your dream?" With this, he stopped over-pitching his service (and presentation) and got a more emotional connection and a more holistic view from his prospects. His business is now incredibly busy and he is expanding.

Your Presenting Style: Best Practice

Whether on audio, video, Web conferencing, face to face, or any other means, you should follow some simple tips for your presenting style:

- Try not to speak for more than 60 seconds at a time.

- Break things up by constantly testing the water:

  - "Any questions so far?"

  - "What do you think?"

  - "Can I elaborate further?"

- Keep an even tone and pitch.

- Get permission to continue.

We have covered a range of Dos and Don'ts for sales presentations in this section. This may seem like a lot of rules, but they are well worth applying to your next presentation, and you might want to start working on a couple at a time until you get a chance to practice and you feel comfortable adding in a few more. In time, these techniques will become part of your natural presentation approach as your skills continue to improve.

E-mail and Marketing Campaigns

Much like newsletters and many of the ideas mentioned in this chapter, e-mail campaigns can be a rich source of leads and opportunity. Linking a campaign to your websites, webinars, videos—and having a strong call to action—is vital.

Here's an example. We were doing some consulting work with a client who sells high-end Austrian furniture. Everything is custom, hand-made, and has a high sales value. The client was doing a monthly marketing campaign that had a reasonable click-through rate to their website of just over 2%. The challenge was the conversion rate. We conducted an assumption-busting interview; we wanted to find out if there was some aspect of their business that the owners might be overlooking that they could capitalize on. We came up with many different elements, but the main aspect was that in Austria, to make this furniture you need a college degree! The mailings were mainly visual, so we added a "How we make X" section and mentioned the need for a degree. The conversion rate increased ten-fold and the click-through rate went to 8%.

The lesson is, never assume. Make your content about more than just the product and service. Target things people are interested in and the types of information they wouldn't get from your competitors.

The following are some websites and products you will find useful in planning your campaigns.

HubSpot. Hands-down, the most valuable source of ideas, discussion documents, lead generation, webinars, and advice is HubSpot. It is much more than just an inbound marketing service (one that helps you get found by customers, by providing relevant content); it combines social media, insight, marketing, mailing campaigns, analytics, and sales automation. It is well worth checking out, and lots of their insight is free. Check the learning center at http://learning.hubspot.com/.

Marketo, MailChimp, Constant Contact. A vast array of options from each of these services who compete with each other: Marketo is a lead-generation service for B2B marketers. Constant Contact helps you create marketing campaigns, and they have solid offerings for social media campaigns for Twitter, Facebook, and LinkedIn. Mailchimp helps you implement e-mail marketing campaigns.

All of these offer free trials and enhanced paid for services to their products. We have been using MailChimp to great effect in launching Phinkit; it is simple and allows you to track what actions receivers make; read the e-mail, delete the e-mail, follow links in the e-mail, etc. You can also send up to 12,000 e-mails per year for free, which makes experimentation without commitment very easy to do.

All of these services allow you to track who has opened the mail, allowing you to make calls based on this knowledge. You can integrate all of this into a social media sales strategy by pointing people to pages, offers, and different media. Mix it up.

Cloud Technology

Amazon, Apple, Rackspace, video, data backup, social media, DropBox, Facebook, social media, CRM, conferencing, banking, hosting, Go Daddy, Microsoft, SlideShare, Salesforce.com, and on and on. Everything is now based on or in the cloud.

You will likely already be familiar with some of these names or types of cloud-based services, but if hearing the word *cloud* in conversation worries you, fear not. It is merely a very good marketing term that everyone jumped on and threw in front of their products. In simple terms, these are companies who will store your files, data, music, video, presentations, and countless other things online, which people can access using logins from anywhere with an Internet connection.

Cloud technology enables us to have a faster-running computer by storing all our data with companies whose services we use. It also allows us to access our files from just about anywhere and from any computer. So far, so good.

Apple iCloud is a great example of converged technology. All of your purchases and content are stored in one place but made available to all your devices (albeit on Apple devices!).

In a sales capacity, cloud-based services can untether you from the office. You can access and manage everything virtually and in many cases via mobile devices, so the days of needing to travel with an Everest-expedition-sized bag are no more. You are now more available, more flexible, and have more tools than ever before because they are made accessible from anywhere, without the need for special hardware or software beyond standard Internet access.

Summary

We've now run through most of the technology—hardware and software—that can aid you in making the sale. The rest is up to you. Use this chapter as a reference point to pick only the ones that suit you, your style and, most importantly, your target market. But don't be afraid to test out new tools. You'll likely not only sell more, but you'll create stronger bonds with customers and gain more time to sell or enjoy life.

Using Social Media to Sell

Does the phrase "social media" concern, intrigue, excite, worry you, or all of these?

If so, this chapter is going to break through all the marketing jargon and do some much needed demystification. We go into detail about which sites could work for you and which to avoid. Social media is a very important and interesting sales topic and is generally being treated in five ways:

1. It is handed off to marketing: "Social media? Oh, marketing deals with that."

2. It is being avoided, as salespeople are not sure how to use it and are not being trained to use it.[1]

---

[1] This tends to be true in larger companies and is being massively confused with brand messaging. Brand messaging is your set of guidelines about communicating as a company, but this has created a fear factor about what you can and can't say, so it is causing non-usage or is taking away individual personality or sales.

3. It is being used, but for disproportionately little return by people who do not like to be asked about, or who are not measured on, results! They are in a fog of thinking that making noise for noise's sake will win out in the end.

4. It is being used with mismatched sales approaches and in inappropriate environments. Does anyone really want to find a business consultant/human resources specialist/anything B2B when chatting with their friends on Facebook?

5. It is being used by salespeople who do know what to do, which site(s) to use, and how to leverage social media to successfully win business.

We cover all of this in this chapter, and we include our view on the benefits and pitfalls of using social media for sales. You should come out of this chapter with a solid understanding of the best fit of social media for you, your industry, and your sales approach.

Here is what we cover in a little more detail:

- Not all "noise" is good
- Your online persona
- Keeping the dialogue moving
- Social media vs. brand
- LinkedIn
- YouTube
- Facebook
- Twitter
- Pinterest
- Phinkit
- Notable mentions and niche sites
- Blog tips and tactics

- Corporate strategies to enable the sales team

- What content to broadcast

- What not to broadcast

Not All "Noise" Is Good

To say social media has skyrocketed in usage, options, and activity is an understatement. We all know it to be true, but what does that mean for buying habits, sales strategies, and which tools and tactics actually work?

It is easy to jump on the social media bandwagon, but why spend hours online on multiple sites just to make noise for the sake of it? That is the inherent challenge for salespeople; if we can't see the direct line of sight to a sale, a new customer, or a meeting, we're not really interested.

There is a general perception that, traditionally, marketing should do the fishing for leads. But, equally true, salespeople then complain about the quality of the leads they get. Social media allows you to draw on your expertise and your personality to bait the hook for catching big fish! Consider this extreme fishing—turbo-charged, targeted, multifaceted lead generation that is completely within your control and allows you to build your profile as an expert on the product or service you sell. Social media allows you to earn the right to market to your customers and prospects, letting them find you at the right time—when they are looking to buy. You may be thinking it all sounds great, but first of all, what *is* social media? Let's take it back to basics.

Social networking sites are the top online destination for North America, accounting for 22.5% of traffic. The average American spends 5.5 hours per month on Facebook and, in May 2011, Americans collectively spent more than 325,679,000 minutes on LinkedIn.

In the Internet age, we are inundated with more streams of information than ever, and the reality is that it is human nature to filter out the excess noise. Not all noise is good! As its popularity grows exponentially, many people have started using social media simply because "everyone else" is using it. And because social media first emerged for personal use, there has been little guidance on how to leverage this technology successfully in the business world.

There are many pros and cons of using social media for sales, and we here identify some suggested approaches to using a number of the most popular and emerging social media sites. It is crucial to ensure the use of social media is relative to your target market, based on your product, customer segmentation and size, and whether you are targeting B2B (business to business) or B2C (business to consumer) markets. We guide you through these aspects to help you cut through the other noise online, reach your customers in a new and timely way, and—of course—increase your sales revenues.

Your Online Persona

Whatever social media you are using, the key is to build a program of delivery for social media messaging and most importantly, remember: don't make noise just for the sake of it. I know someone who uses his business website blog and social media sites to talk about all of his personal issues and his rather "out there" views of the world; this person was a friend of mine and it made me cringe to read this stuff. I couldn't help but ask him: "Why are you doing this?"

He answered, "It shows people who I am."

That may be true, but if your online self reflects opinions that are perceived as too negative, extreme, or simply too strong, this can easily put people off, especially in business. Social media should definitely be about conveying your personality—it is all about the old maxim "people buy from people"; just be careful not to blur the lines too much. It can be easy to get more carried away with your views online, much more so than face-to-face, as you don't have the same sensory cues to indicate the acceptable social boundaries. You may also feel you have to "shout louder" to make yourself heard among the huge amount of "noise" online; this simply isn't true.

You want to portray your best self, and strong views have an opposite, meaning there will be others who disagree and who will not want to work with someone who makes a point of standing on a personal soapbox. Personal views are exactly that—personal. Dial them down in the business world. Your aim is to make sales and earn revenue; reserve the personal opinions and debate for nights out with your friends. Showing your personality can be about what you do in life, what and whom you care about, or it may be the passion and thoughtfulness you put into your job.

Personality is whatever you want it to be and what you are comfortable with.

Many of the most popular social media sites currently available (e.g. Facebook, Pinterest) are designed for interacting with your friends, family, and acquaintances—your personal contacts. You may have a long-established personal profile that you'd like to continue to use. Ask yourself whether it is appropriate to continue using this same profile to promote your business self. It may be, and this will depend on your business and market, but more likely—just as we like to come home at the end of the day and shut off from work—you will want to keep your work self and your personal self separate. This is win-win for everyone. Google+ has made a first attempt at allowing you to organize circles of contacts into groups such as friends and colleagues, and the underlying principle is sound; you only want to communicate certain messages to certain groups. On Facebook, Twitter, and Pinterest, this option doesn't exist so it is commonplace—and recommended—to have a separate business profile which you can use exclusively to promote your work persona.

Whatever sites you use and however you decide to manage your online profile(s), you need to commit to constantly contributing and keeping the dialogue moving.

Keeping the Dialogue Moving

Update your social media pages or accounts with *relevant* content on a regular basis.

My rules of thumb for frequency of use are:

- Blog places—weekly

- Facebook—three times a week (at least once this should point back to my blog or website)

- LinkedIn—five times a week

- Twitter—three times a day plus one or two re-Tweets of others' Tweets

- Other sites—program frequency based on your target groups (e.g., on Pinterest, if you have visual content that appeals to others)

I explain the reasons for these recommendations in the corresponding section for these sites later in this chapter.

To start building your approach for the type of social media messaging you want to use, start by listing your objectives and goals.

Goals

Goals should be oriented by whether yours is a singular endeavor, or if you have a staff or run a sales unit. In the latter case, you can be more strategic in your approach. For example, you could align responsibility for messaging to particular customer types with salespeople selling into those markets:

- Salesperson A will create messages for customer type X.
- Salesperson B will create messages for customer type Y.
- Salesperson C will create messages for customer type Z.

Next, list each social media platform you will use and what your target numbers for each look like. For example:

- 2,000 followers per Twitter account
- 1,000 connections per LinkedIn account
- 500 Facebook page "likes"
- 100 weekly page impressions of your blog
- 200 more website hits

Finally, what is your end goal? Possibilities include:

- Improve brand awareness.
- Increase your number of leads.
- Increase your sales revenue.

- Provide customer service enhancements.

- All of the above!

Now that you understand what you want to accomplish and you have some target numbers to work toward, the next step is to consider the tools you have at your disposal and how you can use them to achieve your objectives.

Objectives

First, consider what you have at your disposal by answering these questions:

- How big is your team?

- What type of business are you?

- Do you have a range of products or services?

Then ask whether you have:

- Multiple customer types?

- Knowledge by demographics?

- Details of the roles and departments of your decision-makers?

- Knowledge of which locations you can sell in?

Last, ask how you are going to accomplish this:

- How much time can you or your team give to a proactive social media program?

- Are the people involved sufficiently trained?

- Do we want to dictate and completely control the messaging or assign content and topics for our people to write? (With the right training, the second option is much, much better. Let people create and sell.)

The last bullet point is of particular importance. Ideally you want a balance between the two—maintaining your strategic approach and also enabling the personality of you and your team members to come through with content based around the activities you've been doing. Shortly we will look at which sites you may want to use and why, but first let's round off social media by comparing it with the concept of brand.

Social Media vs. Brand

Something strange happens when new things come along. We refer to it as "push the button" training, which is simply teaching people the bare minimum of how to use the functions of a product or system.

For example, when e-mail first arrived and people were shown how to use it on a technical level, you might have been told:

- Click here to send an e-mail.

- Click and drag to move an e-mail message into another folder.

- Go here to turn on your out-of-office message.

This is fine in terms of getting to grips with basic functionality, but it doesn't build your understanding of e-mail technology and its potential value to you in your role.

When e-mail first arrived, there weren't any standards of how to behave when using it. There were no answers if you thought to ask, "How should I treat or handle e-mail?" No one said, "Here are the top five rules." So, here are the top five rules for best use of e-mail:

1. Treat e-mail like you would a phone call and respond quickly.

2. Always respond to e-mails within a few working hours, if not sooner.

3. Or, taking this back a level, always respond to an e-mail!

4. Send a bridging message to say you need more time to respond if that's the case.

5. E-mail has people at either end; treat it as such.

Not long after the advent of e-mail, spam began to appear in our inboxes, and so did streams of unrelenting internal corporate communications. E-mail became less of a communication system and more of a time filler—or time killer—as we became inundated with e-mail "noise." Without standards, bad habits became the norm.

The reason we restate this issue using the e-mail examples is because the same is true of social media. It came along, we started using it, but nobody said what to do so everyone made lots of assumptions. Too often that was to pass it to marketing, ignore it, or start collecting loads of names. Standards are important in delivering business messages, but there is a distinction between this and brand communication guidelines.

The whole concept of brand communication in many ways can be characterized as follows: given certain circumstances, you should respond to customers, and advertise or communicate in a way that is in line with the company's culture. This is great in that it makes sense for wider communications, customer service, and for the marketing department—not forgetting the customers. Where the concept of brand guidelines gets skewed, however, is with the use of social media. Let's look at an example to show why this is the case.

While interviewing people during the months of research before launching Phinkit, we started to come across a strange phenomenon when we spoke to salespeople. When we asked "Do you use social media for work?" we usually got one of four responses:

- "I am registered on [social media site X] but I don't use it; I don't know how to."

- "Marketing handles that."

- "I am registered on social media sites, but marketing does most of it."

And our all-time favorite answer, which came up all too often:

- "Sure, I'm registered, but our company doesn't want us saying too much. It's frowned upon."

Frowned upon? Here is this fantastic new medium of communicating and following people online, yet why are employers are actively discouraging their salespeople from using it?

The use of social media has exploded and as a business community we were caught unawares. Typically, the bigger the company, the slower the catch up with using social media, so it tends to get handed off to marketing to deal with. When businesses pigeon-hole social media as a marketing tool, the sales force (or indeed anyone else within the firm) receives no training on social media use. They are left figuring it out for themselves or not using it at all.

Now, before we get an avalanche of complaints from diligent companies and marketers, we do think that for the purposes of developing it as a strategy for use, and in general for brand communication, responsibility within the company for social media absolutely should rest with marketing. However, a change is also needed to encompass the use of social media for sales, business owners, and other customer-facing positions. People in these types of roles should be leveraging social media communication technology, not fearing they aren't allowed to touch it.

On one hand, businesses are saying:

- "Get out there and sell our products. Go and speak to people about our business."

- "Go, sell! Send people e-mails about our service."

- "Write proposals and marketing materials and send them to our customers."

But when it comes to social media (the clue is in the name—this is *social*), businesses are saying:

- "Wait a minute; you can't just feel free to inject your personality and sell like you do the rest of the time. Marketing controls social media use, because they are trusted to say the right thing."

Of course, we are not saying this is true everywhere, but it did come out consistently in our research when we asked this question.

Your success as a salesperson relies—at its core—on your sales approach and personality, whether this is online or offline. The fact is, if you are employed by a business as a salesperson, your employer has already tacitly stated that he believes in you and in your capabilities. This includes the key ability to interact effectively and professionally with clients. After all, you're in the most customer-facing role of all! Whether you are a one-person sales force or part of a sales team 10,000 strong, you should simply view social media as an extension of what you currently do—and go ahead and make as much productive use of it as possible. For Phinkit users, we see this as each person offering insight to their businesses and what they do, mentioning unique and customer-centric good news and simply feeling free enough to be themselves.

The old adage is true: people buy from people. Of course, people buy from brands too. But why leverage only one of these at the cost of the other when the social media platform allows for both?

Let's now take a look at some of the biggest social media sites available.

LinkedIn

As of this writing, 150,000,000 members with average usage time of 180 minutes per person per month (of their active users). At the time of publication of this book, LinkedIn is the biggest professional networking site. Please note the use of the word "networking"; by LinkedIn's own definition, the site is designed to let you connect with past and present colleagues and other contacts and is not specifically for selling. Their top aims are to let you re-connect with contacts and "power your career" by leveraging these connections when you're seeking a new job or business opportunity.

Like many social media sites, LinkedIn has a programmer's heart— technically it works well, but there is no consideration of the people using it. The site doesn't communicate to you other than with automatic messages that are generic and mostly marketing for the site itself. More importantly, the general feeling is that no one expects to be sold to on the service itself. LinkedIn defines itself primarily with the word "connect." Let's think about that word for a moment. Connect. Connecting with other takes you to a certain point, but if we only connect with someone and that's it, it doesn't help thereafter. This leaves people to make their own calls about what the site is supposed to be used for.

All too often, this leads salespeople to a fundamental social media mistake: quantity over quality. The thinking goes like this:

> "OK LinkedIn, what do I do? Hmm . . . let me look up people I know. Ah, Jon London; I know him! Wow, Jon has over 500 connections; let me do the same. If I spend a few hours a week getting to 500 connections—any connections—then naturally, I'll start getting leads."

Pretty much every salesperson we know has thought this at some stage. As a business, LinkedIn—being based around this idea of the word "connect"—*is* about collecting contacts. This leads to lots of spam and lots of invites but not many conversations. Unsurprisingly, recruiters have found themselves a natural niche use for LinkedIn, as they can leverage their contacts' connections, which are visible on the site. Having a lot of connections does, of course, have a value to it, but it is not a sales strategy or a magic formula for leads when done in isolation.

Let's look at what you can do to take things in the right direction for sales.

The fundamentals:

- Your profile should be 100% complete so others have a good understanding of you, your skills, and your experience.

- Your bio should highlight your unique skills, not just a basic, standard list. In effect, you're selling yourself. So think about what really sets you apart.

- Be strategic. Think about what you would like potential customers to learn about you when they read your details.

- Personality is key. LinkedIn is a fairly uninspired site, in many cases because of the perception that it is only recruiters using it for headhunting or gaining business.

- Rightly or wrongly, a judgment call is made against the number of connections you have. Do make an effort to connect with as many people as you can.

- Drive your number of connections with the value of what you offer and of what you have to say.

Establish and build credibility:

- Connect with people you know; it's the first obvious step.

- Join every group that is applicable to your field, industry, and customer audience.

- Search for connections based on job functions, especially those of your potential clients.

- In the connections section of LinkedIn, the "People you may know" feature is a simple and effective way to invite contacts to connect with you and spread your network.

- Connect with industry leaders and see who they are connected with. This can provide a wealth of intelligent data you can harvest.

Sales approaches:

- The approach on LinkedIn is essentially a soft sell. Of course, you can take the mass message and spam route if it fits your sales model, but for most users this is increasingly becoming a turn off in using LinkedIn.

- Start by beginning to comment and socialize in your groups. Your aim is to become known, raise your profile within groups of value, and start to put across your point of view and knowledge. Remember: *No hard selling*.

- Connect with people from the groups in whom you see opportunity. Compliment, engage, and *discuss* with them. Join them on Skype calls; don't interact online alone. You'll be amazed at who people know and what you can achieve.

- LinkedIn members very frequently share their phone numbers on their profiles; if you see something of note, then call the person. For example: "Hi, I just read you comment on LinkedIn; I thought it was great and it really interested me so I wanted to call and introduce myself."

This is highly effective, yet hardly anyone does it. This is because sending a profile update (that may or may *not* be seen) is easier than making a call. Try it out! It is the same principle as we discussed regarding the Internet in Chapter 4. LinkedIn can help you create legitimate reasons to call and make contact, leading to any number of possibilities for new business.

Groups and webinars:

- Starting your own group can have merit but you do need to consider how big the audience could be and what type of group it is. A niche group with a small number of members may be of great value in building relationships and sales leads, but the smaller the group, the more of your attention and care will be needed to keep the dialogue and interest going. A larger group, say with a few hundred or more members, will by its nature have more organic interactions without quite as much effort on your part. Though this is something to bear in mind, the key is to consider the purpose of the group and keep the focus around this.

- A post-sales or post-customer service group is great. It builds up a repository of endorsers you can invite potential customers to view so they can see the upsides.

- Naming a group after your company is less likely to succeed than if you think a bit more creatively. If you have a good knowledge base, make the group about that. Or you can focus the group around your key target market. The worst-case scenario is that you will gain valuable customer insight!

- Start groups that relate to your business. Jonathan has a prospects group and a new VP of sales group because he wants to stay in touch with these people and use social media to do it.

- Webinars are offered left, right, and center, with the presumed hook of "*Free to join!*" That is not a hook. Your hook is offering valuable content, addressing a specific need, or featuring a person well known in the industry—or all three. So if you offer a webinar or some other event, make sure a potential client can see the value.

YouTube

You might not think of YouTube as being a social media tool in itself, but it is a massive component to any social media strategy. YouTube is the world's second largest search engine. It is owned by the largest search engine (Google) and it can carry significant impact for your business.

YouTube defines itself as "a forum for people to connect, inform, and inspire others across the globe and acts as a distribution platform for original-content creators and advertisers, large and small."

Why should you use it?

SEO—Your YouTube content can help with your website's search engine optimization. Not surprisingly, because Google owns it, YouTube content ranks high in what Google looks for.

Popularity—Typically, website home pages appear in search engine results as a starting point. Because it is all about viewing the content on it (and not just the site in itself), YouTube videos appear in your search results as a direct link to the video, rather than to the YouTube homepage. YouTube is also fun to use and extremely popular because video is simple to use and engages multiple senses for a big impact.

Video—Video thumbnails are starting to appear in Google search results instead of standard Web links, something that is expected to increase dramatically. Video is the number one way for people to learn and is the preferred way to view content online.

YouTube channel—It is free to create a YouTube channel. Like a TV channel, this is the place from which you broadcast, and it is then associated to your website to complete your SEO approach. You can upload videos to YouTube without a channel, but if you intend to host multiple videos, it is highly recommended that you set up a channel.

Social Hub—For our work with Phinkit, YouTube serves as a video storage hub. Users can access Phinkit videos, hosted remotely on YouTube's expansive server network, which are seamlessly embedded and played from within our site. Phinkit videos do get independent views from people browsing YouTube, but mainly access to our video content on YouTube is via links from our other social media sites:

- @Phinkit on Twitter is used for posting the latest articles that include a link to a video on YouTube

- The Phinkit.com website itself is designed to show YouTube videos embedded within Memex posts from our Phinkers (users).

- Our Twitter feed is linked automatically to Facebook and LinkedIn, so all updates are streamed and visible to our followers in one go.

What Can I Use YouTube for?

Open your mind. Relax your senses. And forget any other jargon and sayings you can think of! A better question is: What *can't* you do with video?

As a medium, it is just about getting comfortable with its use. We often think of video for business as being a highly produced graphical presentation. However, video can now be easily produced in any number of ways and quality is not paramount. Content is. For sales purposes, as ever, it is crucial that the content holds value. Here are some examples:

1. Vlogging—Video diary of the latest happenings and your thoughts on them.

   What to use: webcam, tablet, cell phone, video camera

2. Presentation—Recordings with a voiceover of presentations, or new content such as changes or additions to your website.

   What to use: screen capture software

3. Special offers—Slides, audio, or "talking head" video of something you have on offer. This could be hosted on your website, sent as part of a mail-out or shown direct to customers on site.

   What to use: webcam, tablet, cell phone, video camera

4. Interviews—"Meet the Team" videos or interviews with industry people or people of interest to your customer base.

   What to use: a room, video camera

5. Animation—Xtranormal is a simple way to do this and it can be a lot of fun. For Phinkit, we have used the Queen template to create an animation, and we have her saying things Her Majesty never would. It is a corporate video, so nothing risqué, but it injects a bit of humor.

   What to use: Xtranormal

Don't overthink these kinds of videos. You can edit everything quickly and once you get the hang of using these technologies, you can even record things on a per-customer basis. Ask yourself what is better:

1. A 40-page proposal document in Word

2. A 2-minute proposal summary on video

With option B, you still send the proposal as well, but ask your prospects to watch the video first. Who will they remember—you, or the competition with their dull Word-only approach?

Quick tip We have all experienced the pain of having a technical hitch in the presence of a customer. If possible, as insurance, have an interesting introductory e-mail when you send video links or content. In the event that the video will not play at the customer's end, they should at least get some basic details from your e-mail message and appreciate what you are trying to achieve.

Facebook

Facebook is the most popular social networking site in existence today. It is designed primarily to help friends connect, share, keep in touch, build their profiles, follow each other's activities, and join common-interest groups. At the time of writing, Facebook had more than 900 million active users— greater than 13% of the world's population! The company has just gone public, and many speculate this will put more pressure on Facebook to deliver profits to its shareholders. Although it is not designed for business use—the site is very much centered on your personal profile and your interactions with friends—Facebook business pages are already available and many companies are trying to find ways to use these in a meaningful way. With the recent IPO, no doubt Facebook will face pressure to look for ways to cater to the business world in order to drive revenue, but at this point we can only guess as to what they might deliver in this vein. Let's have a look at Facebook as it stands today.

Part One

Let me be clear on this right away:

Facebook is not for business-to-business sales.

This is my opinion, but I have studied the subject matter in great depth. So why isn't Facebook for B2B sales?

1. Facebook is for escapism or for keeping in touch with and sharing with friends.

2. Many have tried to use Facebook for B2B sales and many have failed.

3. It takes a lot of time to maintain your best messages.

4. A Twitter hook up with Facebook can be harmful.

5. Get creative and prove us wrong!

Let's consider each of these points separately.

1. Facebook is for escapism. It's for keeping in touch with and sharing with friends.

The one word that defines Facebook is *friends*.

Consider that sentence. Reflect on your own usage. The vast majority are on Facebook to chill out, to catch up, to laugh, to look, to get recommendations, to share, and to enjoy.

In short, someone using Facebook is not there to be sold to and definitely not there to think about work. Nobody goes on Facebook to find sales training or to ask about a business-to-business solution. You don't want someone making you think about work when you are on the site, but you will happily visit consumer brands on Facebook and find out about new things to buy, but this is for *personal* use (more on this in Part Two). The business value in using Facebook is governed by your type of business; as with most social media platforms, recruitment companies can get a lot of benefit from it, while fashion and retail can smash it.

We're not saying you shouldn't use Facebook for business; just make sure it is proportional to the benefit received or as part of a unified approach (such as Twitter integration).

2. Many have tried to use Facebook for B2B sales and many have failed.

Facebook will evolve to incorporate more of the needs of the business world. This is happening now; for example, the BranchOut networking app, despite having a lack of features, is taking off on Facebook, mainly because it is about jobs and career networking. At the time of writing, the Facebook IPO has just kicked off; they have cornered most of the personal networking world, so what's next? An IPO means capitalism to the fore and increasing profit demands. They will be progressively moving further into the business market; this could be great or it could be a major turnoff to their core user base that sees it as a personal networking tool and do not want their work and private lives to become one.

We suspect Facebook will end up somewhere in between the personal and business worlds.

To date, many businesses have tried to leverage Facebook, but there are limited—if any—success stories of B2B companies using it to great advantage. You will also need to consider *how* you use it. Logically, on LinkedIn, you may connect with the people you know in your business life; on Facebook, you start with your friends.

Do you want your friends and family being pestered with updates about your work life?

Are you comfortable mixing work and play? Do you want Saturday night's party to become part of the feed to your work contacts?

You could create a separate ID for work and personal profiles, but expect your friends to send you invites to connect to your work profile and then get annoyed if you don't accept them (trust me on this). You will also need to log in separately to update one profile or the other.

If you create a separate work ID, whom do you invite? Facebook is not a platform with a really open approach to connecting, and you won't want to start with your friends. People you know in your work life might find it weird if you are asking to connect with them because they view Facebook as personal. So this would require everyone to create a separate work ID and profile and do the same thing as you . . .

That leaves you with the option of a Facebook page for your business and page "likes" (and having more page likes helps influence your SEO ranking). This is where many have tried and failed. In this forum, business to business sales simply don't interest people. Plus, you have a new challenge . . .

3. It takes a lot of time to maintain your best messages.

Let's say you set up a Facebook business page. Almost everyone else has done one too! How do you get people's attention? To maintain your page "likes" and have a chance at increasingly your number of page "likes" (remember these are not sales leads, they are just page "likes"), you will need to keep up a stream of updates to those who like your page. This is time consuming and the update messages themselves will need to be quite general as your audience is unknown. Each comment you makes moves everything down on your page. Keep this in mind; when was the last time you did a Google search and looked on page 2 of the results?

Therein lies the problem; your best sales messages need to be repeated so they get prominence and can be seen at the top of on your Facebook business page.

The new timeline design is organized to help Facebook users see their closest friends' content first, whereas previously you saw all of your connections' posts in the order they were posted. By prioritizing your closest friends' posts and displaying these at the top of your news feed (and notifying you specially only when these people have posted something), users now spend even less time exploring the news feed and may miss interesting content that is pushed down the list. To try to get page Likes for your Facebook business page you could buy advertising space on the site, but the cost of doing so must be weighed against the benefit. Ultimately, all you have is the potential for some page Likes; it's hard to calculate the value or benefit of this and even harder to link this to any kind of effect on your revenues.

4. A Twitter hook to Facebook can be harmful.

Linking up your professional Twitter account to your business Facebook profile means that all of your Tweets go simultaneously into your Facebook update stream. This is worth doing *if* you are happy for your Facebook contacts to see your Twitter updates. But it can equally be damaging if you *don't* want this group to receive such updates.

5. Get creative and prove us wrong!

The lack of fit of Facebook for business-to-business sales is only our opinion, so if you have a way to get people interested in B2B propositions on Facebook, then go for it! Our point is that there is an easier way to find business than the mismatched approaches that Facebook currently offers.

Part Two

Facebook is for friends.

Facebook can be incredibly effective for B2C, retail, and personal promotion.

Here is an example of a friend of ours who has been incredibly successful in using Facebook as her main vehicle for success. At our request, Julie Christie explains how she gets results:

> Starting a Facebook business page is the easiest thing in the world. However, making that Facebook business page work for you is not as easy as it may seem. You have to care for your page and give it some love. Like your website, it is another virtual "shop window" for your business, so it is important to make it look great. Drench it with your branding (but be mindful of Facebook's new policies on cover images) and make sure it reflects your business ideals.

Next, you want to build your audience, and there are various ways you can do this. The first and easiest way is to invite your Facebook friends list to "like" your page and ask them to recommend others do the same. Of course, your friends may not be your target market, so make use of Facebook ads and sponsored-stories campaigns to reach specific demographics. You can also run contests to increase your fan base using applications like "Wildfire." Contests allowed me to build up 3500 "likers" in less than five months with my first Facebook business page. Again, read up on Facebook's very strict guidelines on running contests or you risk having your page removed.

Once you have your page looking good and you've built up a decent fan base, then what? It's simple. You must *keep* your current fans and continue gaining new ones. How do you go about this? You *engage* them and encourage them to interact with you regularly. You need to keep your fans interested in you by making your posts worth reading. Post something they will like, something that will encourage them to click that "like" button or, even better, leave a comment. Facebook is clever, very clever. Based on the quality of the content and who interacts with your page, Facebook decides how many newsfeeds it will send your post to. It is possible to have thousands of fans but feature in the newsfeeds of only a few hundred of those people simply because your content is dull and/or repetitive and doesn't grab fans enough to make them engage with you. It is all about getting your fans engaging and interacting with your business page.

With my photography business, Facebook forms a large and crucial part of my marketing strategy. Using Facebook, I am able to show off my work on a regular basis. By showing off my images I can also tag clients in my posts so that my work reaches everyone on their own friend lists on the site. If they like what they see they will hopefully leave a comment and maybe even "like" my page.

I post regularly so that my fans don't forget about me, but not so regularly that I clog up their news-feeds and get on their nerves. I try to post high-quality content with images people will enjoy looking at. I sometimes ask for opinions or stories related to my posts; encouraging fans to comment increases the reach of your post and brings it to the top of newsfeeds.

I encourage my clients to "check in" at Julie Christie Photography when they are at a photo shoot with me. This is a great endorsement for any business—it says, "I'm here with this business and I am enjoying it so much that I am checking in!"

I often offer a little of myself via my business page also. Posting little tidbits about my personal life, photographs of my own children or just about a great book I have just finished often generates more comments and interaction than images I post! This also allows potential clients to see the person behind the business, meaning they will be much more likely to choose me over my competitors since they feel they already know me.

It is easy to be a bit "Me, Me, Me" on your business page. However, I have found that if you reach out to other businesses in your posts using the tagging system, you will be richly rewarded. If you have just read a great blog post and think your fans would enjoy it—share it and tag the writer. If you met someone interesting at a networking event—mention them in a post and tag their business. Much like karma, this will all come back to you and you should reap the rewards!

Julie Christie, Owner, Juliechristiephotography.co.uk

Let's turn our attention to Facebook's slightly younger sibling—Twitter.

Twitter

Celebrity voyeur site or marketing platform?

Twitter is both of those and more. It's a site on which you can interact with friends, businesses, celebrities, track news, carry out marketing, and many more things. A combination of social networking and microblogging, Twitter allows you to connect with and follow others, and send and receive short messages in real-time—known as Tweets. It has been referred to as SMS (or text-messaging) for the Internet.

Using Twitter is also good for SEO. If you send a Tweet and this message then gets re-Tweeted, say, more than 50 times, this can have a positive impact on your SEO rankings.

From sales, the best approach for setting up your Twitter account is to start following people who are in your target market by searching for them using keywords and then following them. Unlike LinkedIn and Facebook, you can connect with most people on Twitter without having to request their approval first.

For example: If you search using the terms "social media," you will get a whole host of industry commentators, bloggers, and lots of people who have noted social media as an interest.

There is a rule of thumb for the math of connecting with people on Twitter; the ratio of people you are following to people following you is roughly 5 to

I. So for every 500 people you follow, you need 100 following you back. Bear this in mind, as following everyone for the sake of it can cause you problems. It is best to take a careful, staggered approach and see who follows you back in return. You can then adapt your approach as you go.

Tweets can be updates, general thoughts and insights, but ideally you should put a call to action in linking to more detailed content as Twitter only allows you 140 characters to get your message across.

You should always use Twitter as hub for other social platforms you use, such as LinkedIn and Facebook. Linking these accounts together is a good time-saver and allows you to reach all of your connections in one go.

Do interact with people you are following and vice versa; re-Tweet their content and then take it from there. Just remember to keep it interesting!

Pinterest

Wow! Out of nowhere, Pinterest has ballooned to the third largest (at the time of writing) of all the social networking players.

Pinterest is a highly visual site, with an almost magazine type feel to it. In effect, it is a virtual moodboard, allowing you to "pin" things you like from around the Web and to connect to others who find the same things interesting. Pinterest has a much higher female user base than other sites. If you have images, videos, or products to share, it can be very useful to start pinning them up online as a way to get people talking about you.

As with Facebook (and indeed any content or messaging you deliver in sales), your Pinterest content should match your audience. The more creative, imagery-based product or business you have, the better Pinterest will fit your business needs.

Start by following others and making some interesting comments, then take it from there. Only put in the time if it matches your customer base.

Keep it creative! Jokes, funny and interesting images, and anything engaging can work really well. Design businesses or cool products are a home run on Pinterest!

Phinkit

Think about every social media site you know and consider the following questions:

- Do they communicate with you?

- Do they advise you how to sell?

- Do they help you find people who are interested in what you have to say? Do they do so every time you post something to the site?

- Did they build the site first and foremost for sales and marketing people's needs?

The answer to all of these is *no*. No other social media sit has been built for sales or marketing, for passing and receiving referrals, for getting ideas, for making sales, or for getting your business voice heard.

I (Martin) am one of the founders of Phinkit. What we have created is a site that is primarily for sales and promotion and will support anyone in helping them achieve their goals on the site. Let's look at a few of the unique features of this site:

BFF

We communicate to people with a fun but serious service: the Business Friend Forever (BFF), which is your business concierge. You can ask the BFF anything you want:

- Ideas for selling and marketing a product

- How to find good connections (and more of them)

- How to get heard or share ideas

- How to put across your personality and passion in what you sell

The BFF provides a truly unique support system based on business skills, expertise, and ideas, not just technical support.

Memex

The Memex is the place you can post and share ideas, writing about your work life, your passions, fun things, opinion, products, services, and customer successes. The Memex posts your content in real-time and is organized to deliver each of your posts to the people who are following you, people you are connected with, people who are interested in your content (by matching interest categories), and also to a general feed containing everything posted by all users. You can also filter what you see in these same ways, allowing you to view messages of interest in different groupings.

The Phinkit site fully supports multimedia, so you can include images and your YouTube videos within your Memex posts.

Check out some examples:

1. A Memex I wrote about "Speed of Response, Quality of Response." Available at: www.phinkit.com/Memex/?b=45

2. A Memex with a video from Jonathan called "Identify your Competitive Advantage." Available at: www.phinkit.com/Memex/?b=234

3. A Memex from "Mr. Creativity," Simon Jack (more from him in Chapter 7): "Content with your Personality." Available at: www.phinkit.com/Memex/?b=67

These Memex posts cover topics that add extra value alongside this book—and all three give more insight on the authors of this book and their services. Please feel free to post your comments at the end of each article.

Phinkit offers a range of features. So beyond simply connecting with others, as on LinkedIn, Phinkit allows you to list and promote your services, interact with your client base, provide referrals, solve business challenges, generate requirements, show what business you are looking for, send and receive testimonials, have an external profile page, and create all manner of value for your business. And if you get stuck, just ask the BFF!

The team we put together to create Phinkit includes people with primary skills sets for sales, marketing, management, creativity, usability, design, IT, hosting, programming, and many more. The reason I mention this is one that was referred to earlier: most other social platforms were started with a team of programmers only, which means they have great technical capabilities but lack focus on people-based and business-based services.

People-based services consider features beyond the technical and consider the person using them. Business-based services think about the needs of business users first in the fundamental design and functionality of the site.

For example, in one day alone we've had Phinkers (users) asking us about:

- How to write an article about their product
- The best way to promote themselves
- How to find a good personal assistant
- How to set up a YouTube channel
- Ideas for Phinkit TV episodes
- How to find a mentor for sales

Phinkit: Social Hub

We have also recognized that no matter how good a service we have built, it is *another* social media site. With this in mind, we have created Phinkit as a social hub, which means you can link your Phinkit profile with your profiles on other social sites. For example:

- When you write a Memex, you can instantly send it to LinkedIn, Facebook, Twitter, and Pinterest.
- If you read something you like on Phinkit, you can share it in LinkedIn, Facebook, Twitter, and Pinterest.
- We also promote the best content in all these social sites and in the "Editor's Choice" section in the Memex.
- You can do everything you need in one place— Phinkit—and that one place is also a fully supported multimedia environment for all your sales needs.
- Feel free to connect with us there: www.phinkit.com

Notable Mentions and Niche Social Media Sites

There are countless other social media sites. Some are very niche- and target-specific groups; others are attempts at cloning LinkedIn or are singular in what they offer (e.g., Web links, pictures).

Here are some of our favorites and notable mentions and what they are for:

- **43 things**: Setting goals online and finding out how to achieve them.

- **Bebo**: 117 million members with a customizable interface, but lost out to Facebook in the popularity stakes.

- **Blogger**: For creating your own blog which is hosted on Blogger's site.

- **Classmates.com**: For connecting with schoolmates, college friends, work or military colleagues.

- **Delicious**: Social bookmarking allowing users to locate and save websites that match their own interests.

- **Flickr**: Social pictures, sharing content, photography-related networking.

- **Foursquare**: Location-based mobile social networking. Businesses, venue owners, and brands can be successful promoting on this site.

- **Google+**: Late entry from the powerhouse that is Google. It makes an attempt to help you manage both the personal and business sides of your online profile, although it is confusing to sell on both. There is not much that's really groundbreaking here other than the awesome Video Hangout feature.

- **MySpace**: Once the dominant social media player, MySpace now mainly caters for a music-focused teenaged user base.

- **Reddit**: User-generated news from around the globe. Users vote to promote news stories to the front page.

- **Vimeo**: With its roots in user-generated content, Vimeo is an alternative to YouTube as a platform for showcasing and sharing your creative videos. Although its reach is not as great as YouTube's, Vimeo boasts that is hosts the highest-quality user-generated video on the Web.

- **Xing**: Popular in mainland Europe, Xing is very similar to LinkedIn.

There are plenty more social media sites, and some very niche ones (knitting anyone?) are very popular and could hold an advantage if they have your customer demographic using them. We have a very open approach to new social media sites because, at a minimum, you can find out what makes people tick and conduct sales analysis. You can also see if there are ways to unearth more sales opportunities, so keep an open mind. It takes only a few minutes to check out a new site or review whether a site is right for you.

Blog Tips and Tactics

Blogs are used for you or your company to educate, find, and feed your following and in the best of all worlds to be considered a thought leader. Some of the key elements of a blog being effective are:

- Be consistent and write at least once a week, if not twice.

- Have a unique voice or perspective that people will be attracted to.

- Include a call to action that leads them back to your website where they have to register their name and e-mail.

- Use provocative subject lines to get people's attention.

- Use great graphics, bullets, and make it easy to read.

- Comment on other people who blog that have a big following to take advantage of their audience and capture their attention.

- Re-purpose your blogs as newsletters to reach your e-mail audience.

- When you blog, write three or four tweets that will appeal to people and have them read your blog.

- Write a blog that brings attention and information to other companies or resources that are helpful to your audience and don't compete directly with you.

- Get used to giving away more information and insights than you are accustomed to sharing.

- Blogs can be video blogs of about 1 to 1½ minutes.

- Find or use a resource that gives you good insight and advice for using key words, meta tags, etc.

Corporate Strategies to Enable the Sales Team

Social media is a tool like telephone calling, e-mail campaigns, and allocation of target markets or customers. As we have mentioned, social media is something marketing can (and should) work on, but it should also be a key part of your sales strategy as well.

The great thing is that you and the sales team you are part of can divide up responsibility for using social media in exactly the same way you would divide up and align a territory or customer base, perhaps even to a deeper level.

Approach

Here's how to go about it:

- First, work out which social platforms your customers use.

- Then subdivide your target customers not just by the industry they work in but also by the job roles they hold.

- Assign target customer groups to each salesperson.

- Assign subgroups within those customers.

What you're aiming for is the right set of messages going to the right target markets. Example: You have two salespeople, James and Grant. Both are selling the same product but they are aligned with different industry verticals. James is assigned to Financial Markets and Grant is assigned to Oil and Gas. On their preferred social media sites, both can join groups for their target industries to reach people in specific companies by following them or sending connection requests (depending on the platform).

Let's say they can sell to contacts in sales, marketing, finance, operations, and directors. They could plan their social media efforts by dividing their week accordingly, with each focusing on his own customer industry:

Monday—Salespeople

Tuesday—Marketing

Wednesday—Finance

Thursday—Operations

Friday— Directors

This accomplishes a few things:

- They are working on different industries, so they are able to cover more ground on social media sites.

- They are not sending the same messages to the same people.

- They can tailor their messaging to each combination of industry and job role, making them more engaging for their audiences.

- They have a daily focus and a clear social media plan in which they can consider the different thought processes of their target audiences.

- It keeps a fresh approach, instead of sending generic messages to a wide group, which gets monotonous.

Remember, social media is a sales vehicle; deploy yourself and your team strategically.

What Content Should I Broadcast?

I (Martin) like to talk about social media as being a vehicle for your personality combined with targeted messages. A business's website is generally fairly static in terms of its content, because it is your storefront and it needs to act as a catch-all for all the different types of people who land on it. Social media means you can provide much more specific content for your audience, and you can also be much more targeted in your approach by tailoring distinct messaging to separate segments of your audience.

As with the "enabling the sales team" that we just covered, you can make social messages much more targeted.

Example: An SEO Business

Let's consider a SEO company that helps companies improve their rankings on key search sites. Their website is generic to cover all customer types: "We cater to all types of businesses and our expertise covers a wide range of business types and industries."

However, with social media they can target various customer groups on the sites that suit them best. Here are some examples of targeted messaging for marketing, business owners, and retail:

> Marketing: "We have just achieved number one ranking on the Google search for a Marketing Design company for seven search terms, including their new product. Helping push this company to the top search ranking has already succeeded in winning new business for this company."

Business Owners: "Here is a fantastic testimonial from Martin Lucas, who runs his own sales training company: 'My results ranking went from page 3 of the search results all the way to page 1 and then to the number 1 spot on Google in just 2 months! I LOVE these guys.'"

Retail: "We recognize that retail businesses now have the power to have their doors open for business 24 hours a day. Customers don't stop looking at 5:00 p.m.; online shops are for online shoppers. We can help keep people who are visiting your online shop at all hours."

Whatever your messages, always remember to show your passion and what you do day-to-day; people buy from people!

What Content Not to Broadcast

Social media makes it easy for you to send out targeted messages. In some cases, it's too easy—and can lead to problems.

The big Nos:

- Religion
- Race and nationalities
- Politics
- Swearing
- Pointless nonsense! For example, "I just made a cup of tea." Remember—*no* noise just for the sake of it!

Social media is mature enough for people to know when they see "noise."If you are a regular user of Facebook, then you will understand or you may be a Facebook noise maker! Business social is not personal social. Keep it interesting.

Social Media Synopsis and Summary

In this chapter, we have covered a lot of detail on how to use social media for sales. It is a huge passion of ours, but equally we recognize that first you must identify which platforms are right for you. If that means using multiple sites (it usually does) then we recommend using one site as a social hub, for example, Twitter or Phinkit, both of which allow you to update multiple sites at once.

You should also recognize that the majority of sites currently available have a programmer's heart. What we mean by that is, taking the example of LinkedIn, which was started by eight programmers, the technology may work really well, but there are no people-based user communications and users are left to figure out the site for themselves. It is the same with Facebook and Twitter.

This lack of guidance and purpose leads to bad user practices; the most typical one on LinkedIn occurs because of the way the site defines itself with the word "connect" but doesn't advise on what to do once you do connect with someone. They actually advise you to look at the connections of the person you just connected with. There are no hints and tips otherwise. This leads to people arriving on the site and thinking the route to making sales is to start collecting connections (i.e., people or contacts). Most people think getting to 500 will magically mean they start getting opportunities.

It doesn't work like that; it is about generating value and taking the time to connect and to do things that matter to those with whom you are connected. It's very easy to tell when people are churning out value-less content simply to "tick the box" vs. those who take the time to think about their target audience and craft interesting, valued content.

Focus and spend time on where you can win and add value!

If you want to know more, connect with us at the following places:

Jonathan

LinkedIn—Jonathan London

Twitter—@jonlondon

Martin

Phinkit—Martin Lucas

Twitter—@phinkit

Using Technology at Each Stage of the Sale

Add Power to Your Sales Skills

This chapter brings together all of the previous chapters by showing you specifically how to use different technologies at each stage of the sales process. We offer tips on best practices and what to avoid. It is important to note that technology is constantly changing, evolving, and offering new options at a dazzling pace—every day brings new tools that can potentially assist you in each step.

Note We will keep abreast of these changes on our website: www.ipgtraining.com

---

We also discuss different categories of technologies that salespeople can use to improve their productivity and time management during a sales process. The impact the technologies will have for you depends on the technology itself, and on how well and often it is used.

Baseline Capabilities

Before we go into the process and technology at each stage, it is important to discuss the three essential areas of mobility, data, and customer relationship management/sales force automation (CRM/SFA). E-mail is discussed separately in the Appendix.

Mobility

I (Jonathan) am writing, from the 6th floor of a hotel in Singer Island, Florida. I have also written parts of this book in Leeds, UK; New York, NY; Umbria, Italy; Ottawa, ON and many more places. I've also written parts while my wife was driving and while I used my headset to dictate into my iPhone while I was driving. Mobility allows us to work as much as we like (and if you are like Martin and I, that is a lot).

For the purpose of this book, mobility includes computing, broadband or private networks, and cloud services. Not using these today (even if you have to pay for them yourself) is tantamount to going into battle with only your bare hands and no weapons. For example, we have been using the cloud-based SharePoint site belonging to our publisher, Apress, to upload, download, and share chapters of this book. We have also used Skype, a free service, to collaborate live. (Martin is in London, Jonathan is in New York, and our editor, Jeff, is in Vermont.)

A Story

Martin and I were recently training employees at a company that was transitioning from selling print advertising to digital advertising. Approximately 300 people were trained, and true to the stereotype of older salespeople, most did not have a smartphone to use and demonstrate their offer digitally. They had screenshots and pictures instead.

When we gave them a homework exercise to create their own Twitter and Facebook pages, their resistance and fear were palpable. One of the salespeople (an excellent salesperson at selling print advertisements) was so naive about technology that when I suggested she increase the size of her e-mail font from 10 point to 14 point, she told me she couldn't because she was using a very small laptop.

I tell this story because it is a dramatic example of how misunderstood and underused technology is, even by people who sell technology. They sometimes don't even know how to use it, or use it at the most rudimentary levels. If you haven't already invested in a smartphone, or set up some accounts on Twitter, Facebook, or LinkedIn, YouTube, please do so. You will have better sales tools to do your job.

So from this point on, Martin and I could be anywhere writing this book—and we probably are (Figure 6-1).

Figure 6-1. Texting from spring training game with Jonathan's brother Jack.

Data

There is very little, if anything, that you cannot find on the Internet. Take people: As of May 11, 2012, there are more than 150,000,000 users on LinkedIn and more than 800,000,000 on Facebook. According to the website UnderstandingBigNumbers.com,[1] Google handles more than one billion—that's 1,000,000,000—searches daily. That doesn't include searches through Yahoo, Bing, and other non-US search engines.

There are huge databases that you pay for that are intended for the sales world. Some of the most popular are Hoovers,[2] LexisNexis,[3] OneSource,[4] The List,[5] and Sales Genie.[6] These are all excellent for searching and getting specific information however you need it. For example, if you want the names of all VPs of sales in New York State and New Jersey, it will give you all the names they have. Depending upon the company or level of service, you might also get their phone numbers, e-mail addresses, social media addresses, and more.

Using the words "sales list" in Google search (see Figure 6-2), brought up many million more names.

---

[1] Entry from August 17, 2011.

[2] www.hoovers.com

[3] www.lexisnexis.com

[4] www.onesource.com

[5] www.thelistinc.com

[6] www.salesgenie.com

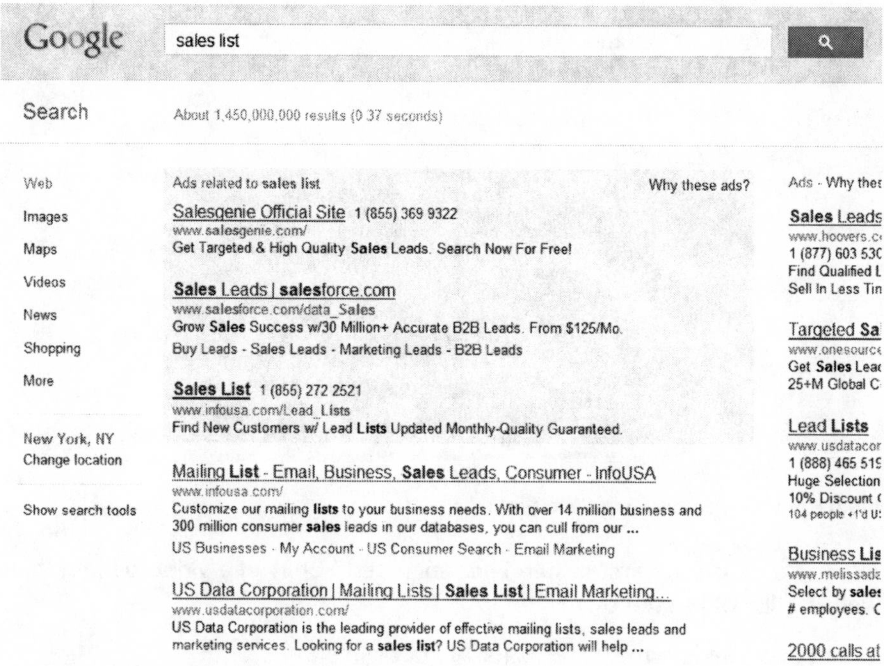

Figure 6-2. Google search for "sales lists."

These data via Google (you should also search with Bing, Yahoo and others) can also be accessed for situational or micro scenarios. For example, when I am meeting with a person and/or in an industry I am not familiar with, I will search for a website for that industry or job position to get familiar with the trends and language they use.

Another scenario is if I want to brush up on CFOs, the terminology they use, and the world they live in, I type in "cfo terms." I come up with Figure 6-3.

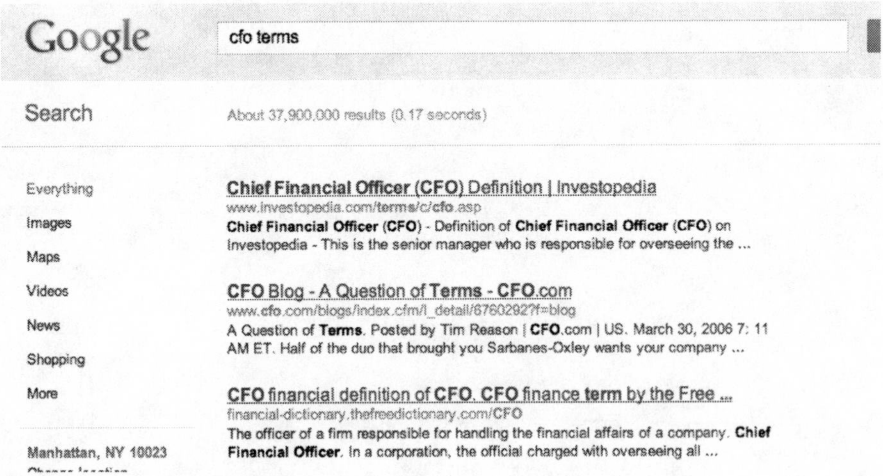

Figure 6-3. Google search for "cfo terms."

When I click on the first result, I get an added bonus of a video definition as well as a list of related terms.

When I search "cfo measurements," I get Figure 6-4.

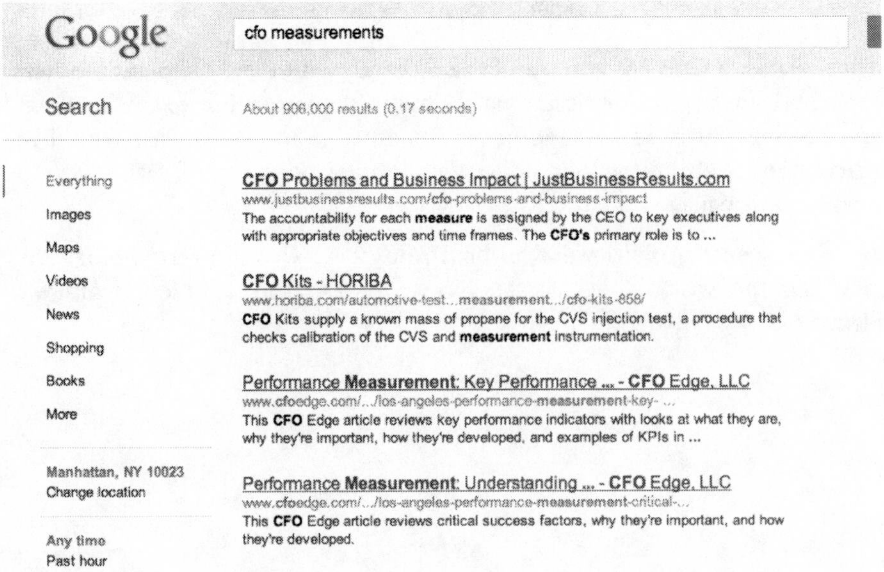

Figure 6-4. Google search for "cfo measurements."

It took me about 15 minutes to do all of these searches, and read what I needed to feel comfortable meeting with a CFO. If you are a more analytical person, or like doing research, it might take more time but it is well worth it.

Having more information and knowledge will demonstrate your credibility, confidence, and competence to the prospect, which has always been an essential element of sales success.

CRM (aka SFA: Sales Force Automation)

Customer Relationship Management (CRM), also known as Sales Force Automation (SFA), is like the control center, the mothership, the heart of your personal or company's sales operations. It is where all your sales, prospect, activity, and customer information should be. Some companies integrate back end functions (billing, ordering, etc.) as well, but that is not part of our discussion.

One of the first, and very popular, CRMs was ACT. I (Jonathan) have been using ACT (now called Sage ACT) for decades. At first I used it to simply keep track of contacts and reach out to them. I used it to remind myself of when I had to follow up and how.

The CRM world has progressed exponentially. Today these basic functions and so much more can all be done for you via your CRM of choice (Salesforce.com, NetSuite, Goldmine, Salesnexus, SugarCRM, Landslide, and many more) or lead/demand-generation services such as Eloqua, Marketo, Genius, Pardot and many others.

Let's fast forward to today's CRM capabilities to see what they can do for you. As you will see, CRM can do a lot more than just keep track of names and activities. It can also:

- Integrate leads or information about a company, prospect, or person directly into your database.

- Allow everyone you want to include to have access to your data so others can collaborate about a deal or respond to a service problem.

- Send out a single or series of e-mails to one or many people.

- Integrate "chat" functions so people can see when they are online and chat with each other.

- Integrate your chosen sales process so it provides tips to sell better and aligns with your forecast process for better forecasting accuracy.

- And more . . .

CRM is as essential a tool to selling effectively as a hammer is to a carpenter. It is available for use by one person or an enterprise. The level of functionality and services you use will vary based on needs and budget. In addition to those already mentioned, there are many Web-based CRMs for you to use. (You'll get about 42,500 results when you type in that term on Google.) Ironically, most companies have trouble getting salespeople to use a CRM since most salespeople are averse to any form of "administrivia," even if it is automated.

Just for reference, Jonathan's company, IPG, uses Sage ACT for the enterprise, Hubspot to host its website, and Constant Contact for its mailing services. IPG is transitioning to Voodooviral.com as well for sending out a series of video e-mails and to keep track of prospects' interaction with them.

The stages of the sales process have been detailed in Chapter 3; in Chapter 6 we move into more specific ways of utilizing the three essential elements of technology—mobility, data, and CRM/SFA—at each stage as well as other relevant technologies for you to use. For the reader's reference, several of the tables in Chapter 3 are used here as well.

Stage 1. Profile Territory and Assignment

As mentioned in Chapter 3, having a territory, assigned accounts, or even an individual account is like having your own business or franchise. You need to understand what you are selling and then analyze your territory to see where the business opportunities are most abundant. Conversely, you can analyze your territory and see which of the elements you offer will make you the most money (see Table 6-1). If you work with partners, you need to decide on whom you want to work with and/or where you might have to recruit additional partners.

Table 6-1. Overview of Stage 1: Profile Territory and Assignment

Stage 1 Goals:
• **Research territory and generate leads based on target profiles.**
• **Identify sweet spot.**

Actions	Technology	Resources
• Research territory. • Research companies. • Leverage channels. • Create target account list. • Enter into customer relationship management (CRM)/sales force automation (SFA).	• D+B/Hoovers • OneSource • LinkedIn • Salesforce.com • Vertical databases • Lexis/Nexis	• Other salespeople • Marketing and product management • Internal database • Library • Competitive Analyst

Skills
• Territory management   • Channel management

In this stage of the sale, you are profiling your territory or assignment, which could be geographical, by vertical/industry, by application (HR, finance, manufacturing, sales, etc.), by assigned accounts or a combination of these. This is best done via the multitude of databases that are available.

Some of the databases are free, but the best are available on a paid, subscription basis. They all attempt to provide the most up-to-date and accurate data, which you can search and sort in as many ways as you would need. The most important thing to do at this stage is to profile your territory by searching and sorting the database by location, SIC code, size, public or private status, and titles of the people you want to sell to.

Figure 6-5 shows a screenshot from OneSource's iSell that demonstrates the kind of information they offer.

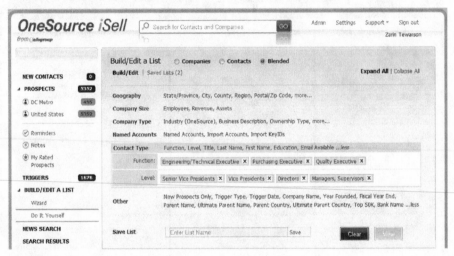

Figure 6-5. OneSource's iSell portal.

As you can see, you can search for prospects with all kinds of variables, and even make lists that will automatically search with your criteria without requiring you to enter the search terms each time. Of course, the narrower the search (i.e., the more variables involved), the fewer companies will be shown.

A salesperson would want the phone number, title, and street and e-mail addresses of the contacts to be able to start the next stage, prospecting. This information can be downloaded into a flat file (a plain text or mixed text and binary file that usually contains one record per line, also known as a csv file) or Excel file, and then merged into your CRM, a letter, or e-mail template to target one person or many at the same time.

Google and LinkedIn

You can also use Google (and/or Bing, Yahoo or others) to do simpler searches and get good information, but the information is not as easily used because it cannot be downloaded in as usable a format.

You can use LinkedIn and search by different variables. Depending on your type of membership, you can reach people more directly. You can also create a group based on the information and invite people to join. For example, if your territory was Akron, Ohio, you could ask LinkedIn to give you the names of all the companies or people in that area. You could then invite them to join your group. If I (Jonathan) were selling to the dentistry market, for instance, I could ask for the names of all dentists in my territory and then start a group called "Dental Practices Group for Akron." The same functionality is true of Facebook and other social media databases.

> **Note** IPG just created a LinkedIn group called "New VPs of Sales" because they are one of Jonathan's main targets and he wants to capture their attention as best he can. He is providing relevant information to encourage them to join and interact with him and each other.

Figures 6-6 to 6-7 show some screen shots from the basic version of LinkedIn. First, I searched with geographic criteria (Figure 6-6).

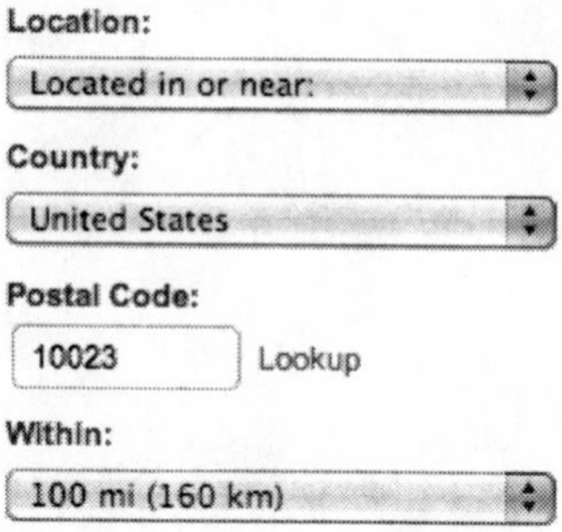

Location:
Located in or near:

Country:
United States

Postal Code:
10023   Lookup

Within:
100 mi (160 km)

Figure 6-6. Searching LinkedIn by geographic criteria.

I then asked for VPs of online media, in all companies, regardless of my connection (Figure 6-7).

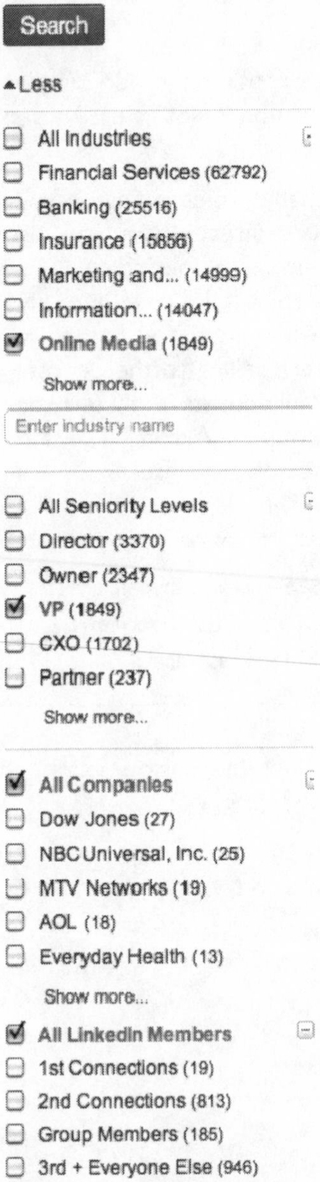

Search

▲ Less

- ☐ All Industries
- ☐ Financial Services (62792)
- ☐ Banking (25516)
- ☐ Insurance (15656)
- ☐ Marketing and... (14999)
- ☐ Information... (14047)
- ☑ Online Media (1849)

  Show more...

  Enter industry name

- ☐ All Seniority Levels
- ☐ Director (3370)
- ☐ Owner (2347)
- ☑ VP (1849)
- ☐ CXO (1702)
- ☐ Partner (237)

  Show more...

- ☑ All Companies
- ☐ Dow Jones (27)
- ☐ NBC Universal, Inc. (25)
- ☐ MTV Networks (19)
- ☐ AOL (18)
- ☐ Everyday Health (13)

  Show more...

- ☑ All LinkedIn Members
- ☐ 1st Connections (19)
- ☐ 2nd Connections (813)
- ☐ Group Members (185)
- ☐ 3rd + Everyone Else (946)

Figure 6-7. LinkedIn search for all VPs.

In the end, I received a list that showed I was already connected directly with 19 people with the characteristics I was seeking, and I was only one connection away from 813 other people.

Figure 6-8 shows the results of a request for VP of sales (the title I really want to sell to).

Figure 6-8. LinkedIn results for VP of Sales.

There were 17 direct and 305 secondary connections. I can save the search and get weekly updates to the group via e-mail.

In just a few minutes, I was able to see the following:

- There are many possible contacts but I am connected with only 17 directly.

- I have to be more aggressive in contacting others. Being a secondary connection with people doesn't mean I don't know them, only that I haven't reached out to them directly.

- There are groups for Online Media I can join to supplement my previous searches. (There were 4 with more than 14,000 members, many of them redundant.)

On the downside, to reach out to the people in these searches, I would have to do so individually. Or I'd have to join one of the groups, hoping the people I want to reach are members. Or I'd have to start my own group and invite people to join. There is no way to capture all the data, as I can on OneSource, and then do a mailing or e-mail all of them at once.

Data Mining and Analytics

More sophisticated users and organizations use data mining and analytics to notice trends as soon as possible. LinkedIn itself uses its database to see how much hiring is occurring in different geographical areas and industries to align their sales organization with these trends (you can also use government databases like the US Census to see such macro trends).

Companies use data and analytics to understand trends and tendencies of their prospects and customers by hundreds of characteristics (age, income, gender, season, previous purchases, etc.) to create their offers and focus their sales team. These capabilities are available on both a group and individual basis.

Once you have selected the companies and industries you want to sell to, start entering the data into your CRM. This can be done automatically if your CRM integrates with any of the databases. If done automatically, you will be able to access the data as described and use it for a mailing to your prospects of choice. Your records for each company you mailed it to will be updated for you, and, depending on the level of sophistication of your CRM, or other systems, it can alert you if somebody read or opened your e-mail. If not, your CRM can automatically send a second mailing and update you as well. If this doesn't reach your intended recipients, you'll need to send your message manually.

Lead-Generation Tips

Below is an approach we have used for years that has helped us in both good and bad times to be as successful as possible:

- Pick three verticals/applications/industries as your primary focus. You can experiment with a fourth every quarter to see what the potential is. Identify the companies that you want to sell to in these categories.

- Experiment quarterly with another one (if you have the capacity) that you think might do well. These could come from a sale somebody in your company made that is repeatable, an industry that is growing, etc.

- Don't exclude names of accounts that you know but may not be in the three verticals you are focusing on.

- Everyone wants to sell to the biggest companies, regardless of their or the company's ability to do so. Be realistic about how well you are positioned and what your real strength is. This does not mean you shouldn't try to land the biggest accounts, but don't fool yourself and make those targets the largest part of your efforts.

By using technology to identify and support your efforts to sell into your sweet spot, you are giving yourself the best chance to win as much business as possible.

Stage 2. Prospect and Gain Access to Key Contacts

It is best to think of prospecting as a form of marketing. There are many technologies available today that can enable a salesperson or organization to prospect or market themselves. It's also important to prospect/market all the time, and for the same reasons companies advertise all the time: to build awareness and stimulate people when they are thinking about, or ready to buy, something you are selling. Though they aren't interested on Tuesday, they may be on Friday, or if not this quarter, next and they may prefer a more visual medium to text. Table 6-2 outlines actions and resources for preparing for and contacting a prospect.

There are two basic types of marketing: branding and targeted. Branding is the reason companies advertise on TV, radio, billboards, newspapers, online, in taxis, in elevators, and pretty much every possible place they can. It is intended to create awareness of a brand, product or company, so that when people are ready to buy something, they will be favorably disposed and inclined to buy from that company.

Table 6-2. Overview of Stage 2: Prospecting and Gaining Access to Key Contacts

Stage 2 Goals:		
• **Prepare for and contact prospect.**		
• **Prequalify and obtain first meeting.**		
Actions	**Technology**	**Resources**
• Analyze selection criteria.	• LinkedIn	• Other salespeople
• Establish call objectives.	• Salesforce.com	• Marketing and product management
• Identify value of your offer.	• Vertical databases	
• Identify key contacts.	• E-mail	• Internal database
• Create prospecting message and delivery mechanism.	• Desktop video	
	• Streaming	
• Prequalify once appointment is confirmed.	• Social media	
Skills		
• Gaining access to power (aka prospecting)		
• Objection handling		

Targeted marketing, on the other hand, is intended to get a specific message to specific kinds of buyers, hopefully when they are beginning to think about a purchase or in the sales consideration funnel. For example, if you were to see an advertisement or get an e-mail about a car when you were actually in the consideration process, that would be good timing for the advertiser.

As mentioned in Chapter 3, there are several steps in the prospecting stage of the sales process. We focus primarily on steps 1–4 and 9 of this process since these are the steps best enabled by technology.

1. Build a Strategic Territory Plan

This has been covered in the preceding pages. The first step in prospecting is to narrow your search to the most likely potential customers. Using database services geared to salespeople gives you the biggest bang for your time and money. Depending on what you are selling, you can also use databases or online information that can tell you where people are moving in or out of, or where the youngest or oldest population is.

For example, I (Jonathan) worked with a client who was selling security technology to K–12 school districts, so his company needed to know which areas had the greatest number of children or where the most schools were being built. Another client was selling into the construction industry, so they needed to find where the government was lending the most money to build roads, bridges, and other types of infrastructure. They found data under the Freedom of Information Act and from H.U.D. (Housing and Urban Development) to determine where the money was going, and, in turn, where they should be spending their time and money selling. I also worked with a company that sold remote surveillance systems and decided one of their target markets would be churches that could use their systems to protect everyone from any inappropriate behavior. They then found a list of all the churches and archdioceses in the United States.

2. Initiate a Multipronged Attack

This step is all about identifying the best positions/titles/functions to contact once you have chosen your vertical industries. In general, in a B2B environment, there are usually four to five departments or functions in an organization that can probably benefit from your offer, including:

- Finance

- Executive

- Functional (HR, sales, manufacturing, etc.)

- IT

- Procurement

Of course, different industries have different functions that may limit you. For example, when selling to the government, healthcare and education verticals in particular, there are often more centralized or regulated models for an organization to buy things. Federal government sales need to abide by Government Securities Act (GSA) rules or an existing contract that has been awarded to a specific company or companies. If your company doesn't fit into either of these, it makes it much more difficult to sell to the government. Large companies may force you into selling only to the procurement department, limiting your ability to penetrate an account.

If this is the case, you can play by their rules and see where it gets you. If you don't succeed, then you might consider talking to other people in the company to influence the main buyer, or someone else who might be able to act on his or her own, if necessary, and if your offer is really compelling. It is very doubtful that if the general counsel or CFO said he or she wanted something, procurement would say, "No, you can't have it."

Using the database of your choice, search for the titles and names you want to sell to. We (Martin and Jonathan) search for several titles, including VP of sales, VP of channels, VP of customer service, VP of HR or training, and CFO, because they can all benefit from our services.

You should also use your own connections and contacts to see if you or an acquaintance knows any of the people, specifically, or in the companies you want to sell to. Social media such as LinkedIn or Facebook, Pinterest, and even MySpace (if you are in the music or entertainment industry) are good for this. Of course, if you are using a database you pay for such as Hoover's, The List, OneSource, or others, you need to refer to these as well.

3. Never Cold Call Again

This step, recall, is all about creating legitimate reasons from the prospect's perspective to call a potential client.

There are so many different technologies and ways to use technology during this step. Remember, the most important thing to do is keep yourself aware of things that are happening in the categories (industry, profession, geographic area, etc.) and companies you decided on in step 1 of this 9-step process, preferably before everyone knows about them and the event becomes a fait accompli.

A perfect example is reading a blog or online news piece suggesting that a client might be having troubles with the company's lawyers or ad agency. If you are a law firm or ad agency, that would be an amazing time to reach out to the client with a proposal for your services. You could then call all clients of that law firm or ad agency to see if they are having similar problems.

Some of the events you might want to be aware of in the accounts you want to sell to include:

- *Changes in positions.* I, Jonathan, look for hires of new VPs of sales. You want to look for the key positions you want to sell to. If one company hires somebody from another, that means there is an opening at the first company. You might have two places to call and not just one. You simply go into Google Alerts and type in "VP of Sales."

- *People updating their biography on LinkedIn or elsewhere.* The two biggest sales I made in 2011 were the result of bio updates by two people I know. One was an individual I hadn't spoken to for almost 10 years, and the other for about 5 years. Both became VPs of sales and I contacted them to offer my congratulations. Then I asked when would be a good time to touch base. Each responded accordingly, and I made substantial sales in a relatively short timeframe.

- *Company expansion.* They might need a variety of services, domestic or international.

- *Hiring plans.* If they are hiring, they are probably making money and might be in a better position to spend. Or, if you are a recruiter, they may need your services.

- *Moving.* Companies that move need phone systems, moving services, furniture, architectural services, etc. Salespeople in such areas would want to know of any plans to move.

- *Mergers and acquisitions.* They may be acquiring a company you are already doing business with, or a company you already serve may need more of what you offer.

- *Good or bad earnings.* You can call about either one. Either they may have more money to spend, or need to save money. Both are opportunities.

- *Bad experience with current vendor.* How do you find out about this? Blogs, LinkedIn groups, company-sponsored forums, etc.

- Can you think of others for you and your industry?

There are many sources of data online that compile information and will send you alerts. Google Alerts is one of the best and it is free. You can enter company names, terms, events, and job title changes and Google Alerts will send you an update daily or weekly.

Figure 6-9 shows what comes to my e-mail every week. I review it and decide which items I want to respond to. I also invite each person to my R.E.A.L. Selling LinkedIn Group and my Constant Contact e-mail list.

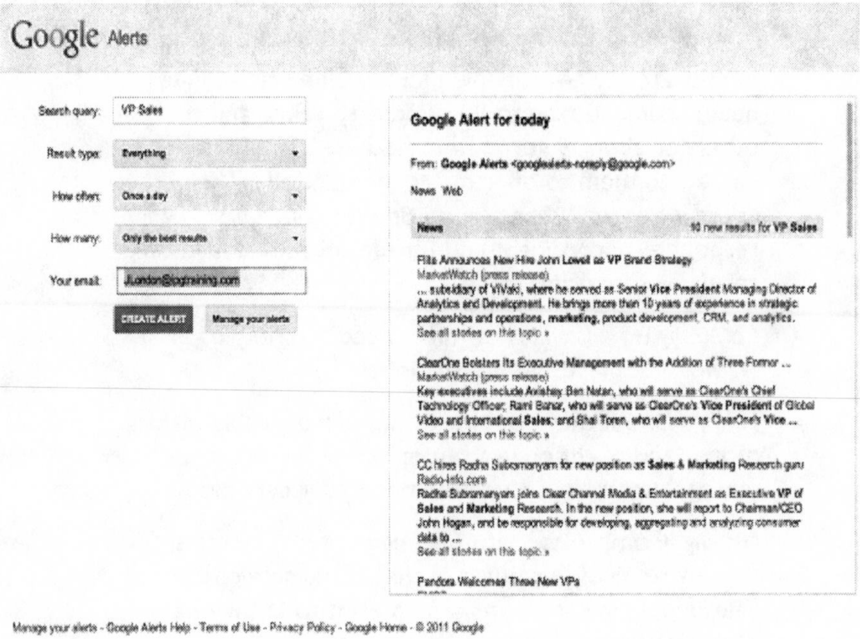

Figure 6-9. Google Alerts for VP of Sales.

Joining LinkedIn groups that are pertinent will also notify you of changes. (See Figure 6-10.)

LINKEDIN SAVED SEARCH UPDATE

We found **2 new results** that match your saved search "VP Sales 100 mi (160 km) 10023":

Saved Search Results
• View all new results

Figure 6-10. LinkedIn group saved search update results.

RSS feeds from blogs or websites that you want to follow will keep you informed as things are happening. Several databases, such as iSell from OneSource, will let you know of developments in your targeted accounts. iLantern.com can do the same. These might add to what you get from Google Alerts or be presented in an easier to use format that can be integrated into your CRM.

As part of your marketing/prospecting effort, you can also reach out to people with information that may not lead directly to a sale, but that is relevant to them, and in doing so will keep them mindful of you when they are considering, close to deciding, or ready to buy something you sell.

For example, I use different sources of information in verticals I want to sell to and when I see something interesting, I might send it to an individual or a group I belong to. In particular:

- I sell a lot to the "new media" category, so I get feeds from sources such as IAB and MediaPost that I send to people. I even get feeds from my competition so I can use some of their information to help clients or prospects.

- IBM and major consulting firms publish brilliant research papers on trends in an industry or position (CMO, CFO, etc.). I send links to people who I know can learn from and use the information to perform better in their positions. They also make me an "expert," so I have more credibility than my competition.

Note One of the reasons executives agree to see salespeople is to learn things about their industry, competition, or other to help them make smarter decisions and be more competitive.

Using all these methods, you will never have to make a "cold call." You will always be messaging and reaching out for a reason that is relevant to the person you are trying to reach. This will help you get more appointments.

▓ **Remember** The best reason way to get through to somebody is with a referral, since it lowers people's resistance and immediately creates trust. If you do have a reference, ask the reference if she knows what the person you want to reach is focusing on and what you should say. You can also ask her to introduce you and suggest to the person that he take a meeting with you. This almost guarantees you and the prospect will meet.

4. Use Different Methods to Contact People

How do you get in touch with prospects? In as many ways as you can and whatever works best. For companies, technologies that can be used include TV, radio, Internet, online advertising, e-mail, social media, blogs, video (streaming or seminars), webinars, whitepapers, e-books, Twitter, and others. Individuals can also use all of these except TV (unless they are extraordinarily aggressive and/or well funded). These can be used individually or in combination. For example, I know salespeople who have created their own Internet radio shows to attract people to them and what they are selling. Options here include:

- www.internet-radio.com/
- www.blogtalkradio.com/

Both allow you have your own radio program over the Internet. You can then invite people to the show, get their names and e-mail addresses upon entering, and start building your following. The quality of the show will appeal to attendees who will invite others, etc. What you can do to get your message in front of someone is limited only by your imagination.

There are a myriad number of websites and companies that can educate you on the best way to run your own online ad campaigns, or improve your search engine optimization (SEO), including Hubspot (hubspot.com), Pardot (pardot.com), Marketo (marketo.com), Eloqua (eloqua.com), and many others. There are thousands of consultants who can help with this as well. YouTube has great tools to help with any video campaigns as well.

Jonathan tried to do this by himself for 3 years and it didn't work out. He finally hired Precision Marketing Group, LLC, to help him bring all of this together. The activity on his website has increased fivefold in less than 12 months. Hubspot is currently hosting his website, and they also offer a great service.

Here are some examples of how to use technology to reach people.

E-Mail: There are many companies that will allow you to send e-mails as a series that addresses the "persona" (basically a profile of a type of person or job description) of the person you are trying to sell and their decision-making or evaluation process. For example, a household with two working parents and two children younger than 5 might be interested in certain things as their children grow older or services that help them juggle their busy lives. You can use e-mail to maintain awareness. These are called "drip campaigns," and they keep people mindful of you so that when they start considering the need for your type of service, they will reach out to you. The e-mails can be a combination of many things, including text, video, and/or links to data on your website. Remember, you can also use more targeted e-mail as described in Chapter 3.

Blogs: To survive today, companies and individuals must have blogs (short for Web logs if you don't already know). In sales, blogs are used primarily as a prospecting/branding initiative. They can be text or video, which is becoming easier and more popular. You use them to create awareness and "mindshare." You can repurpose them to send to a specific prospect if you know a person has a particular interest in your blog's subject. It has become so common that there are even blogs for blogs. Wordpress.com is the company whose technology platform is used most often because it has a lot of tremendous capabilities including content management, ability to integrate multimedia, an inherent design that makes it more search engine friendly, and more. It is also free! Google, Posterous, Tumblr, and others offer a free blog service.

Let's say somebody was interested in reading about or finding a "sales expert" and used the search term "sales blogs" on Google. As of May 2012, they would have come up with 151,000 names.

As you can see, there are an overwhelming number of blogs devoted to sales. With better filtering and knowledge of how to use Google search, you can get a smaller, more useful number. Using "blogs for sales" reduces the number significantly and is more useful. You should also search the Web for tips on using Google search or go into Google's help pages directly to get better at this.

One way to get your blog noticed is to invite prospects and customers to receive the blog as it is published and updated. When you add entries, they receive notice automatically. You can also post new entries by letting people know through your LinkedIn status, Twitter, or by mentioning it in a newsletter. The idea of the blog is to provide a continuous stream of information and insights that keeps you top of mind for prospects and customers, so your marketing of each piece needs to be ongoing. For more blog tips, see the sidebar.

So the question isn't whether you need to blog, but how to get your blog noticed. Go to www.ipgtraining.com/sales-tips-blog/ to see Jonathan's blog.

MAUREEN CONDON ON BLOGGING

Maureen Condon, a Principal at Precision Marketing Group LLC (precisionmarketing.com) in Boston, offers the following advice about blogging.[7]

Your business blog can have a tremendously positive impact on your sales process. Here are six benefits you can expect to achieve with a quality blog:

Position yourself as a trusted expert in your field.
Your prospects want to know that they are engaging with the most qualified expert possible. Blog posts that illustrate your industry knowledge and experience can build critical credibility among your target audience. These may include general pieces about best practices, things to consider and questions to ask, and more specific posts about customers you have solved problems for and things you've learned on the job.

Tip: Give, give, and then give some more. Do not be afraid of giving too much information away in your blog posts. Your audience will appreciate content that offers honest value, and they will remember you when they are ready to buy.

Guide prospects strategically through the sales pipeline.
Many of your prospects will start the buying process with online research. A well-optimized blog will drive these people to your site at the early stages of their decision making. By mapping out the path you'd like prospects to take to convert to a paying customer, you can create content that guides them through your pipeline successfully. Perhaps they start by reading a post on how to choose the right provider of your product/service, which guides them to download a buying guide, which triggers a demo invitation.

---

[7] © 2012 Maureen Condon. Used with permission.

Tip: Integrate your sales process with your blog strategy so you can offer up relevant content at each stage of the buying cycle.

Stay top of mind.
Your blog offers an opportunity to put valuable content in front of your audience on a regular basis. Ideally, your prospects will subscribe to your blog so your posts appear regularly in their email or RSS feed. But for the many prospects and customers who don't subscribe, your blog posts can be linked to from your e-mail newsletter, tweeted, posted on your Facebook page, and used as updates on LinkedIn. These updates keep you visible with the audience you want to engage.

Tip: Leverage every blog post you create in all of your other distribution channels— newsletter, website, social media, etc.

Inspire desired action.
If you've mapped out your sales process and know what you want prospects to do as they travel through your sales funnel, then you can use your blog posts to trigger desired actions. You may know, for example, that prospects who complete a certain questionnaire are more likely to buy than those who don't. Why not publish a post that teases some of the questions in your questionnaire and then invites readers to complete it?

Tip: Include a call to action after every post you publish, but keep the blog post itself educational in nature. People will stop reading your blog if you use it to sell.

Build lasting relationships.
Blogs are especially powerful in their ability to help companies create and sustain relationships with prospects and customers— people do business with people they know, like, and trust and your blog is great place to become known, liked, and trusted. The best blogs create connections by allowing the writers' personalities to shine through in the posts. Your firm may have one or several people who publish posts, and after a while, your readers should be able to recognize who is writing without looking at the byline.

Tip: Encourage your blog writers to share stories about their family, hobbies, etc. within the context of their posts and allow them to put forth their opinion and create a distinct voice for themselves in your blog.

Attract new prospects.
As your prospects do online research about your products, services or industry, you want to show up in their searches. Your blog can pull new people into your site by offering up the right content at the right time—when they are searching and in the mindset to learn more. To make sure you show up in relevant searches, make sure you optimize posts strategically and publish fresh content consistently.

Tip: Think about three or four big ideas that your prospects will care about/do research on over the course of the year. Then create several blog posts—and other content—around these ideas to publish throughout the year.

Online Advertising: Anybody who is willing to spend money—whether individual entrepreneurs or companies—can start advertising online. The most common and popular are:

- PPC (pay per click) with Google, Bing, and Yahoo.

- Banner advertising with Facebook, LinkedIn, and other social media platforms.

- YouTube, Vimeo, Ustream, Blinkx, or others where you can have video advertisements.

It is a simple equation for PPC. You set a budget and the maximum you are willing to pay for someone to click on your ad (which should then link the person to a particular place or landing page on your website). For example, you can say you want to spend no more than $100 per month, with a maximum of $10/click.

Jonathan's wife, a psychoanalyst, started using Google's PPC a few years ago with a limited budget. She gets a many of her patients from her online presence and referrals. She also has her own website with videos of her speaking or being interviewed. She sets herself apart because of the quality of her online and personal presence, so people who are considering some help would be more comfortable with her.

Banner advertising is usually based on a CPM (cost per thousand). That means that for every 1,000 people who see your ad, you will pay a certain amount. Again, a person can click on your ad and go to a specific place or location. CPM will get you more exposure but with less specificity.

Martin has done marketing campaigns on LinkedIn and Jonathan has done the same with a Google PPC campaign. Our experience is that unless you have deep pockets, and do it properly, you probably won't get the results you want. You need to have a more targeted market, which can be accessed via social media and SEO (search engine optimization), and costs less. Many companies will use PPC as a way of building up their SEO and social media interaction and then reduce their expense once the SEO is working the way they want it to.

You might want to use LinkedIn to target a particular industry or title, while Google is more general and directed to a larger audience. For example, if you are announcing a new product or service (you can be an individual entrepreneur or salesperson for a company) you can place an ad in either of these media to make people aware of it. Or if you want to get to VPs of sales (Figure 6-10), you would target your ad to that audience (recall Figure 6-10 earlier of my actual search LinkedIn).

You can update your status to let people know of new services without spending anything, although some consider this inappropriate since updates are meant to be more subtle.

Please understand that these services cost money and you need to decide whether this is the best use of your budget for marketing your services. You can use social media for the same purpose, via blogs, Twitter, Facebook, and search engine optimization, without having to pay per click.

5. Craft Effective Messages for Voicemail or E-mail

Creating effective messages does not require technology but delivering them does. This is where you would use your own individual e-mail system or work with a lead generation system such as Eloqua, Marketo, Pardot, and others.

You can create video messages using your own camera, software that can record you such as Camtasia.com or Quicktime on your Apple, or myriad other offerings. Voodoo Marketing is excellent for sending and tracking your video e-mails. A service called VYou is also available for you to capture and interact with people using video messaging.

■ **Note** Remember, the key to any voicemail or follow-up e-mail message is to leave a message that is relevant and intriguing without necessarily leaving the whole message. That way the prospect might call you back (probably not) or be more receptive the next time you reach out.

---

6. Get Past Gatekeepers

Executives still have executive assistants, yet most still check their own e-mail, so e-mail is a very good way to get past the executive assistant. Combined with a referral or a current event, and formatted properly (as shown in Chapter 3), it is an unbeatable weapon. You can also use a technology called a telephone and call early or late when the executive assistant may not be around. Asking for the assistant's help and support using e-mail, video, etc. is the foundation if you don't get to the executive directly.

7. The Moment of Truth: Three *Musts* When the Prospect Picks Up the Phone, Opens Your E-mail, or Views Your Response

Again, the structure of credibility, benefits, and close for appointment is something created best by you. The delivery of the message is done in the same way you craft an effective e-mail or video mail. If you are following the blogs, tweets, LinkedIn groups, or updates of a person or company, you can respond to those as a way of getting to the person you want to reach.

■ **Note** If you go to http://www.ipgtraining.com/sales-training-videos---podcasts/, you will find samples of good video and prospecting messages.

You can also start using e-mail to get people involved in contests to see if they will respond or to be more interactive as opposed to using plain text or HTML. Trying different combinations will help you find the best way to use e-mail in combination with voicemail.

8. Anticipate and Handle Objections to Your Offer

We don't have much to add here regarding the use of technology except to remind you the best way to handle an objection to your offer is to address it before the prospect says something. Perhaps you can do this through the subject line in your e-mail. For example, if you know they are using a competitor you can have your subject line say, "Because You Are an XYZ User" or, if it is the end of the fiscal year for them, your subject line could be "You Probably Don't Have Any More Money." These are examples of formatting vs. technology, but hopefully they help.

9. Always Follow Up Appropriately

It is unimaginable to prospect today without some form of automation—whether it is a simple list management function, Excel, or dedicated software such as ACT/Sage, NetSuite, RightNow, Landslide, Salesforce.com, or countless others.

You must automate your prospecting to manage all your activity, especially your follow-up.

As mentioned in Chapter 3, you should also vary the time at which you follow up and the method. Social media is now allowing you to make connections you never could before. You may use some of the more unique ways described earlier in getting to people, or through some colorful graphics, using video or animation just to mix it up and appeal to different people in different ways. Video e-mails, attaching a YouTube video, and sending e-cards or e-vites are examples.

There are many companies that can now automate your e-mailing or marketing process. Voodooviral.com (especially effective for video e-mails) and Constant Contact (constantcontact.com) can do this by automating the timing and the type of mailing sent to your prospects vs. your needing to figure it out or doing it yourself.

Finally, you should use technology to analyze the effectiveness of your different types of prospecting or marketing. Again, there are thousands of companies that can do this for you, including several we have already mentioned. Search for "sales pipeline analytics" or "sales analytics" to see what is available.

In appexchange.salesforce.com there are more than 85 companies offering "pipeline management" tools and 24 companies offering "prospecting" tools. In a Google search there are about 68,700 results for "prospecting software" These tools will help you analyze which of your prospecting and marketing campaigns are working best and least effectively.

If you take advantage of the ideas in this chapter, you will now have more meetings of a higher quality that put you in a better position to win more deals. You are in the best place you can be for the next stage, meeting with prospects.

Stage 3: Meet with Prospects to Discover, Qualify, and Influence

The initial meeting with a prospect used to be confined to meeting in person or over the phone. Now there a multitude of technologies that can add video, including Web conferencing and streaming (see Table 6-3).

The same process of S.PRI.N.G. dialogue discovery (see Chapter 3) should be used regardless of the medium. There are some great and free desktop video capabilities including Google, Skype, Tenhands, iChat, and others. Companies that allow you to share, demonstrate, and collaborate while offering video include GoToMeeting, WebEx, AdobeConnect, iMeet, and more. Chapter 4 describes all of these options and more.

There are also companies that allow you to chat with a prospect when they come on to your website. The most popular is LivePerson; it allows you to have as short or lengthy a chat as needed to qualify or sell a prospect. Many of Jonathan's customers use this with great effect.

Video is available for a fee from the major manufacturers and their resellers including Cisco, LifeSize, Vidyo, and others. A Google search for Web conferencing brought up thousands of choices. Not all have video, but many do. These services are also becoming available on your iPad or tablet so you can take have these meetings wherever you are (as long as you have a good Internet connection and good lighting).

Table 6-3. Overview of Stage 3: Meeting with Prospects to Discover, Qualify, and Influence

Stage 3 Goals: • Discover, qualify, and influence.		
Actions	**Technology**	**Resources**
• Understand the current situation. • Build rapport and show expertise. • Define priorities including a compelling event. • Qualify time frame, decision process, decision criteria, budget. • Plant seeds and create traps for competition. • Get commitment for a next step that favors you. • Analyze selection criteria. • Establish call objectives. • Identify value of your offer. • Identify key contacts. • Identify key business drivers. and pain points. • Address business problem you can solve.	• LinkedIn • Salesforce.com • Vertical data bases • E-mail • Desktop video or web conferencing • Streaming • Social media • Laptop • iPad or tablet • Wireless	• Management • Pre/post technical support • SMEs (subject matter experts) • Brochures • Case studies • References
Skills		
• DiSC • S.PRI.NG dialogue • Presenting • Objection handling		

We do most of our selling using Web or video conferencing. When I send an Outlook invitation to confirm a meeting, I always give people the Web conferencing information, which includes video via Skype or Adobe Connect.

Using Web or video today can give you a real competitive advantage, or a disadvantage if your competition is using this technology and you are not. Having video can let you see prospects' mannerisms, or whether they are distracted. You have more control of the meeting. You can therefore use DiSC more easily because you are given more information.

Figures 6-11 and 6-12 are some examples of what an initial sales meeting via webinar (in this case Adobe Connect) looks like:

Figure 6-11. Selling to two people. Jonathan is talking to two people from PEER1 over video.

Figure 6-12. Interacting with seven people simultaneously in different locales. Jonathan is presenting to six people from iMediaSalesTeam.com, a DBA of Iverson Media and Communications LLC.

You should always do some research about the company, industry, and person/people you are meeting with. By being as knowledgeable as possible, you—and remember, people buy you first—will be more impressive and influential because you are more of an expert.

A real example is when I (Jonathan) was meeting with a company called PEER1 Hosting. My goal was to sell his sales training program to the VP of sales. Here are several easy ways I prepared for the meeting:

First I used Google Alerts (Figure 6-13).

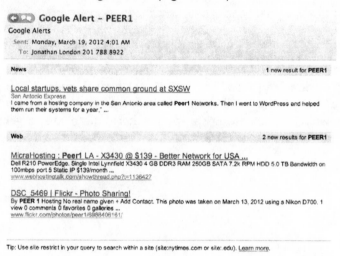

Figure 6-13. Google Alerts for PEER 1.

Google Alerts informed me that PEER 1 just opened a new, environmentally friendly data center in the UK, a fact I will use in my S.PRI.N.G. dialogue.

Then I check LinkedIn to see if I know anybody in common with the person I was meeting with. I then called those people to see if they could give me some insight into the prospect.

In this case, I talked to my friend X about PEER 1. He told me that it is a great company with a great service, but it needs to increase its presence in the enterprise market to be more competitive with the biggest competitors. Next, I went to their website to see if they had press releases (Figure 6-14) or are emphasizing anything in particular. I learned they are doing great things in the UK and are also hiring—good signs:

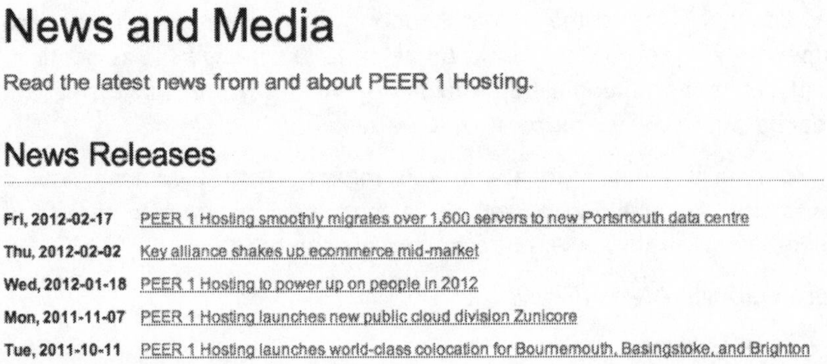
News and Media
Read the latest news from and about PEER 1 Hosting.
News Releases
Fri, 2012-02-17 PEER 1 Hosting smoothly migrates over 1,600 servers to new Portsmouth data centre
Thu, 2012-02-02 Key alliance shakes up ecommerce mid-market
Wed, 2012-01-18 PEER 1 Hosting to power up on people in 2012
Mon, 2011-11-07 PEER 1 Hosting launches new public cloud division Zunicore
Tue, 2011-10-11 PEER 1 Hosting launches world-class colocation for Bournemouth, Basingstoke, and Brighton

Figure 6-14. News releases for PEER 1.

Then I viewed blogs (Figure 6-15) to see what people were saying (a search for PEER1 using Google's blog filter got 16,500,000 hits). I learned that people love their offering in the SMB (small-medium business) market but don't know them well in the enterprise space where there are larger opportunities and their services are just as good.

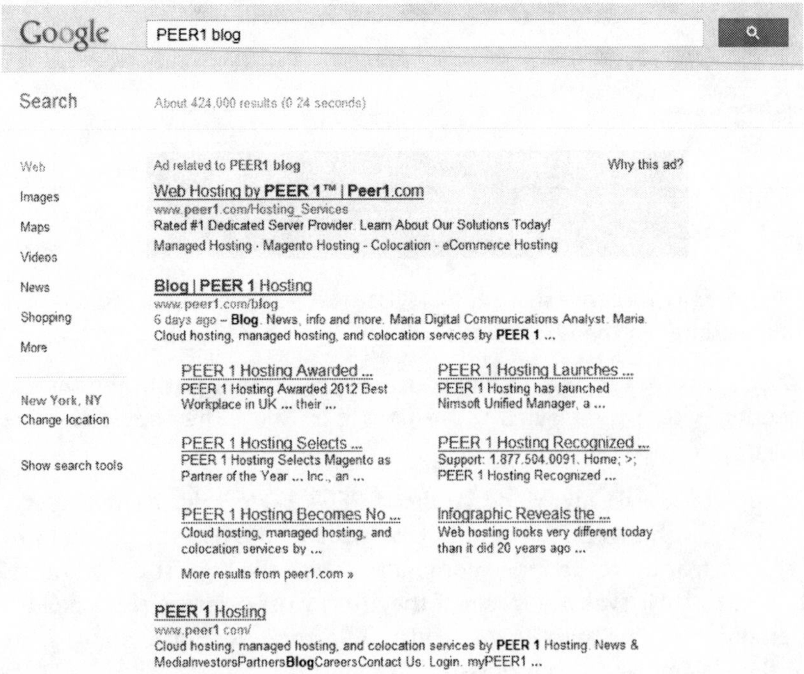
Google
PEER1 blog
Search
About 424,000 results (0.24 seconds)
Web
Images
Maps
Videos
News
Shopping
More
New York, NY
Change location
Show search tools
Ad related to PEER1 blog
Why this ad?
Web Hosting by PEER 1™ | Peer1.com
www.peer1.com/Hosting_Services
Rated #1 Dedicated Server Provider. Learn About Our Solutions Today!
Managed Hosting - Magento Hosting - Colocation - eCommerce Hosting
Blog | PEER 1 Hosting
www.peer1.com/blog
6 days ago – Blog. News, info and more. Maria Digital Communications Analyst. Maria. Cloud hosting, managed hosting, and colocation services by PEER 1 ...
PEER 1 Hosting Awarded ...
PEER 1 Hosting Awarded 2012 Best Workplace in UK ... their ...
PEER 1 Hosting Launches ...
PEER 1 Hosting has launched Nimsoft Unified Manager, a ...
PEER 1 Hosting Selects ...
PEER 1 Hosting Selects Magento as Partner of the Year ... Inc., an ...
PEER 1 Hosting Recognized ...
Support: 1.877.504.0091. Home; >; PEER 1 Hosting Recognized ...
PEER 1 Hosting Becomes No ...
Cloud hosting, managed hosting, and colocation services by ...
Infographic Reveals the ...
Web hosting looks very different today than it did 20 years ago ...
More results from peer1.com »
PEER 1 Hosting
www.peer1.com/
Cloud hosting, managed hosting, and colocation services by PEER 1 Hosting. News & MediaInvestorsPartnersBlogCareersContact Us. Login. myPEER1 ...

Figure 6-15. Blogs for PEER 1.

I was better prepared for my meeting and was able to weave all this information into my S.PRI.N.G. dialogue. Doing all this led to me to making the sale and having a very happy customer.

■ **Note** Doing deep research can help immensely when prospecting since it will give you very relevant topics and problems you can help prospects deal with.

You are now ready to assess whether this is an opportunity you want to engage in or walk away from.

Stage 4: Confirm Fit and Decide to Engage or Not; Begin to Develop Team and Sales Strategy

At this stage, you should analyze and compare the information you have to decide if you want to engage and what your chances are to win the business (see Table 6-4). A version of your "ideal opportunity" (a list of the elements involved in a sales opportunity where you win most often) should be the basis of comparison and can be automated via an Excel spread sheet or integrated into your CRM/SFA.

Table 6-4. Overview of Stage 4: Confirming Fit and Deciding Whether to Engage or Not

Stage 4 Goals: • Decide to engage, confirm fit. • Begin team building and strategy.		
Actions	**Technology**	**Resources**
• Match information from initial meeting to determine if it is a real opportunity and your chances of winning are good enough. • If you decide to engage, start building team and strategy to win the deal.	• LinkedIn • Salesforce.com • E-mail • Desktop video or web conferencing • Streaming • Social media • Laptop • iPad or tablet • Wireless	• Management • Pre/post technical support • SMEs (subject matter experts) • Brochures • Case studies • References • S.C.O.O.P. strategy sheets • Previous sales • Sweet spot profile
Skills		
• Resource management • Team selling • Selling strategically using S.C.O.O.P.		

An example might look like this Figure 6-16, taken from our strategic selling methodology called S.C.O.O.P. (see Chapter 3), which is integrated into Salesforce.com with our Appexchange Partner (www.white-springs.com). The scale is 1–10, with 10 being the best and 1 being the worst.

Strengths & Weaknesses		View Competitors
Strengths (1-10)	Us	Internal
Technical Fit	10	0
Positioning with DM	10	0
Geographic Fit Inc International	9	0
Existing Happy Customer	0	0
Pricing or ROI Advantage	5	0
Circle of Influence Supports Your Company	8	0
Industry Expertise and References	9	0
Cultural Compatibility	4	0
Have a Coach	8	0
Resources to Execute and Win	6	0

Figure 6-16. Decision-making criteria in deciding whether or not to engage.

Additional criteria for deciding whether to engage might include:

1. Knowledge of the decision process (people involved) and your alignment. Are you well or poorly positioned?

2. Decision criteria and fit. Are their criteria for making a decision a good fit for your offer?

3. Knowledge of decision-maker's priorities, gain, and fit. This is essential because you can do great work with everyone but if it isn't relevant to the decision-maker, then you are wasting your time.

4. Length of time involved in opportunity. If you came in early, you might have influenced the criteria or developed good relations. If not, you are usually not in the position you want to be in.

Some criteria can be weighted to be more important than others. For example, alignment with the decision-maker, having a coach and others might be 1.3% more important than cultural compatibility.

Hypothetically, if your best score could be 130, any score above 65 would give you a 50% chance and you might decide to compete. However, if the items are 65 or above but the items with greater importance show you at a disadvantage, you still might not engage. Anything below might mean you walk away and find something better.

Another option is using an Excel spreadsheet (Figure 6-17). You can define more easily whether there is a real opportunity to sell to:

Compelling Event Assessment

Rep Name _____   Assessment Date _____
Company Name _____   Potential Revenue _____
Decision Maker/Power _____   Projected Close Date _____

Dimension	Question	Yes	No	Don't Know	Comments
Internal pressure	Is there any **internal pressure and/or initiatives** to specifically deploy a POS System by a certain date? If so, please provide in the comments section.				
	Has a date or timeframe been set for a solution to be "**in place**" (e.g. beginning of fiscal year)?				
	Are there competing projects for the funds available?				
	Is the POS system the **highest priority** among competing projects with the company?				
	Has the Power **openly committed** to a result that is tied to this project by a certain date?				
External Pressure	Is there an external event/forces/requirements that is prompting the power to investigate alternative POS Solutions?				
	Is the current POS system negatively impacting current business requirements, needs and pressures?				
Personal Impact	Does our Coach and/or Power stand to benefit personally if an improved POS solution is approved or deployed by a certain date?				
	Is the pain associated with status quo greater than the pain and risk expected with this change?				
	Are all the personal wins by stakeholders associated with this project greater than the possible risks (Implementation, Operational, Financial, Talent)?				
	Has the decision maker or key influencer personally committed to the success of this project by a certain date?				
	Have there been negative personal effects related to the company's POS System capabilities?				
Consequences of Inaction	If they do not go live on a new POS Solution by a certain date, are there consequences?				
	Are there hard, soft, political, or personal costs of **doing nothing**? If so, please document in the comments section.				

Figure 6-17. Compelling event assessment using Excel.[8]

Assuming you wish to compete, you then need to build a team and/or follow your internal processes. You should schedule meetings with these people throughout the sales process using your e-mail (Outlook, Google Calendar, iCalendar, and others). When you meet, be sure to integrate video and Web conferencing when appropriate and see if you can include team members outside your company (partners, customers, etc.) more effectively using these same technologies.

---

[8] Used with permission from Sales Benchmark (www.salesbenchmarkindex.com /bid/81016/Will-This-Deal-Ever-Close-A-Compelling-Event).

Many companies offer software that allows teams to communicate and collaborate easier, more effectively, and for less or no money. These include SAVO (not free) and the collaboration or Web conferencing software mentioned earlier.

Most browsers today have their own version of Instant Messaging (IM) or chat that you can use to communicate and collaborate with people on your team. If you are using Salesforce.com, you can use their integrated version called Chatter.

Other CRM companies may have similar functionality. Salesforce.com with its app partners, including IPG (in partnership with White-Springs), allows electronic access to members of a team so they can visualize, contribute to and discuss a strategy via IPG's S.C.O.O.P. (strategic – comprehensive – optimized – online – planner) process (see Figure 6-18).

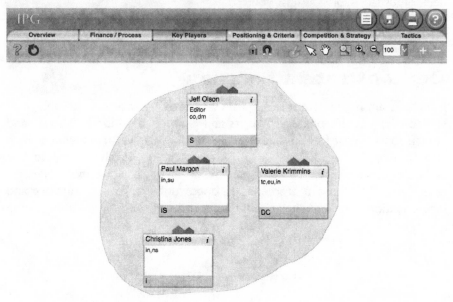

Figure 6-18. Salesforce.com image of key players using S.C.O.O.P. in a sales opportunity.

They say a picture is worth a thousand words. By having a visual of the people involved, their relation to each other in the decision and the roles they play (DM—decision maker, in—influencer, fn—financial, etc.), it is easier to collaborate and strategize an opportunity.

Finally, if you are using CRM as a tool that can help you close business, you should update it to accurately reflect where you are in an opportunity. This way, team members can have a real-time awareness of what is happening and the appropriate course of action, if any, they should take. As mentioned earlier, most salespeople resist doing this, and we believe it hurts their ability to sell more effectively, especially when there are larger, more complex deals.

If you have decided to pursue an opportunity, and have chosen a strategy, then all the subsequent actions should align and support your chosen strategy. For example, if you have chosen a "head on" strategy, where you are clearly and substantially in a position to win, all of your actions should be aimed at speeding up the sales cycle and closing the deal ASAP. Why? Because when you are in that good a position, anything that delays a decision usually works against you.

Stage 5: Present, Propose, or Demonstrate a Solution

If there is any stage of the sales process where you can take advantage of technology, it is this one. Our clients and prospects are local, national, and international. Regardless of their location, if we cannot meet with people face to face (even if they are in the same city), we always try to use technology to make our presentation, proposal, or response more effective (see Table 6-5). It is a tremendous opportunity to create rapport and differentiation that will help you win more business.

Table 6-5. Overview of Stage 5: Presenting, Proposing, or Demonstrating a Solution

Stage 5 Goal:
• **Present, propose, or demonstrate solution**

Actions	Technology	Resources
• Provide a formal proposal or presentation with your unique solution. • Demonstrate the solution, showing off capabilities and return on investment (ROI). • Align above with information from S.PRI.N.G. dialogues and other sources. • Address priorities, needs, decision. process, decision criteria • Set traps for competition • Provide initial pricing • Align with your strategy • Trial close and/or gain next step to put you in position to win	• Desktop video or Web conferencing • Streaming • Social media • Laptop • iPad or tablet • Wireless • PowerPoint or other like offering • Screen capture • YouTube or other video • Online images or photos	• Management • Pre/post technical support • SMEs (subject matter experts) • Brochures • Case studies • References • Presentation planners • Channels • S.C.O.O.P. strategy sheets

Skills
• Presentations and demonstration • Team selling • DiSC • Objection handling

The basic technologies—some elementary—have already been mentioned but bear repeating:

- If presenting to an individual or a small group using a laptop or tablet, make sure you are projecting to a large, vivid screen.

- If you can, use a HDTV or projector to project a larger image.

- Use Web conferencing (the ability for people, in remote locations, from their PC, Mac, or mobile device to share information, view a presentation and interact with it simultaneously). The more sophisticated Web conferencing products also include video conferencing and audio conferencing, allowing you to show them your presentation and "force" interaction, which helps you stay in control. Jonathan is selling to a large social media company and has made three presentations using Web conferencing. He has not sent one proposal prior to any conference and he has much greater interaction and effectiveness.

  We have used PGi, WebEx, Microsoft, TenHands, Adobe, Citrix GoToMeeting, Glance, and others. There are literally hundreds of providers of this service.

▓ **Note** Too many salespeople send people proposals too early, and they are losing out on an opportunity to present a powerful presentation. Their customer set has conditioned them to do this and they need to push back a little to get more actual or virtual face time.

WEB CONFERENCING FAUX PAS SCUTTLES DEAL

Web conferencing allows you to share information on your screen (like a PowerPoint), but never forget that you are sharing *everything* on your screen. Jonathan heard a story from a customer about a salesperson who was trying to sell him something and sharing his screen to show him a PowerPoint. Unfortunately he also had his internal chat on and his manager "pinged" him to see how the demo was going. The salesperson started saying things like, "We got this one in the bag," and the manager was saying, "Great, let's close this baby." My customer was so amazed that he started to play with them by pretending he wasn't seeing their conversation and asking questions like, "When can you deliver this?" and "How much does it cost for a large number of users?" After seeing the comments in the chat box, he had no intention of buying anything.

- Video conferencing. There are hundreds of vendors who offer high-quality video conferencing on many different platforms including mobile devices, computers, roll-about room systems, and expensive, integrated "continuous presence" systems. They allow for multiple participants, and they can provide good-to-HD quality depending on the quality of your camera, amount of bandwidth, and processing power.

My favorites are:

  - Vidyo (Figure 6-19) for the desktop and corporate environments. Vidyo is an enterprise offering that consistently provides high-quality video that more commercial services like Skype cannot.

  - Skype (Figure 6-20) for free or low cost (even Oprah uses it). I use it all the time when I am on the road to talk to my family, friends, prospects, and customers *for free* or for 2 cents a minute if you are calling a land line. The quality is usually excellent.

▧ **Note** Web conferencing services offer the ability to share any information on your computer or any application with others. Video conferencing allows you to see others you are in conference with, either on your computer, tablet, or on a larger screen. Most good Web conferencing services now allow you to add video conferencing as well, so you can have both at the same time. Video conferencing vendors offer some Web conferencing as well.

Figure 6-19. Web conferencing via Vidyo.[9]

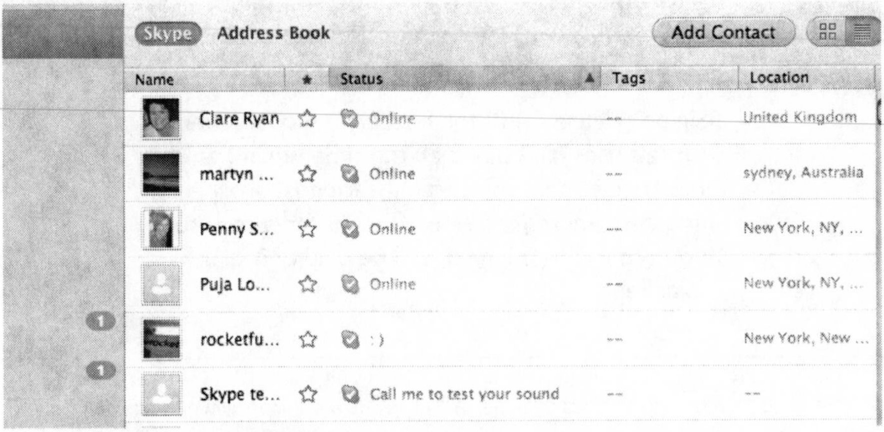

Figure 6-20. Skype address book.

■ **Note** Chat is a great thing to use. You and the other people on your team should chat with each other to provide ideas and information to make your presentation better. Please make sure the prospect cannot see you chatting with each other.

---

[9] Used with permission from Vidyo.

- Microsoft's PowerPoint (and Apple's Keynote among many others). It is almost embarrassing to mention PowerPoint in this day and age but it is amazing how many people don't know how to use it, or how to use it properly. It is an extremely powerful tool. We are well beyond the days of just having words on a slide. PowerPoint lets you integrate urls, videos (from your laptop, Web, or YouTube and similar offerings), streaming, music, quizzes, tests, etc. All can make your presentations more interesting and memorable. Here are some tips to make your presentations jazzier.

Use pictures and images in witty ways. For example, Figure 6-21 shows the "elephant in the room."

Figure 6-21. The "elephant in the room."

Cut Words. Don't have too many words or bullets on any one slide. Which one is more inviting? (See Figure 6-22)

Other Good Questions:

- Tell me more? Why is that the most important? Why now?
- What are the business drivers? Who is the executive sponsor?
- What is the link between these priorities and business priorities?
- What have you done to address this priority?
- What is working well?
- What isn't working well?
- What are the greatest pressures you have to deal with?
- What are the consequences of success or failure for you, your dept. and the company from a financial and business perspective?
- What are the key measurements being used for you and your organization?
- How well are they being met?
- What would you like to be able to do that you can't today?
- What would you like to stop from happening that is interfering with your success?
- How are you using networks to address these priorities?
- Who else benefits or is impacted by these priorities?
- Seed questions:
    - Tell me about .....
- Gain: How do we make you successful? Define success?

My Role
- Teach
- Remind
- Crowd Control

Figure 6-22. Limit the number of bullet points in a presentation.

Use no more than four bullets. However many bullets you have—and try not to have more than four on one slide—don't show them all at once. Build them and use interesting ways to do so (see Figure 6-23). That way, people can't read the slide and not listen to what you are saying:

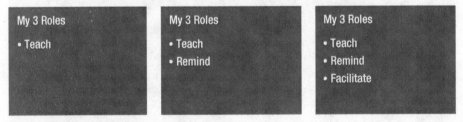

My 3 Roles
- Teach

My 3 Roles
- Teach
- Remind

My 3 Roles
- Teach
- Remind
- Facilitate

Figure 6-23. Building bullet points.

Use pictures instead of words. Famous author Seth Godin suggests that you not even to use words, just pictures. Here let's replace the words in the above slides with pictures to show the difference (see Figure 6-24).

Figure 6-24. A picture is worth 1,000 words.

Pictures create more emotion and tell a story more effectively. Too many people make the mistake of using too many words that people don't remember. A picture is more vivid!

Slideshare, Rocketshare, Prezi, Articulate—all are later-generation technologies that are designed to provide more functionality and work more effectively on the Internet. For more on how they work and their capabilities, please go to:

- www.slideshare.com

- www.rocketshare.com

- www.prezi.com

- www.articulate.com

Screen capture allows you to capture and store whatever you are presenting from your computer. This is excellent if you want to capture the best presentation for distribution to a large audience or if you want to capture a specific demo or presentation and send it to people who cannot attend live.

Proposal writing software. A standard requirement for salespeople is to have a standard proposal that you can modify to meet the specific requirements of your customer or prospect. Simple cutting and pasting of boilerplate materials can make it easy to create good proposals. Companies such as Qvidian, captureplanning.com, proposalsmarts.com, and sellbold.com all offer technology to help you write more effective proposals.

Tinderbox.com is a Web-based tool that can help you with your proposal generation by automating the creation, management, and tracking of your proposals. Since it is Web based you can access it—and any of your proposals—from any browser.

Depending on the complexity of your product and service, you might want to find software that automatically configures your proposed solution and prevents technical or pricing mistakes. There is an old joke: How can you tell the difference between a used-car salesperson and a person who sells telephone systems? Answer: A used-car salesperson knows when he or she is lying (not very complimentary to car salespeople). The point of the joke was that selling phone systems was so complex that you thought you were telling the truth, when you might not have been.

We were using these configuration tools as many as 25 years ago with companies like ROLM, PictureTel, and BT. We are also working with companies in 2012 that sell very complex solutions and *are not* using a sophisticated configurator. This is wasting a lot of time in creating proposals, fixing errors, and responding to customer problems because solutions are misquoted.

Figure 6-25 is a shot of us using Vidyo to present to UK and San Luis Obispo from New York City. Such presentations can be very powerful.

Figure 6-25. Jonathan using Vidyo to present to people from Shopatron in remote locations.

If you have done a good or great job presenting, you have taken a major step in winning business. You now have to continue working your strategy, which we discuss next.

Stage 6: Work Strategy

Working your strategy can be a very short or a very long timeframe depending on the complexity and breadth of your solution, the customer's timeline, delays within and outside of anyone's control (economy, personnel changes, etc.), and more. When it is a short timeframe, it is easy to stay on top of the deal because it is top of mind for everyone and is probably on your forecast, so it is being closely watched. It is when the timeframe is longer that you have to be more mindful of using technology to keep on top of the deal.

For example:

- You can use Google Alerts to keep you abreast of things happening at the account you are trying to sell to.

- You can invite prospects to webinars or send them video information about subjects pertinent to their decision.

- You can use monitoring RSS feeds from their blog, being on LinkedIn, or using Twitter (just to mention the most common and popular technologies) as legitimate reasons to reach out to them.

- LinkedIn can make you aware of changes in key positions that could work for you or against you.

Many of the technologies outlined in stages 4 and 5 should also be used, especially conferencing and collaboration to communicate internally and with the customer. You should also use CRM to keep your team updated and strategy tools like S.C.O.O.P. to update the status of a deal with team members.

Table 6-6. Overview of Stage 6: Work Strategy

Stage 6 Goal:		
• **Work the sales strategy.**		
Actions	**Technology**	**Resources**
• Using S.C.O.O.P., meet more often with team as the decision comes nearer. • Person in charge holds team accountable to execute on actions, including executives. • If using a "Change the View" strategy, begin ideation of the "Change the View" tactic. • Continue to develop the coach. • If there is a dramatic change in circumstances (either good or bad) evaluate a strategy change and supporting tactic(s).	• Desktop video or Web conferencing • Streaming • Social media • Laptop • iPad or tablet • Wireless	• Management • Pre/post technical support • SMEs (subject matter experts) • Brochures • Case studies • References • Presentation planners • Channels • S.C.O.O.P. strategy sheets
Skills		
• Selling Strategically/S.C.O.O.P. • Team selling • Objection handling • Time management		

Make no mistake, however. You need to stay mindful of developing your coach and communicating so he or she can keep you aware of what is happening. Add personal social medial like Facebook to get closer with coaches. Stay on top of them and their companies using Google Alerts and other feeds so you can reach out to them with relevant technology. Put their company name and the names of all the top executives into Google Alerts to see if anything is happening or changing in their company. You can also put their industry type or top competitors into an alert for the same reason. Having done this, technology cannot be your coach. If the deal is big enough, you must *visit* the key prospect regardless of how far away he or she is. Don't use technology as a reason not to. Face-to-face meetings (especially if the person is in a remote, difficult location to reach) builds relationships and trust. It shows a seriousness and level of attention that can give you a competitive advantage.

Use scheduling technology to schedule follow-up meetings with your team. The closer you get to the decision date, the more frequent these meetings should be. Don't abuse your privilege, but don't feel uncomfortable demanding the right amount of time. These meetings are sacrosanct so hold your people accountable. Having said all that, you can record these meetings so people who can't attend (usually executives) can review the meeting at their leisure.

Assuming you have executed your strategy properly and all the pieces fall in place, you will be chosen as the vendor of choice and be ready to negotiate.

Stage 7: Negotiate and Close

Most prospects don't negotiate with you unless they want to do business with you. Don't lose sight of this fact, because these same prospects will do everything they can to get the best deal possible for their company. Table 6-7 outlines actions and resources for negotiating.

Table 6-7. Overview of Stage 7: Negotiating and closing

Stage 7 Goal: • **Negotiate successfully and close.**		
Actions	**Technology**	**Resources**
• If not done already, deliver terms and conditions. • Put team together to negotiate. • Meet with the prospect's negotiating team if not done so already. • Establish negotiation strategy.	• Desktop video or Web conferencing • Laptop • iPad or tablet • Wireless	• Management • Legal • Channels • Finance • Sales ops if special deal required • S.C.O.O.P. strategy sheets
Skills		
• Selling Strategically/S.C.O.O.P. • Negotiations • Objection handling		

Unless (a) it is a very simple request or small deal, (b) you are negotiating with a customer you have worked with for years, or (c) there is no competition, try never to negotiate using e-mail. We point this out because it is becoming a bad and common practice among sales teams.

Surprisingly there are not as many technologies that are specifically designed to assist in formulating and deploying a negotiating strategy. There are only seven companies in Salesforce.com associated with the term "negotiating" and six with "negotiate." Moreover, very few companies show up in a Google search.

You can therefore use one of the companies mentioned. You should continue to use the Web and collaboration tools to communicate internally and with the prospect. You should also use any pricing/configurator tools you have when you need to adjust your solution/s. However, if it is an important negotiation the best approach is still negotiating face to face.

Using these technologies in the way that is best for you will help you differentiate yourself from the competition and win more business. Table 6-8 summarizes how you can use technology at each stage of a sale. Feel free to make notes for yourself in the "Tips and Differences" column.

■ **Note** Chapter 3 contains some negotiating strategies.

Table 6-8. Summary of Using Technology at Each Stage of a Sale

Stage	Technology	Tips and Differences
1. Profile territory or assignment.	• D+B/Hoovers • OneSource • LinkedIn • Salesforce.com • Vertical databases • Lexis/Nexis	
2. Prospect and gain access to key contacts.	• LinkedIn • Salesforce.com • Vertical databases • E-mail • Desktop video • Streaming • Social media	
3. Meet with prospects to discover, qualify, and influence.	• LinkedIn • Salesforce.com • Vertical data bases	

	<ul><li>E-mail</li><li>Desktop video or web conferencing</li><li>Stre. ming</li><li>Social media</li><li>Laptop</li><li>iPad or tablet</li><li>Wireless</li></ul>	
4. Confirm fit and decide to engage or not; Begin to develop team and sales strategy.	<ul><li>LinkedIn</li><li>Salesforce.com</li><li>E-mail</li><li>Desktop video or web conferencing</li><li>Streaming</li><li>Social media</li><li>Laptop</li><li>iPad or tablet</li><li>Wireless</li></ul>	
5. Present, Propose, or demonstrate a solution.	<ul><li>Desktop video or Web conferencing</li><li>Streaming</li><li>Social media</li><li>Laptop</li><li>iPad or tablet</li><li>Wireless</li><li>PowerPoint or other like offering</li><li>Screen capture</li><li>YouTube or other video</li><li>Online images or photos</li></ul>	

6. Work strategy.	• Desktop video or Web conferencing • Streaming • Social media • Laptop • iPad or tablet • Wireless	
7. Negotiate and Close	• Desktop video or Web conferencing • Laptop • iPad or tablet • Wireless	

Using Technology in Managing Your Sales Team

Sales management is about guiding and inspiring people to be creative with how they sell. To accomplish this, managers need to be open minded and creative in how they manage people as well, like introducing new communication technology to help teams share new ideas. In this chapter, we explore advantages technology can bring when managing a sales team or sales unit, or for managing teams virtually. Much of what we discuss applies to management in general, but by nature the sales force needs more inspiration and encouragement and tends to work in a more widespread geographical distribution.

READ THIS CHAPTER EVEN IF YOU'RE NOT A MANAGER

You can read and act on the ideas in this chapter even if you don't manage people yourself. It will still help you:

- Understand and help your line manager.

- Improve your internal profile with the ideas you introduce.

- Develop certain skills if you want to become a manager.

- Close more sales!

Inspiring Leadership vs. "Passing the Buck"

Leadership in sales is about inspiring, motivating, and driving results. Depending upon the salesperson's DiSC style, how long they have been in their jobs, and how competent they are, inspiring them as a sales manager can be more or less critical. And everyone is different. Jonathan worked with a woman—let's call her Bernadette—who was one of the best salespeople he had ever worked with. She needed less teaching than some of her colleagues. But Bernadette did need lots of attention, because that is how she did her best work. Jonathan would use all kinds of ways to provide this, including chat, video, and talking on the phone or in person.

"Pass the buck" management can undermine efforts to inspire your team, especially in larger corporations. In "passing the buck" a manager passes on his or her responsibilities to someone else, often without any notice. For example, your sales director asks you to do something and you simply pass this on down the line to your team. It could be any action, like reporting or setting sales objectives or priorities. Whatever the request, there are far too many managers who just accept what they're being asked to do by their superiors, or who pass along an instruction but do not explain to their teams why something is being requested of them—usually because they haven't asked the questions themselves. That is not management and it is certainly not leadership. It can become CYA (cover your ass) management at its worst. That does not mean you don't need excellent organizational and reporting skills, but first and foremost you need to be present with your team to make sales happen and deliver on your targets.

With or without technology, you can inspire your team. The further distanced you become from the day you stopped selling and became a manager, and the more distance you have from your team geographically, the more risk there is that you will lose touch with the realities and challenges of being in a sales role. Theory and abstraction can overtake the reality of doing the job your team is executing on a daily basis. But maintaining high levels of engagement with your team will temper this.

How do you inspire people?

- Share ideas.

- Obtain new technology for your team.

- Suggest new ways to sell.

- Teach new ways to close.

- Introduce change.

- Offer detailed explanations where necessary.

- Pay attention to them in person or virtually.

We explore all of these in this chapter.

Your approach to sales management in general can also be inspirational. For example:

- Never assume everyone sees or understands things the same way you do. Explain everything clearly; it creates buy-in, and honesty can motivate people to work harder for you.

- Just because someone isn't asking you to pay attention to him or her, or is doing well, doesn't mean he or she doesn't need to be attended to.

- People don't want to show their vulnerabilities, so you need to make it safe for them to do so.

- You are in your position for a reason; you have a great deal of experience and you see the bigger picture, so share it! This point is becoming more and more important as people are overwhelmed with data. They need a leader to sift through all the information, cut through clutter, and give them direction.

- Paying attention to the smallest details can make all the difference in improving performance and sales.

Here's an example on the last point. I (Martin) was once working on a sales consulting and training opportunity. I identified a problem: Because the company had a geographically disparate sales force, it had a great deal of difficulty getting salespeople to focus on product training. The training was carried out weekly for 1 hour and the content was good but no one was paying much attention. As part of our proposal, we offered bite-sized recordings of training with mini-quizzes to be used for reinforcement after the initial training sessions.

This was very simple to put into practice. But no one else was doing it, and we had a very agile approach that was different from that of the competition. Our approach was so successful that it resulted in the same method being repeated in training their management team as well. We now include this option with all of our proposals, offering an additional and unique element beyond that offered by most of our competition. After adding the range of technology we employ, this approach means we can react quickly with a variety of solutions. Paying attention to what seemed like a small detail—that the length of the original training videos was too long for their salespeople to digest—provided an opportunity to offer a meaningful and successful solution.

As a sales manager, you can help your team identify key details that can accelerate their success in a particular deal and how to leverage these details to their advantage. If something works well, as a manager you can replicate this success easily by sharing best practice using the technologies at your disposal. We discuss sharing best practices in further detail later in this chapter.

▓ **Bonus content!** You can read about another simple management approach—L.E.E.D (Listen, Empathize, Execute, Deliver) on Phinkit.com: www.phinkit.com/Memex/?b=46

Using Technology from a Manager's Point of View

As a manager, you should consider technology as a tool you can use to help measure and develop your team. Of course, how and why anyone uses technology should also have a customer benefit, but your perspective needs to have an added dimension: How can the technology help you manage and develop your team, and make everyone generally more efficient?

You can apply the use of technology in a number of ways, and you can categorize various types of technology in terms of management benefits or goals, such as time to get a new employee onboard, time to identify a bad hire, and early indicators of success or failure for a person/team. There are also sales benefits such as reducing the time to close deals, reacting quickly to customers, managing (and shortening) the sales cycle, and reducing travel time and costs. Understanding what tools to use and when is the key. The ultimate reward is having something that delivers on all of these goals at once.

An example:

One of our contacts works in sales for a global business information provider. She was based in London and managed key accounts located all across the U.K. From the time she joined the company, she was targeted with conducting eight face-to-face meetings with clients every week, because the sales management team believed this was the most effective way to close business. Unsurprisingly, this resulted in a lot of travel time and costs, much "dead" time spent traveling during which she could not work to her capacity, and generally longer sales cycles because booking in meetings around a travel-heavy schedule often delayed things more than was necessary. She became frustrated with this approach when her customers could not get the time they needed with her, delaying deals or forcing them to seek out someone who could respond more quickly. In the meantime, her sales revenues were plummeting as she struggled with the practicalities of achieving the eight weekly face-to-face meetings.

Having previously worked in sales of conferencing and collaboration tools, she proposed the use of Web conference calls as an alternative to the strict policy of face-to-face meetings. Not only did it drastically reduce her travel time and costs, but it also allowed her to shorten sales cycles by attending more meetings in the same timeframe. She was quickly able to restore her principles of speed and quality of response. In fact, she was able to conduct more than the targeted eight meetings per week, hold more engaging and interactive meetings with clients, and turned her performance from 15% behind her sales revenue target to 104% simply by replacing some of her face-to-face meetings with Web conference calls.

Exercise

Let's imagine you want to sell more through new approaches, like virtual selling, and you want to review your team's performance. Your team is located all over the continent and each member has accounts equally widespread.

Your categories are:

- Increased sales
- Virtual selling
- Performance reviews

If you look back at the list of technologies covered in Chapter 4, you can begin by selecting the best tools to help you accomplish these goals and ensure your people's knowledge and competency during the process.

An example:

Web conferencing—will it support your goals?

- Increased sales—Yes
- Virtual selling—Yes
- Performance reviews—Yes

You know Web conferencing is a great fit and now you just need to pick the service you want to use. You can use the technology itself to train your team faster and better. For performance reviews, you can use live Web conference calls or recorded meetings that you review later (for the latter, you will want to choose a service with recording capability).

Whatever technologies you decide your sales team should employ, you are responsible for briefing them on what they should use it for and how. This doesn't have to be the technical know-how (i.e., the functional training); the key is to communicate how to use it for sales, plus strategic insights and best practices. In the case of videoconferencing, this might include:

- Preparing and loading all content before the meeting starts

- Treating the Web conference like a physical meeting room

- Using a mix of multimedia content to keep the presentation interesting

- Understanding that pace and tone are critical—that your voice is much more important when body language isn't in play

- Knowing that you can show anything—documents, presentations, images, websites, videos, or audio clips— and how best to do so. Do not restrict your ideas to slide decks (many people do, but there's a reason for the expression, "death by PowerPoint")

The functional training can be carried out by the Web conferencing provider. Your job as manager is to show them how to sell using these tools and to offer ideas for discussion. As a leader and manager, use the tool as much as possible internally so people get used to it. Also, give access to everyone once you decide it would be a useful tool. Many companies try to keep costs down and buy fewer licenses than they need. This frustrates people and diminishes usage, which defeats the purpose of using technology.

BUY THEM THE TOOLS THEY NEED!

Jonathan has a customer with more than 20 salespeople whose job it is in part to prospect actively. To this end, they use OneSource, which allows them to see who has visited their site, regardless of whether they have filled out any forms. But they have only one license for it, meaning they have to go to the one person who owns the license for information or not use it all. As a result, the salespeople don't use it all, leading to missed opportunities.

What's Good for You Is Good for the Team

This rather strange phenomenon has been encountered so many times that it is worth mentioning: Many sales management teams use a number of different virtual meeting technologies (e.g., conferencing, collaboration, or video), to join team members for internal meetings, but they do not make the simple connection of getting their sales force to leverage the same technologies to engage with their customers!

If these tools deliver enough value for you to use them as a manager, why shouldn't your salespeople also be employing them? The most common use of virtual meeting technologies is for sales teams holding weekly team conference calls, but often the salespeople themselves do not have their own conferencing accounts that they can use with their own customers. Quite simply, this makes no sense.

Note Make sure your people have access to all the same productivity-enhancing sales tools—like videoconferencing—that you do.

However, we have some insight as to why this may occur. Meeting technology is too often pigeon-holed as being useful for one-to-many person conversations only. In other words, you need three or more people before you think of holding a conference or Web call. Traditionally, any one-to-one engagement has been done simply via a direct phone call. But why? It is a completely false notion that this is the only way; we sell ALL the time using virtual meeting technologies in one-to-one situations. The benefits are the same whether you have one person at the other end, or ten! You can still close deals, deliver presentations, manage the sales cycle more quickly, be more attentive, react more quickly, and reduce the need for travel; there is no rule that says you need more than two people on a call to gain the benefits of these collaborative technologies. Get your team working virtually—they will sell more, have more satisfied customers, and close deals more quickly.

One last point on this is that as your customers and prospects get used to a mix of face-to-face and more regular technology-based meetings, innovation and creativity become much more acceptable. Imagine being able to strike while an idea or opportunity is hot, rather than delaying while you try to coordinate schedules to find time for a face-to-face meet: "Hi, Mr. Customer. I have a great idea about how we can help you; are you free to jump on a quick WebEx call, or could we schedule a call in the next day or two?"

As your contacts get used to this more flexible and time-sensitive approach, you can develop a closer, more collaboration-based relationship with your customers. That is not to say you will never meet with them in person, but in a fast-paced world where everyone's time is precious, the ability to be responsive and quick off the mark by using virtual meeting tools means you can focus in on new opportunities for your clients as they arise and your relationship will change and develop into a consultative partnership.

Collaboration and Sharing Best Practices

Sharing best practices is vital to developing your team's skills. The way your salespeople collaborate and share ideas can raise the entire output of your team. No matter how good a manager you are, your team members are the ones out there on the ground doing the job, and their insights are highly valuable. The question is: How can you build and share these insights among team members?

The following are some themes you should include in your team training/sharing activities on an ongoing basis to encourage collaboration:

- Deals of the week/month

- Ideas of the week/month (e.g., tips for closing, a new prospecting approach)

- Sales messaging of the week/month

- Customer solution of the week/month

- Run contests for the best demo, interview, most unique use of a technology, etc.

PictureTel, now Polycom, held a worldwide sales contest for the best demo—over videoconferencing, of course. We did the same thing for the best demo at NBI (no video at that time, however). These kinds of events bring out the competitive spirit and ingrain the desired behavior.

TAKE SOME CHANCES

Many managers wait to get permission for all kinds of things they don't need to. Our advice is to make decisions on your own and take charge of what you want to have happen. If you have an idea, use it in your own region. For example, if you want to create a blog for the sales team, do so for your own team first. The best way to validate an idea is to show the value of doing it.

In the forgoing I suggested weekly or monthly options, but you can tailor the timeframe to one that makes sense for your team, as it will vary by your average sales cycle and the frequency of your sales. Now, so far there is nothing here you could not do in face-to-face meetings or without some additional technology, and that is fine; these are basic sales-management concepts for sharing ideas and there is nothing dependent on technology to carry it out. You can, however, take this a big step forward by employing collaboration technologies. With any best practice, the most important thing is reinforcement—it' s creating insight that people can revisit and that new team members can access at any time to get up to speed.

Without an additional layer of technology, sharing best practice happens at a single time and place—say, your monthly team meeting—and is dependent on everyone being there and remembering the detail. It's a bit like the days before VCRs and DVR (digital video recording) technology—if you wanted to watch your favorite program on TV, you had to be physically present at the time it originally aired or miss your chance.

The whole concept of best practice is to create ongoing, repeatable success. Why then is it mainly carried out as a one-off and infrequent presentation? Possibly the worst example of this is at annual sales kick-off days, in which great ideas may be shared but crammed into a 15-minute timeframe and slotted among a packed full day's agenda, which everyone subsequently forgets. It's a waste of great information and learnings; why relegate the sharing of best practice to a once-a-year event simply because you've got your whole sales force in one big room? In reality, sales teams are broken down into smaller groupings for logical reasons—e.g., by territory, industry vertical, customer size, or type—and for these reasons, your best practice can (and should) be tailored at this more focused level to begin with. And to add the capability to develop ongoing success and improve your salespeople, you need a means to build, improve, and reinforce best practice over time.

The solution is incredibly simple: record it. If some of your salespeople have insight to share, you can ask them to simply sit in front of their laptop and record the content and video of themselves. Or, if you're on a team call, you can record the call and make the recording available to your team afterwards. The same goes for Web conferencing calls; you can simply record on the fly. Alternatively, you could record a video with your salesperson in an interview format, either virtually or face-to-face. However you choose to do it, the next step is to take all this great insight and put it onto a shared drive, intranet, sales portal, CRM (Customer Relationship Management) system—whatever you have at your disposal. Much like recording your favorite TV programs with TiVo, you can access them anytime and watch them over and over again.

■ **Note** Affordable software from companies like Articulate.com and others allows you to set a deadline for when your salespeople need to watch something and then offer a quiz or test they have to take with a minimum score to pass. All is recorded and reported for your benefit.

You can accomplish sharing of best practice by using other types of technology as well. For example, you could collate your team members' brilliant ideas and store these on a SharePoint, Wiki, or an internal blog accessible to your team or even the wider sales force. There are plenty of technologies out there to help you share ideas and best practice; as a manager your job is to facilitate this for your team.

Everyone will respond well to shared best practice. Why?

- Learning from one's peers is highly effective—your salespeople will be learning from like-minded colleagues facing similar challenges.

- It is something your salespeople can access anytime, as often as needed and on their own time.

Once you have built up a knowledge base, you can present it to your peers and management; it goes over extremely well, especially if there is no formal knowledge-management system in place, which is unfortunately often the case.

A word on this—you may be lucky enough to work in a business that offers knowledge-sharing systems for its sales force. I have seen some great centralized intranets and portals for sales teams that provide access to the tools you may use in your daily role—order forms, pricing sheets, product databases, sales and marketing collateral, and even value propositions. While these are invaluable, there is a distinct difference between them and the best-practice sharing among your team that we've been discussing. The knowledge-management site is more likely to be static (or updated on an infrequent basis—usually once a year) and is designed for the whole sales force. We have already established that your team faces unique challenges, and it goes without saying that best practice evolves more than once a year! You might use your knowledge management system to store your ongoing best practice information, but to reiterate, the key is to develop, improve, and reinforce continually, so it's more about facilitating and recording these conversations so they can be accessed again after the fact.

Better and Faster Recruiting with Technology

This is as much of time-saving tip as anything else—when recruiting, it is tempting to simply do a quick sift through CVs or resumes and then set up face-to-face interviews. This can be incredibly time-consuming, as CVs can often fail to convey enough about a candidate (especially in terms of "fit" with your team) and most of the screening process has to occur during time-consuming interviews in person. It is not at all uncommon to carry out dozens of interviews before finding even a remotely suitable candidate. To save time and dramatically improve the recruitment process, we add a simple step between reading CVs and the interview stage, which is to conduct a 10-minute recorded meeting, ideally on a video call, but audio calls can work just as well.

> **Note** Be sure to check your local laws about recording conversations and always tell people
> you are recording the event. In most cases, the service will automatically announce to all
> participants that recording has begun.

This is a slight variation on a standard telephone interview and the reason we do it is to save time by getting to know a bit more about the candidate before scheduling a full interview. In particular, you will get a better sense of the candidate's personality and approach to his or her work, something that is difficult to get simply by reading his or her history on a piece of paper. Taking this a step further, by adding the recording element, you also have something you can review afterwards, and this is where technology allows us to take things a step further.

When you are conducting an interview, you are talking with the candidate and asking questions, so you are not reviewing 100% of the time, and it is only natural that you miss things. It is surprising what you can pick up by listening back to a meeting and, if you have recorded using video, observing mannerisms and body language. These additional nonverbal cues can be invaluable in helping you reduce the time and effort to find the right person for the job.

You can also have more people interview a candidate, regardless of anyone's location. Or you can do team interviews in the same way.

As an aside to this section, many salespeople don't sell themselves well on a CV, so consider relying on an intuitive impression once in a while. The greatest salesperson I ever hired was dreadful at CV-writing and giving interviews.

Finally, if technology skills are an important job requirement, you can see how comfortable your candidates are using it or react to it.

Failsafe Selling

Reinforcement of best sales practices was mentioned earlier in this chapter but not specifically in a management context. This is a fantastic thing to do, especially for new team members or those who need to improve. It also is a great time saver for you. Failsafe selling is a way that, as a manager, you can reinforce best sales practice.

If you recall from our discussion of failsafe selling in Chapter 4, a salesperson's approach can be improved when selling virtually, because other people—such as subject-matter experts—can join on customer conference calls and give input to the meeting and feedback to the salesperson using tools like online chat on-the-fly during the meeting. Because you can have side-conversations online and you are all getting a sense of how things are going, you can modify your pitch as the meeting proceeds. From a management perspective, the principle is simple. The use of virtual collaboration technology allows you to control the sale in a way that is not possible face to face. You can conduct live development with your salespeople—improving their sales technique on-the-spot—and help control the sale.

Let's say, for example, that your salesperson is busy presenting and so is not fully listening, or is over-talking or could be doing something in a better way. By using the online chat feature of the conferencing tool, you can send him an instant message (or if you're sitting beside him, giving him notes or visual cues) so you can change and guide the pitch as you go. This is highly effective, both with new or more experienced salespeople, and the best part is that you can better reduce the risk of losing a sale than is possible in a face-to-face meeting in which it is harder to control things without looking like you are correcting the salesperson and thus surfacing mistakes.

Managing Virtual Teams

Whichever technology you decide to use, consistency is important. Weekly team meetings can be conducted easily and are a great way to keep a geographically diverse sales team engaged with each other on a regular basis. Working from home is becoming more and more popular, especially for salespeople aligned to geographic territories, but being home-based can be a lonely existence leading to a feeling of being disconnected from the office hub where often relationships are fostered and knowledge is imparted almost by osmosis. Conducting regular one-on-one meetings as well as group collaboration is essential in overcoming these challenges.

Many sales managers record and send ideas and sales inspiration out to their teams on a weekly and sometimes daily basis. It's very efficient, as you can make the recordings in your time and the team members can listen to or watch the recordings back in their own time.

▓ **Note** Start using social media internally. You can set up your own private Facebook or LinkedIn group to communicate. Let people use it as creatively as they do on a personal level.

Some ideas you might want to use for recorded content:

- Daily target: Let's focus on X today; Jonathan closed a great deal last week by doing X.

- Competitions: The first person to close today is awarded $50!

- Sales inspiration: Let's take a look at how Martin got six appointments in just an hour's work.

- Push a product or service: The company wants us to move 100 units of Product A this week. And if we do . . .

- Big deal insight: We just won the business of customer X; here's the story about how that was achieved.

- Google+ results such as role changes or industry news: Jennifer Jones, who had been in charge of purchasing for Company X, has moved over into the logistics department. Now we'll be dealing with . . .

- New or existing testimonials: We received three new testimonials last week . . .

- Collaboration and best practice previously recorded with your team: I want everyone to watch Steve's meeting with Company Y (find it here). We'll go over the highlights in detail next week . . .

Remember our often-used tips for sales management—these are as applicable to your general approach as they are to your use of technology to share best practice:

- Don't overthink things.

- The small things, or things that may seem obvious to you, need to be shared; never assume people see things the same way you do.

- You are likely to be in your position as a sales manager because you have a wider strategic vision, ideas, and experience. Share them!

"All Hands and Feet" Calls

This is a term for a weekly meeting called by a sales manager, or more often a VP of sales, with the entire sales team to update everyone on key items, give them clear direction, or bring positive attention to a person. It used to be done on the phone but now it can all be accomplished via Web or videoconferencing and recorded. More people can also participate in a more engaging way.

Work Effectively with SMEs and Partners

We partner together to work on any number of things, not least of which is selling and sharing different prospecting strategies and ideas for our customers.

Now, consider where we are each based:

- Martin is in London, UK.

- Jonathan is in New York, USA.

Depending on our work with customers, we may see each other only a few times a year in person. Almost all of the rest of our joint work is conducted virtually, using some of the collaborative technologies we discussed earlier. Both of our businesses are classified as SMEs (small- to medium-enterprises) and we both have backgrounds coming from—and selling to—medium-to-large corporations. We mention this because we want you to consider how we manage to work so well together and with our partners (and customers!), despite being based on opposite sides of the Atlantic Ocean. Partners don't challenge us about meeting with them face-to-face; they accept the global nature of what we do and how we do it. Meeting in person is fantastic, but we are doing quite well almost entirely without it. You shouldn't be constrained in your thinking by geography or approaches that were always sold as standard (such as face-to-face meetings), mainly because they were the standards when you had no other choice! Nowadays, with all the technology available, things are much different and there are plenty of options.

If you have partners in business, SMEs you want to utilize, internal contacts, experts, or other business units you want to engage with, then technology (e.g., collaboration, conferencing, and sharing tools) enables all of this in a time-efficient manner.

To give you an indication, here are the things for which Jonathan and I might use technology in a typical month (either together or as separate activities):

- Skype calls to continuously to check in with each other while writing this book

- A videoconference to deliver a 2-day training program

- A WebEx (Web-conferencing call) to collaborate on a presentation for a sales pitch

- Five project management calls with a customer about an ongoing piece of consultancy work we are doing

- Mailchimp e-mail marketing tool to send five messages out to Phinkit users

- Xtranormal to create a fun video for Phinkit (http://youtu.be/OLXhHYYgsjE)

- Delivery of a sales webinar for Jonathan's LinkedIn group

- Wrote a blog on Phinkit about the journey and the challenges of writing this book

- A three-way conference call to discuss the best keywords to target for Jonathan's business with our SEO (Search Engine Optimization) expert

- Sent more than 50 personal e-mails from Google+ information for prospecting

- Used Ten Hands HD video for regular meetings with our technical team in Phinkit (three times per week)

- Interviewed and recorded three customers in person to create video testimonial content for use in selling

- Created an electronic newsletter

- Countless introductory meetings via Skype, Ten Hands, WebEx, and audio conferencing

Employing these technologies in your day-to-day work very easily becomes second nature. It is not difficult to do and we don't think in terms of technology; we think about solutions and the speed needed to accomplish everything we need to do. You just need to apply logic to what you need to achieve and then weave in the best way to get the job done.

Speed of Response

We have previously mentioned the creative use of technology to impress and inspire people. As a manager, you should also encourage the use of technology as an agility tool—something that makes you faster and better than the competition. The more a customer or prospect feels valued, the better; this goes without saying. One way is to make your contacts feel valued is to create an environment where everyone works on the customer's terms, rather than their own. In practice, all we mean by this is using technology to do things as quickly as you can to impress and delight customers. Start with phone and e-mail; these are the technologies we utilize most often and unfortunately it's all too easy to become complacent with them. A simple thing like acknowledging a customer's e-mail right away—especially if you can't respond in full immediately—is a rarity (unfortunately) and your client will appreciate the quick response and commitment to a timescale.

You have to live and breathe this approach yourself, demonstrating a great speed of response with your own actions; treat your salespeople as you would expect them to treat their customers. You are there to support your team and show them the best possible way to achieve their goals; leave the ego behind and lead by example. Be the best you can be and your team will aspire to the same level of excellence.

Using Technology Like a Meeting Room

If you are hosting a customer at your business premises, you would prepare the meeting room in advance by setting up chairs, organizing projectors or screens, testing the presentation works, checking that any refreshments will be provided, and positioning everything else accordingly.

The same is true of using technology for virtual meetings. You should carry out exactly the same preparations. This standard must be set by you as a manager, with your team following suit:

- Ensure all conference call dial-in phone numbers and access codes are sent out to all participants well in advance of the meeting (if possible, at the time the meeting is booked into their calendar).

- The lead salesperson should be on the call 15 minutes before the meeting starts in case anyone else comes on early.

- Everything should be tested to ensure it's working as expected.

- Presentations should be uploaded in advance.

- Everyone who is joining the call (other than the customer) should be briefed to come on 5 minutes beforehand.

This practice should be employed with all technology you want your team to use; your team should have a clearly understood approach to using each piece of technology to sell and deliver a good customer experience. That policy comes from you; if your team members are not told of these standards, they will create their own and you will end up with the classic "standard" along the lines of the way people treat e-mail. That is to respond as and when you feel like it, when instead you should be following the speed of response, and the quality of response noted throughout this book, to impress your customers.

Don't concern yourself about being an expert on how to use every piece of technology. It's not about that; it's about setting the bar for the right way to do things to impress clients and sell more.

CREATIVITY FOR MANAGERS, BY SIMON JACK[1]

Technology brings a whole new dimension to sales approaches. But to make the most of its potential, you have to go beyond the instruction manual and instead focus on how best to use it as an engagement tool. As technology presents a wide array of additional options, the same old methods are no longer going to cut it. It's going to take creative thinking to stay competitive.

Creativity is simply the search for alternative methods to achieve a desired outcome. Without it there can be no change and no progress. But it is not enough to just tell people to be more creative; it can be very easy for people and processes to become bound by structure and stuck in the way they have always been done. You often need to break out of the default ways of thinking and encourage new attitudes and habits.

Embedding creativity is both a top-down and bottom-up process. If people are going to willingly adapt their approach, they first have to firmly appreciate what the benefits will be and also have the belief that they can achieve them. But relying on a bottom-up creative movement alone will only get you so far. For managers, there is a need to continually reaffirm the requirement for creativity and instill an assurance of permission to try.

Here are some tips to help make creativity a core part of your sales success:

- *Lead the way.* A positive and flexible attitude sets an inspiring example for others to follow. Opening yourself up to questions and accepting opinions demonstrates you're willing to accept new ideas. Conversely, those who are domineering and set a precedent of always being right are more likely to solicit and receive answers people think they want to hear. This can lead to a situation where ideas never advance beyond an existing comfort zone.

- *Reward creative effort.* One of the major reasons people are not more creative at work is they do not believe it is part of their role or feel their efforts will be to no avail. If you reward only creative results, this raises the bar and can put people off trying for fear of failure. However, if you reward all creative effort, you encourage the voicing of any ideas in a judgment-free environment.

- *Suspend judgment to spot positives and useful concepts.* Many ideas are killed before they've had a chance to reach their true potential. Encourage people to ask "how else" and "what else" to explore other alternatives for achieving the benefits of seemingly flawed ideas.

- *Always remain inquisitive.* Never let yourself stay contented with success long enough for inertia to set in. Ask questions such as "How can we use this new technology to transform a process?" and "Does technology exist that might make this process more effective?"

---

1 Founder, www.creativeencounters.co.uk. ©2012 by Simon Jack. Used with permission.

- *Give people the option to experiment with technology to understand the benefits themselves.* Do not force them to use it. People don't resist change; they resist being changed. Also, using technology for its own sake can result in frustration, abandonment, or disdain. Technology must always add value to what you do.

- *To accelerate the uptake of new technology, a creative manager will leverage success stories and quick wins.* This will catalyze the early adopters to inspire others, thereby creating a strong network of change agents.

- *Finally, lighten up where possible.* Creativity more naturally occurs with a sense of playfulness. There is no need to be boisterous; just a little levity in your own style shows you've taken the time and consideration to really engage with people, leading to a more fertile atmosphere for creativity.

Technology is merely the tool. It is having the presence of mind to use it most effectively that sets people apart. Those with the sales acumen backed by creative attitudes will always come out as the winners.

Author's note: Simon Jack himself has used technology to interact with a wider client base. He has developed a course called "Discover Your Creative Genius" using Kwiksta, an e-learning authoring tool. Not only does this add value for existing customers, but it also extends the reach of such a service to allow Simon to engage a wide variety of people in a way that was not possible before. You can preview the course at: www.kwiksta.com /kwiks/CreativeEncounters/discover-your-creative-genius.

Setting Challenges

A fun way to get people engaged with using new technology is to set challenges. Note the use of the word *challenges* instead of *targets*. You want your team to feel like they are trying something different or aspiring to achieve a small challenge—they have plenty of targets already.

Examples of challenges you could set:

- The first person to create something using a new technology (e.g., a video testimonial).

- The best presentation using a new technology created in the next two weeks wins the team trophy.

- The first close using a new technology.

- The best idea for selling with technology.

It should match your personality and behaviors so it feels realistic to your team, but inject a bit of fun and the results will be better.

Summary

Whatever technology you decide to use for you, your team, and ultimately your customers, always remember that the way it is used will be positioned by you. This will continually evolve but standards, ideas, and the reasons to use these technologies are all within your control. Quite simply, lead by example; this is the best way to show how effective these tools can be.

Technology is only as good as what you use it for.

The New Landscape

The Merger of Sales, Marketing, and Customer Service and How Technology Facilitates the Change

While the sales cycle itself hasn't changed much over time, the context for selling and who does what and when absolutely has. In the training and consulting that we conduct, we are continually surprised by one simple observation:

Salespeople do not understand or take advantage of their position of power.

This is partly due to the changing face of business and how the role of sales has evolved in the past 15 years. Whereas in the past *all* salespeople would write, create, and produce the end-documentation (e.g., proposals, e-mails, and various other types of content) delivered to their customers—and, most importantly, adding their own personality and passion to their work— this is no longer the norm. In many cases, the lead is generated by marketing, and the proposal is generated by the same department or by a customer support department without much, if any, input by the salesperson.

In this chapter, we discuss the convergence of sales, marketing, customer service, and technology, and also remind you that as a salesperson you have much more power—and responsibility—to influence, control, and indeed make the sale happen than you may realize.

Let's consider a few examples of how you can effect your power as a salesperson. Difficult economic times, coupled with the continuous drive for efficiency that has dominated business behavior for more than a decade, can often fuel decisions that make sense on paper but not in practice. Let's look at some of these "paper decisions" that appear to promote efficiency but can actually reduce top-line sales.

Paper Decision One: Marketing Controls the Brand

Far from promoting efficiency, putting all the power into one department can have the effect of narrowing the sales pipeline.

Example: Brand Confusion

We recently conducted sales training for a FTSE 50 organization. Part of the objective for this training was to enlighten and motivate the various sales teams to the challenging—and changing—world in which they were operating. We wanted to get them to build their thinking around what mattered to their customers, to help them evolve from commodity selling to consultative selling.

One of the many things we presented was a simple and highly effective approach to e-mail communication: We suggested that they themselves run a mail merge to their own prospects (in this case, using Mailchimp). We didn't expect the shocking response, a staggeringly needless example of siloed behavior:

Sales:

- "We can't send prospecting e-mails!"
- "Are we even allowed to use this Mailchimp thing?"

Then, the response from marketing:

- "WE control the brand; why are you telling sales to send the customer e-mails?"

It's hard to believe, but in this case the marketing team was convinced that it alone should be contacting clients via e-mail. We cleared up this misconception with the following e-mail to marketing and sales team leaders:

> *You have created an environment where your salespeople are not sure what—if any—communications they can send when prospecting. We are not talking about the brand or the brand message; this is simply about using the best format when prospecting.*

This company had invested such massive authority in their brand messaging that they'd lost sight of who was—and who *should* be—delivering the message. This had been going on for years and no one had ever questioned it enough to empower sales.

Why hadn't anyone at this company questioned who should be delivering which messaging to customers? It is a painfully simple trap to fall into: time is precious to all of us and we can happily fill up our time with the things that concern us in our own roles. In this case, the sales team was busy with all manner of activities—but not necessarily doing the right ones. Marketing was busy delivering campaigns that (as it turned out) no one was happy with, but then sales wasn't consulting with marketing about the messaging. The longer this kind of situation goes on, the more it becomes a case of siloed behaviors: "Sales doesn't do X; marketing handles that." This quickly paves the way to a descent into the blame game. There aren't enough people saying "Sales and marketing work together to deliver that."

The moral isn't as simple as the consequences of marketing or indeed sales having exclusive ownership over certain tasks or processes; everyone has a set of skills but not everyone understands how they can have input into each other's activities (e.g., sales to marketing and vice versa). Consider how things are being done now and whether you are getting to provide the right insight to your customer messaging.

This works both ways, so the flipside is that marketing should be intrinsically aware of the challenges faced by sales and interested in understanding the reasons behind these. Marketing's brand guidelines are not product or service guidelines. In some markets, it's not uncommon for sales to become over-dependent on marketing to generate sales leads, and presentations and pitches as well. But there is a clear distinction between the roles of sales and marketing. As a salesperson, your job is to know how to sell, and you should know your customers better than anyone else in the business and, as such, your insight into the content of the messaging directed at your customers—and who should be sending it—is vital.

How Sales and Marketing Can Work Better Together

A very effective for sales and marketing to work together is for sales to be responsible for prospecting into certain named or target accounts, using marketing materials if that suits them, while marketing is responsible for creating a more general awareness.

Marketing will often have a telesales team that can prospect into any account that isn't named by the salesperson. This works well on two levels. Salespeople maintain responsibility for their largest opportunities and stay sharp doing so. They also lessen their dependence on marketing for their success.

Which leads us straight on to . . .

Paper Decision Two: The Sales and Marketing Void

I often refer to *voids* in business as a means to explain the problems that can arise when business areas are defined too rigidly or operate with no overlap, creating silos. Within an organization, information silos can easily develop in which there is little or no communication between them. They act as independent entities making independent decisions, with a high potential for inefficiencies because silos ignore the wider goals of the organization.

Marketing does not exist solely to produce content for sales merely to pass directly on to their customers. Consider this idea in conjunction with how you behave toward your customers and what messaging you are sending them. Let's say you routinely send out the same piece of collateral any time you receive an inquiry. Ask yourself why you are sending that messaging. Are you truly delivering value or simply ticking a box because you're too busy or because that's what you're "supposed" to do?

■ **Note** Standard marketing collateral is good up to a point. Add your own content to personalize it for both the target and the situation.

It's far too easy to settle into a churn mentality: "I'm busy; where is that standard PDF to send?" You end up sending the same exact marketing or product brochure to every potential client. Sure, if you send large enough volumes of these, eventually something will stick, and you may even hit your targets with this high-volume, low-value approach. But it is much more likely that the standardized messaging won't resonate with most prospects; it wasn't designed with them in mind, so how much impact can it really be delivering?

The answer is a case of working smarter; I call this the 5% Difference.

The 5% Difference is added value provided by the salesperson—sales content, a call to action, a line relating to his or her specific customer—that makes a small but important difference to the standard marketing message. Let's see how the 5% Difference helps. Under typical circumstances:

- Marketing is doing its job producing collateral—tick.

- Sales is doing its job by passing this on to the customers—tick.

So what's the problem?

In many cases there isn't one. Sales are coming in, marketing is producing good content, and leads are forthcoming. However, the best organizations create an approach in which sales and marketing harmonize, not just by a notion of togetherness, but by recognizing that every customer is unique and as such deserves to feel she is being treated that way.

That's where the 5% Difference comes into play: The more you can customize or personalize content, the better. As a potential buyer, I am always inundated with brochures or standardized marketing documents that do not talk about *me*—the buyer, an individual with specific needs—but only about the business or the product (i.e., the seller). This issue is not limited to marketing documents; a similar issue exists with websites, social media content, and other mediums—some of which are more suitable for personalization than others.

How can we address this? What does it mean?

Example: A PDF Is Not Fort Knox

A few years ago, I (Martin) took over the running of a sales unit that had a high ratio of accounts to salespeople. The accounts typically consisted of small companies spending small amounts and large companies also spending small amounts while also spending a lot with other providers. We were tasked with retaining the existing business and identifying larger opportunities to then drive forward and close more sales.

There were literally thousands of opportunities in the marketplace but very few were being identified by my team. I concluded this was mainly due to a "list" mentality; there was so much to do that the majority of this team of 26 salespeople was dealing with potential customers by reflexively passing them standard PDF after standard PDF.

I needed the team members to pause and consider what they were doing and instead start using their skills. Otherwise, we might as well disband the sales unit and reassign the members to the Customer Services call center. Where was the value sales should have been delivering?

1. Recognize Your Strength

After reviewing the marketing materials (which were all fine, if a little bland), I took two actions. The first was an exercise to remind people of their position of power. I asked them to fill out the following form. (I recommend you do so as well—you'll find instructions below it. It might be best to set this up as a spreadsheet so that the fields expand as you write.)

Exercise in Recognizing Your Power as a Salesperson

Customer	Product	You

First, start with the Customer column.

Action: Write down everything that matters to your specific customers.

- Why do they need what you sell?

- What matters to them? Customer service? Response times? Account team? Locations? Buying criteria? Features? Functions?

Think from the customer's mind but never assume the customer's reasons for buying. If you don't know the answers to these questions, enter a question mark—this will identify the gaps you need to fill in by speaking with your prospect.

Second, move on to the Product column.

Action: List everything your product offers along with the reasons why someone would buy it *from you*.

Then write down everything your product does that the competition's products don't. In other words, what are your product's unique selling points (USPs)?

Now, note all of the USPs of your pre- and post-sales processes, materials, training and support—basically, anything that is of value.

Third, fill out the You column:

Action: Finally, write out all of the things you have within your control that you can effect, create, or change.

Note that you should always tag the items within your control with the actions "write," "create," and "respond."

For instance, let's do at a mini-exercise looking at the conferencing market in which I (Martin) used to work:

Customer	Product	You
• Less travel • More advanced technology to replace old • Improved training • More product features	• Feature rich • Different product options combining audio, video and web • Scalable	• Proposals • Multimedia demos • Training delivery • Messaging to the customer • Travel consulting

The product's features and benefits sell it to only a certain extent; it's up to you to create the rest of a winning value proposition so you can secure the business! By mapping out each opportunity this way, you are tailoring your pitch to the customer's specific reasons for buying, how your product meets these needs, and creating additional value using your extensive knowledge of both the customer and the product.

Let's look at each column in a bit more detail:

The Customer column gives you perspective and time to think about something we often need reminders about: Customers. Consider what matters to them—not to you or to the competition. Habitually, we often sell against the competition instead of with our own strengths—one of which is to listen. And if you do that well, you're halfway there.

The Product column adds an understanding of what you have in your arsenal, how strong your position is, and what you will need to cover with the customer to showcase these items.

The You column is the real difference-maker; it's what *you* can do that is the difference. People buy from people, and this includes what salespersons create, write, deliver, and/or change themselves—what they bring to the sale, what they personalize for the customer and this particular sale using their sales expertise combined with knowledge of the client and their specific needs.

This is a very straightforward exercise that effectively produces a map of the opportunity and, when done diligently, you will help you uncover better opportunities and find different ways to approach the same tasks you carry out regularly in your role as a salesperson. The very best salespeople understand this and they write extra content. They go the extra mile, often in the simplest ways—an extra phone call, a commitment, a change to language—everything makes a difference and it is all within your control.

2. Build on Strengths

My second action was to present a simple proposal to marketing. I knew they were good at what they did and I didn't want to change that; I wanted to build on it!

I requested that everything they provided to sales as PDFs be converted into an amendable format. I told them, "I want my salespeople thinking for themselves. What we have from you is a strong library of brand, product, and service content. What I want to add is a customer-by-customer focus."

It took some persuasion because, naturally, we all tend to be rather defensive about our own work and we subsequently create voids of behavior and ownership, and this was no exception. But marketing soon understood where I was going and the team was very helpful in supporting the idea.

3. The 5% Difference

I then introduced the 5% Difference to my sales unit. Here was my pitch:

I want to make one simple change. We are all working very hard and doing everything correctly except for one thing: when we see an opportunity, we are not following through with a conscious effort to show our understanding of what is important to the specific customer.

From now on, all prospects we speak to will get something from us that shows we understand them as individuals.

We now have customizable content, which has a great design and does a good job of selling the product and the support we offer. What we are going to add is simply a line or two including:

- *An offer*
- *A reference to their industry*
- *A reference to their needs*

The 5% Difference idea is simple: you take the existing material and add an extra 5% that is completely centered on the customer and his or her needs. That's all it takes.

Over time, we rolled out this approach to all areas of the sales content. It wasn't just about PDFs—it was about all content, technology, presentations, webinars, training, and anything to which the customer is exposed. Everything you do should have the minimum consideration of "how do I make this matter and relate to *each* customer?" Marketing content is as good you make it; the 5% Difference is made by what you do with it once you get it, or with what you create yourself. Nobody in your organization knows what your customer wants better than you.

As a result of this strategy being put into practice across the sales team, we went from running at 87% of target and losing £100K (US$154K) per month to achieving 123% of target in only 8 months.

Leveraged correctly, such as in the preceding example, technology provides a means to achieve this type of success. However, the main message is to understand your position of power as a salesperson. If you want to excel, then listen, research, and create. It will win you more business.

Paper Decision Three: The Idea of Customer Service as a Department

We all need to rethink the concept of the "Customer Service" Department.

In no way are we suggesting a business should not offer customer service and support. Customer service is a vital part in any business and should be delivered proactively in all business interactions and, of course, reactively whenever a customer initiates contact. Our concern arises from the idea of salespeople passing issues away to be handled by another part of the business. The same goes for salespeople using service management as an issues drop-box.

The saying "The customer always comes first" should be significant to you. As a salesperson, you should have ownership of delivering this experience to your customers, both by controlling communication and by caring about the outcome. The business world is by and large driven by efficiency, and that can often mean the desire to hit challenging targets and statistics that demonstrate "good" customer service response times can end up prevailing over true customer focus and can actually prevent good service.

■ **Note** It can't be said enough: The customer always comes first. Recognize that efficiency and process can sometimes get in the way of customers.

You may think, "that's just the way it is," but having challenged this maxim in our careers, we have both been successful by going the extra mile to anticipate and resolve customer issues and prevent dissatisfaction. I genuinely believe that customer care and service should be the main consideration for any go-to-market strategy. Exemplary service will always retain customers and create more opportunity. If there is one thing salespeople can control—no matter the size of the company—it is the care that they can put into their work.

Example: Use Follow-up Calls to Demonstrate a Service Mindset

One of the first things I (Martin) do when I have a new challenge or role in sales is to look at the customer service. To illustrate, I'll use a conferencing example.

I took over a team that was account managing conferencing services for some of the largest banking and corporate companies in the UK. Most of the accounts were running large-scale conference calls of 500+ people. The account managers were holding monthly meetings with the decision-makers but they weren't speaking to the people in charge of these calls, who were just as powerful and great potential contacts because they were senior people within the business. I added a process for calling the person running each large conference call just before and immediately afterward. The aim of these introductory and follow-up calls was for the account managers to introduce themselves, make suggestions, and find out how the call went and if anything can be improved in the future.

By adding this activity, in one account alone we increased the spend from £10,000 to £50,000 (US$15,400 to $76,900) per month, a new milestone.

Our contact and care allowed us to earn the right to start introducing new ideas and improvements.

We're not suggesting businesses shouldn't measure customer service call center statistics, but rather that there are different levels of customer service. Stats such as number of calls answered, number of issues resolved, average call time, and so on, are *quantitative* measures of customer service and are of value to the business internally. But high volumes of calls answered or issues resolved don't necessarily measure what "good" customer service looks like to your customers (i.e., externally). While it's difficult to put in place similar *qualitative* measurement and targets for "good" customer service, there is another level beyond Customer Service call stats. This is where you can really make a difference in your role as owner of the customer relationship.

The reality is: People are *not* the same as "users"!

- A user is a statistic, a number.

- A user is treated as a classification; e.g., a non-user, an infrequent user, an average user, a frequent user, a power user.

- A person is an individual with a level of expectation.

- A person is someone who will feel a certain way about the interactions he or she has with your business.

- A person is someone who will say good or bad things about his or her experiences.

- A person can either recommend or criticize you.

- A person is someone who makes decisions.

- A person is someone to be impressed every time you interact with him or her.

- A person is someone who can buy!

Whether or not you are using technology to speak with or meet with someone, make sure to treat her *as a person*, with individual problems and goals. You shouldn't assume that the root of one customer's problem is the same as another's. The underlying issue may be very different even though on the surface the problems may appear similar. The same is true for sales objections and issues; never assume the issue is the same because you have heard it before. Every company or salesperson can improve significantly with a simple change of mindset. I often think about this by considering the following questions:

- How would I want to be treated?

- What would impress me?

The answers:

- I want to be listened to.

- I want to know they understand my challenges.

- I want to be confident that they understand my industry.

- I want responses that are personalized to me (or to put it another way—anything not churned out by a machine).

Though it seems like a cliché, the first is the most important: "I want to be listened to." Salespeople do not spend enough time really listening; they hear just enough to respond (or respond about their product), but often not enough to genuinely understand what is important *to the customer*. If this is a problem for you and your team, consider a sports analogy. For every shot a player takes, he has to make four passes first. This works in sales, too: for every statement you make about your product, ask four questions before hand.

I (Martin) was recently interested in purchasing a web-hosting solution and all one company's salesperson did was talk *at* me about what the competition could not provide. All I wanted was to better understand how their service works. I also wanted to communicate to the salesperson that I had certain criteria for reporting and control panel capabilities. The salesperson started off well but soon defaulted to talking at a level beyond my technical understanding about a competitive field I did not know well. I became incredibly frustrated, and as a result, I didn't buy. I signed up with one of their competitors instead.

Customer service is not just responding to complaints; it begins and ends with sales and how much the sales unit and individual salespeople care about understanding the customer and delivering the best sales experience.

Sales Should Drive the Business and Control the Touch Points

Your customer's experience should begin and end with you. Even if the customer has researched your company, the point of sale—or more accurately, the first contact with the prospect to initiate the sale—should be treated as the beginning of the "customer experience." Your company and service are going to be only as good, or not, as you are in your initial call. The more we flow all customer issues through the salesperson as the key point of contact, the better. This does not mean you have to do other people's jobs; it just means you position yourself as the main point of contact. For customers, this means they have a single go-to person—you—to call regardless of what they need. They don't have the distress of trying to locate the right department, moving between unfamiliar areas of the business to find the right person to help them with their query.

Routing everything through you brings a range of benefits for the sales team and company: by acting as the key contact, you remove the need for customers to self-service their queries. You can be highly effective at resolving issues by leveraging your knowledge of the customer, the product, and your excellent internal relationships (discussed in the next paragraphs). This delivers a much better customer experience, helping retain business, and at the same time building a better and wider understanding of customers, their business, and any potential opportunities.

It would be wise to adopt the same approach with your *internal* customers as well—those, for example, who can produce sales materials for you or expedite your orders. Their buy-in to you as an individual can mean all the difference when you, in turn, need to get results for your customers. I don't know a single highly successful salesperson who didn't start by selling well internally.

Your internal customers can include almost anyone in your organization, but it is good to start with people in the areas of the business you will need to interact with the most in your day-to-day job and get them on board with what you're doing. They may vary depending on your specific role and also on what you sell, but in most cases your internal customers will consist of people in:

- Marketing/Customer Communications

- Implementation/Project Management
- Service Management/Customer Experience
- Operations
- The Executive Team

Developing a strong working relationship with as many of these groups as possible will put you in a stronger position to deliver the best possible experience to your customers. Since the support of these teams is paramount to your success, make sure you spend time getting key areas of the business engaged with the innovation and creativity you bring, such as a new style of presentation, an idea, or a new way to sell.

You can use many of the technologies we've discussed to bring your internal partners into customer conversations or internal briefs. Use your Customer Relationship Marketing, for example, so it alerts you and others to changes and keeps people up to date all the time. The use of conferencing is also highly effective, especially as a tool to demonstrate why you need something and what is driving the customer, and to show that you have thought of all the possibilities. The more your internal people understand your approach and have engagement with the customer, the more they will do for you and be prepared to respond to urgent requests.

The following example shows a great way to leverage your position of power and give something extra.

Example: Implementation of a Conferencing Solution

While selling a business-wide, multi-user conferencing solution, we introduced an implementation plan that allowed us to onboard customers more quickly than we could previously. The customer onboarding process is the key period after their first purchase from you, laying the foundation for a long-term and mutually beneficial business relationship (or not!). Although the implementation plan was a good start, I felt there was more to be gained.

What was it that our buyers—in particular, the decision-makers—wanted?

In this case, the decision-makers were in the IT department and had two main concerns:

1. Price. Although audio conferencing is a productivity-based service, ownership was held by the IT department, which regarded it as fairly commoditized. This means that despite being distinguishable in terms of its attributes (such as unique features and brand), the market doesn't perceive the qualitative differences and treats the product or service as virtually equivalent no matter who provides it. When this occurs, the only distinguishing factor in the eyes of the buyer becomes price. In this instance, the IT department was interested in our proposition only if we could compete on price, and one other thing.

2. The risk involved in switching providers. Would changing to a new provider carry any risk that could in turn make the decision-makers look bad? They wanted absolute assurance that changing providers would be smooth and problem-free, and that they'd get extra care during the process.

Our competitor in this bid was selling simply up to point of the client making the purchase decision, but not on what would happen after the decision was made. Their proposal was based on a number of "ifs":

-   If you switch to us, we will provide an implementation plan.

-   If you switch to us, we will brand your user literature.

-   If you switch to us, we will e-mail the users.

Our marketing team provided some great insight: the essence of "If"-based selling means you are asking the decision-maker to imagine what something *might* look like. Conferencing is not a traditional IT purchase because it is a hands-on service utilized by end-users. IT isn't in control of the implementation or support of the service, which is provided by the supplier. So they are typically not familiar with the potential pitfalls that can occur while switching providers. They are still, however, responsible for the purchase itself and what happens afterward, and they rely on the conferencing supplier to do a good job of the rollout and switching end-users from the old to the new service as smoothly as possible.

Because they were looking at price and risk as the key factors in making the buying decision, we started to consider not just "what is it they want" but "what else are they not getting to see?" How could we make our proposition really come alive for them and reduce the risk of change?

1. We added something important to the implementation plan: we would call each individual user to introduce him or her to the new service and help with any questions.

2. Before the first customer meeting, we amended our existing marketing materials via a simple process whereby the salespeople would insert the client's logo, and then we asked them to write content into the introduction that they thought would be of interest to the customer.

With the buyer having a commoditized view of conferencing services, the differentiator here was to ensure the customer was proven to have made a good decision that would not cause any problems in execution. We were offering to ensure the transition was 100% painless by doing all of the direct engagement with end-users during the rollout.

We also increased their usage of conferencing many times over because we showed them how easy it was and what they could use it for. It vividly exemplifies that technology is the answer only if you know how to use it well and often in your business. They saved money by not traveling as much, had greater productivity and communications around projects, and we increased our earnings.

Many salespeople outside of our unit couldn't appreciate the simplicity of what we were doing for a very simple but baseless reason: they considered it beneath them to spend time phoning end-users; they felt they should be spending their time with the "more important" decision-makers and budget-holders. The typical response was, "I'm too busy to call end-users." With revenue from conferencing being driven by usage, it was ironic that other sales teams couldn't see the obvious value of engaging directly with the users and how this could drive usage and revenue figures. By understanding this connection and making the effort to contact end-users directly, our team started seeing revenue from uptake and usage of the service four times more quickly than before. What's more, our deal closure rate of 60% was significantly above the industry average of 27%.

The secondary gain was that we had now amassed details of the direct phone numbers and job roles of more or less every person we would want to contact within each customer's business—including end-users of the service. All of our sales teams were being told to expand their contacts within their accounts, to find new contacts, speak to people in more areas of the business, and so forth. By contacting all of the users of the conferencing service, we were doing exactly that! Their first contact with us was with a person who could react and discuss business with them— conversations that went way beyond IT-based discussion points.

The company I (Martin) worked for at the time adopted this as their standard approach, and later they ultimately moved the end-user calling to a specialist (junior) team that they created anew to handle this element of the customer experience. Ten years later, this is still unique in the industry and the competition still hasn't understood its value or adopted the appropriate behaviors to support it. This is another good example of why it's important to think about the difference between *people* and *users*.

This strategy delivered a further personal success for me as well—I was invited onto the Regional Leadership Team shortly afterward and also asked to implement this approach across all of the sales units in the company.

I've never considered myself too good, too senior, or too experienced to avoid doing something that will make the difference for the customer. It's an approach truly worth considering, as it will result in closer customer relationships. If you also take the time to do some research and use the tools we have mentioned, you will identify more and better opportunities. Add to this an attitude based on *what is possible* instead of just accepting "how things have always been done," and you will be surprised how the little things can make all the difference in your success.

We've gone into detail examining ways in which you can leverage your power as a salesperson to increase your sales and ensure you hit and exceed your targets. Now let's look at some of the fundamentals you can use to make this happen.

The Fundamentals

The topic of fundamentals is very interesting and covers a vast range of areas; "sales fundamentals" can be summarized as the behaviors, knowledge, and tools you need to employ on a daily basis to ensure that you are successful as a salesperson. Whenever I embark on a new sales challenge or change of role, I make sure to review the fundamentals before doing anything else, including:

- Sales tools
- Sales content
- Customer touch points

Sales Tools

We define sales tools as every piece of content, presentation, technology, marketing messaging, customer service, value propositions, and call scripts at your disposal. This is certainly not an exhaustive list! You should review and amend it frequently to build up your own library of capabilities. Ideally, your sales unit should be doing so as a whole; knowledge management/sharing systems are a brilliant way of creating a centralized repository of sales tools and a forum for salespeople to exchange challenges, ideas, and learnings (these are sales tools as well). I tend to start by reviewing the non-sales content because it gives you valuable insight into how well synchronized the different areas of the business are. While you do this, keep a handful of questions in mind:

- Is a call to action on marketing and customer lifecycle messaging being sent to customers?
- Are your contact details included in the messaging?
- If marketing is using webinars and other collaboration technologies, are they including you and are you attending the calls?[1]

---

[1] It constantly disappoints me how little time some salespeople put into experiencing the messaging their customers receive from their business. In sales, we readily complain about the quality of leads, but very rarely attend or influence content at the front end. It seems senseless when you think about how backward that is, so why waste time chasing leads you don't know enough about?

- What video content is available? What are you trying to achieve with it? It the content delivering what it's supposed to? Is anything missing?

- Is the website great? Does it have enough sales messaging in it? Are the links from the site (live chat, phone numbers, e-mails) coming into sales, where appropriate?

You need to complete the journey to make sure everything around you is set up for your success. No business is perfect, and you can influence some things, but not all. Identify what you can influence to improve your own sales capabilities and focus on those aspects.

■ **Note** Focus on things you can influence in the sales process. Don't waste time where effort and action won't help much.

For example, ask marketing to conduct the same webinars they normally do, but with you in attendance. Then make a personal guarantee at the end: "I will contact each of you tomorrow." The danger with relying too much on technology is in expecting it to replace part of the sales role and assuming it will do the work for you. The reality is that after a webinar, often nothing will have changed from a sales perspective; very few customers see webinars as being different from e-mail (and letters before it). You still need to ensure the next steps will happen by following up directly with each customer. The technology—in this case a webinar—is the introduction; people still need to feel like individuals who are valued, so this is the point from which you should take over.

Sales Content

Something you can have complete control of is the content of your sales materials. Clearly, each company has specific guidelines about including certain content and company information, but you are in control of your success and you should leverage your power here as a salesperson—especially considering the explicit understanding you have of your customers. This is where your personality, knowledge, listening skills and use of technology come to the fore. You should use this book as a reference; once you know what you want to accomplish, consider the customer type and which technologies to use through the sales process, and then build your content around that.

We encounter more and more big companies that are either streamlining Request for Proposal (RFP) responses by employing dedicated specialists, or have a single proposal template for the business to use. This can work well, but never take it as a strict rule; you should always add your own personality, approach, and—most importantly—customer understanding. Salespeople should create more, and use their skills and knowledge to inject additional value. The best ones already do.

For example, anything you present as a proposal can easily be recorded. You can get an amazing response from this, especially if you include a simple line in the e-mail or phone call to say, "I know presentations like these can be time consuming, so I recorded two five-minute summaries of the proposal that you can play back at your convenience."

A simple exercise is to consider five different customers you know well. Think about the customer's specific situation, priorities, goals, needs, and gain. Bearing all this in mind, write them a tailored and winning introduction to your business. My top tip is to start with everything you know about them, and weave in your content around this.

The alternative isn't appealing: I (Martin) recently conducted a technology consultation project in which one bidder sent a proposal of 63 pages (despite being asked for 25 pages max—his first mistake) and the content was so obviously generic that the customer was mentioned only in a "find the company name and replace" context. At no point were there any statements or content specifically about the customer; the salesperson has made it all about him—his day, time, and product. Don't make the same mistake—being "busy" is not the same as being smart.

Customer Touch Points

Customer touch points are every interface between a customer and a business, including people (whether in person, over the phone, or online), systems, offerings, marketing, ads, websites, and many more. For sales, technology can greatly facilitate interaction with customers, but equally, the original reason for deploying a technology can get lost over time or not revisited, especially when new tools become available and other priorities arise.

You might think it's not your job to set up or provide guidance to customers on how to use the technology that you're using to sell to them (e.g., web conferencing), and we agree. However, if your customers come into contact with a particular tool that is a touch point during the sales process, it's your job to know what that technology does, how it works, and whether it does the best for your customer and for you.

Let's look at an example from Martin's experience:

Customer lifecycle auto-emails

What:

Our customers were being sent e-mails periodically with the messaging changing for each person based on his or her level of engagement, usage, purchases, and behavior over time.

Why:

The idea was that customers should receive relevant messages at the right times to drive them toward additional products and services, which encourages greater usage revenue or purchase frequency and increases their spend with us.

The Issue:

The calls to action were not changing. The products were evolving, but the messaging from the operations, marketing, sales, and product teams was not. The reason is that none of these teams were approaching the issue from the correct perspective. Our CRM system (which was delivering the customer lifecycle messaging) was a few years old and the marketing team had moved on to newer, "shinier" things despite the CRM system being the tool for the main communications seen by *every* customer. The Operations team was not involved in the process, so they weren't feeding in any issue resolutions. Sales saw it as "just a marketing tool," and weren't sure of the value it delivered.

Change:

I became a champion of the solution and started contributing to the message copy, adding personalization such as the account manager's direct phone number and e-mail address (it was previously a generic number and no e-mail, which was inconceivable, as we were communicating with them by e-mail!). We coupled this with the inclusion of calls to action (such as attending webinars, contacting us, or looking at the website) and new product information, while shortening the copy and adding more links to our website to allow people to access our multimedia world seamlessly.

Over time, all salespersons had influence over *their* copy, which is exactly what it was: messaging going out to their customers all the time. Previously, they had not been viewing the automated messaging as an opportunity. They also didn't realize their position of power; no one had considered how they could leverage this tool. Marketing was not disturbed—why would they be? We were changing just that extra 5%—not the 95% they had built with their expertise—and their statistics also improved because we were making that 5% Difference.

Make Sure You Get Access to Higher Authority

Sales tends to engage, or be pigeon-holed with, one main customer contact once a sale is made, usually the person responsible for running the project. This can become problematic if the person is resistant to any ideas you have that might cost money. It could also be a problem if they don't have the authority or the right DiSC style (see Chapter 2) to do so. Or the person might not be around when an important decision needs to be made. As early as possible, customer service should have at least three names of people to contact, preferably at higher levels of authority, whom they can reach out to if they hit an impasse with their main contact. This has to be done carefully, but sometimes it is the only way to get important things done for the customer.

Sales, marketing, and customer service are involved in the same endeavor— they all provide services for the customer. The difference is that you own the customer relationship for your business, so everything ultimately comes back to you. If you are happy with the messaging the customer is receiving, then you are in a better place. This is equally true for new business, as your standards and service delivery set the tone for customer interactions. Know your position of power and use it, and remember to always explain what and why you want to review or change any process, tool, or messaging currently in use and be mindful of other people, the work they may have put into these things, and also their particular DiSC profile.

Understanding DiSC Internally

The "light bulb" moment for DiSC normally comes within the first 20 minutes of the training session. We start by looking at famous people and some buzzwords by DiSC type as a warmup.

The aim is to become familiar with a few fun and obvious examples of DiSC behaviors; we then want the salespeople to start relating this to their work environment. We consider their internal colleagues and get them to try to guess their own DiSC style and that of their head of sales/VP of sales, so they can better understand their boss. Once we start discussing different ways to interact with their boss and understanding what drives them the "light bulb" goes on.

We call DiSC "getting out of your own way."

Consider that phrase for a moment. We all have default behavioral patterns; gaining an understanding of your own behaviors, and in turn, those of others, is essential. Not everyone will like doing things the same way you do them, or talking the way you do, nor will they necessarily view their priorities in the same way as you view yours.

Selling internally using DiSC is not only vital; it is also great practice for selling to customers. You will need to learn to adjust your content, message, and approach according to your DiSC profile and that of your audience.

Example: Never "High D" a High D

You'll recall that people with a high D (Dominance) score can be described as demanding, forceful, egocentric, strong-willed, determined, ambitious, aggressive, and pioneering. Quite a lineup! The saying "never 'high D' a high D" is a phrase we commonly use; if you have two high Ds, yourself and someone else, and you don't adjust your approach to them, it can lead to, stating it diplomatically, high "tempo" (or aggressive) meetings. I personally experienced this with one of my previous managers; we continually clashed about any number of topics and ideas, and I came to realize this was because we were both high Ds—aggressive and impatient. In the main, we got on well, but at certain times we really clashed. Once I understood DiSC theory, I adjusted two aspects of my behavior when interacting with this person:

1. I learned when to be quiet.

2. I went in to our discussions with a range of choices and options in mind, not just a single option that he might oppose right at the outset.

By adjusting my approach to his DiSC profile, I managed to negotiate with him to get the decisions I wanted (and in about a fifth of the time!), while avoiding needless heated debates.

Whether you're selling internally or externally, it is the same idea. You probably do this to a certain extent already—most people do—and if you really understand the DiSC model, you'll be able to use it all the time and very easily for all aspects from content, to time spent, to presentation. Everyone wants things done their way and to suit their style.

It is becoming a more popular theme in companies to create "pods" or teams of people from different functions that are responsible for the customer. Using S.M.A.R.T. goals (see Chapter 2) to align themselves, sales, marketing, and customer service meet as needed to be sure everything possible is being done to ensure customer satisfaction, which in turn becomes greater loyalty and revenue for you and your company.

Summary

We have covered how to avoid thinking of sales in the traditionally siloed way. As a salesperson, you have both the power and technology at your disposal to strive for the ideas to control your own destiny. Applying logic and reviewing your customers' requirements on an ongoing basis, maintaining key touch points, and constantly adjusting and adapting throughout the journey can win you lots of business. In the next chapter, we'll take these learnings another step forward by examining how you can build value with some even more customer-centric thinking.

Selling to X

As we approach the end of this book, we want to add some further value and thought around your strategy for winning more business. In this chapter, we consider in more depth a subject we have mentioned in various scenarios throughout the book:

- The importance of considering your customer types

- How they prefer to be sold to

- What else should you consider in selling to them

- Matching technology to industries

It is important to think about who your buyers are, and to always put yourself in their shoes. The more technology-based approaches, innovations, creativity, methods, and skills you have, the more you can react, adapt, and change to each opportunity that arises.

This chapter is designed to get you started with some new thinking, but don't let it stop here. Make it a habit to stay abreast of developments in technology—your career will benefit from it. We cover some ideas that are generally applicable but, unfortunately, there are far too many business types for us to cover them all separately. Use the ideas here as suggestions for how to approach your profession and take action tailored to your current and potential customers.

Here's what we cover:

- What do we mean by putting yourself in the customer's shoes?

- Use "just enough" technology.

- Match technology and content to your customer's market and role.

- Speed up and control the sales cycle.

- Reach out to specialists.

- Add decision-makers simply and quickly.

- Use technology that gives the customer control.

- Remember: The more time customers commit, the more business you will win.

- Sell to a user base.

- Treat every prospect as unique.

- What is technology? A definition.

What Do We Mean by Putting Yourself in the Customer's Shoes?

This approach has served us better than anything else we have undertaken in our sales careers. It's not difficult, and when executed well it allows you to make calls on which technology to use, how often to meet with your customer, and how to customize your sales pitch.

For each sales opportunity, all you need to do is take a small amount of time to carefully consider things from the customer's perspective and plan each stage of the sales process accordingly.

Think about:

- What matters to the customer?

- Are you delivering what you agreed to at the start?

- Whose agenda are you working toward?

- How can you impress the customer further?

- How can you innovate in your approach?

These are all great things to keep in mind throughout the sales process, and the crucial element should be about whose agenda you are working toward. The answer to this should always be the same: the customer's. Deadlines are often put in place for a reason, but regardless, it is all too easy to put things off; to reconfigure agreed on touch points; or to become complacent and miss deadlines, even just by a day or two. You may think, "What does it ultimately matter?"

It does matter! You can't impress customers by being average. Put yourself in your customer's shoes or contemplate how would you want to be treated if you swapped places; if you were the customer, what would impress you? Find out the answer to this, and do it. You probably have everything you need to know from asking yourself just that one simple question.

Bearing this in mind, you will need to act on it using the correct amount of speed of response, quality of response, technology, and innovation. This can vary depending on the individual you are selling to, the product or service you are selling, and the industries you are selling into. We look at this further later in the chapter. However, speed and quality of response should always be at the forefront of every interaction you have with your customer. Put simply, this can help you win business.

Here's an example. Several years ago, the CIO of a large retailer was looking to install videoconferencing into 13 regional offices and HQs. The problem was, it was expensive and he couldn't get a business sponsor. To his, and our, relief, a new CEO came into the company and was intrigued by the CIO's ideas. He asked us to put together a demonstration showing the CEO how he could enable several of his objectives via video. We had only 48 hours to get our demo together. Fifteen minutes into the demo, the CEO said, "I like it. Let's get it." Thirty days later we installed more than $1 million in equipment. This was a vivid example of a response combining speed and quality.

▓ **Remember** Speed helps you win business.

Putting yourself in the customer's shoes can also help you craft the right messages to communicate with her. Don't use technology just for the sake of it. Combining the use of technology with your creative sales skills and thought processes to flow into everything you do will help you tailor your approach for each customer and, in turn, increase your sales. The reason we find this method so effective is that it causes us to stop, to think about the customer, and, most importantly, it enables you to innovate even in my most stressful and busy times. You will become increasingly conditioned to it over time, so it is a constant process of evolution. Try it, and keep trying it until it is second nature.

Use "Just Enough" Technology

This book is about using technology to work smarter, sell more, and advance your approach to help you win more business. This is not to say you should completely change the way you work, but you should endeavor to make adjustments to improve what you do and increase the range of tools you have in your armory for selling, connecting with people globally, and achieving your goals.

When selling, you should use just the right amount of technology needed to win the business; for some markets this will mean using lots of different types of technology throughout the sales process, and for others, it will mean using very little. Regardless of how much or how little technology is used, always ensure the technologies are being used to support the activities required to carry out the sale. They are there to serve a purpose and even technology-savvy customers don't want to see technology for technology's sake, so use it appropriately.

The right amount of technology may also depend on your market. Let's explore this next.

Match Technology and Content to Your Customer's Market and Role

Certain markets and customer roles will by default respond better to different sales approaches, and this is exactly the same for technology.

What you need to consider is what makes the most sense for the market you are selling into—that is, your customer's market. Video works well for all markets—it's the most popular media format—and will continue to grow in value as producing your own video content becomes increasingly easier and more accessible. This is also true for video conferencing; what used to cost $20,000 for a room equipped with the necessary technology to conduct conference calls is now available as a free, secure service right on your computer desktop (or your smartphone or tablet). It will take time, but video, Web, and conference calls will continue to move toward becoming the default way of communicating.

■ **Note** Although this seems very basic, if you do decide to bring video into your sales arsenal, please remember that the camera on your device has the same limitations as any other camera. Make sure that your light source is in front of you, not in back, otherwise you will be a dark shadow that nobody can see.

There is a straightforward way to look at matching up technologies to specific markets with a simple three-column view.

- The first column notes the markets you're selling into.

- The second column identifies the role of the person you're selling to.

- The third column names how the person in this role and market typically prefers to be sold to, based on these factors.

For example, let's consider social media sales. We have completed the table below based on our experience:

Market	Decision-Maker Role	Sales Approach
Training	Marketing	Visuals, innovation
Training	Sales	Results, customer experience
Retail	Sales	Customer experience
Retail	Business owner	Numbers, technology
B2B	IT	Technology
B2B	C-level	Results, ownership

Figure 9-1. Social media sales worksheet

Doing this easy exercise gives you a reference point for your product. For example, we know that if we are going to sell to a training company and the contact is in marketing, we can create a personalized video showing him results but also weaving in our own research as well as ideas that are unique to the customer.

Equally, in the same scenario, if we are going to see the same client but both sales and marketing will be in the same meeting, we would change tack and use a video combined with testimonial content in the presentation to appeal to the preferences of everyone in attendance.

The main takeaway from this is to ensure you use the techniques you think will work best for your audience. For a varied group, you may have to take a broader approach, appealing to as wide an audience as possible or recognize when you will need to use different tactics to appeal to different attendees. Lots of salespeople stick to using just one approach, and though that can be effective, it's the same as using one single sales pitch regardless of who your audience is, which wouldn't make sense. Hopefully, you are already shaking your head and thinking, "I would never do that; I'd tailor my sales pitch to the customer in front of me!" It's the same with your choice of the tools you employ during the sales process. Make sure you choose those appropriate to each specific customer and opportunity, using what you think would impress them or make them feel the most comfortable.

The same approach is true of the content that you use. What is appropriate may differ depending on the market you're selling into. Consider the volume of content you should deliver—should you use less than usual? More? What type of content will have the best effect? Visual? Factual? Let's look at a few examples.

Examples

Finance: For contacts who are in finance, you would want to use more content and make it fact-based. Typically, they will want to be thorough, ensuring they have all the facts and checking for accuracy before they make a decision.

Sales: Salespeople want to get results but are generally higher risk-takers and want to make decisions more quickly. It is common to see a preponderance of High-D and High-i behavior styles in sales. So less content is better—keep it focused and get straight to the point, giving just as much as is required and no more. Salespeople will ask for more information (if needed) to make their decisions, and you can respond specifically to those points as they are raised.

Matching your approach to the market and the role of the buyer will greatly help you sell in the right way, spending the appropriate amount of time creating content based on your target audience and their preferred way to be sold to.

Speed Up and Control the Sales Cycle

The longer the sales cycle, the more you will want to control the process and keep your customer committed to making the decision throughout. During longer sales journeys, bear in mind that it's not uncommon for your prospects' priorities to change as they juggle multiple projects and initiatives over time. You may need to work at keeping them engaged all the way through. Sharing regular updates, both with virtual meetings and via recorded content, is a quick and enjoyable way to get things across to your customers and keep them up to date and engaged throughout the process.

For example, while working on a recent consulting project, I (Martin) recorded video updates on the latest progress with the project as well as sharing some new sales ideas that I had and sent this to my main contact. The ideas weren't part of our main remit, but I usually do this kind of thing to provide added value and people do appreciate it. Plus, tactically it can get you more contacts and business in both the short and longer term. In this instance, the client was a global engineering firm and I was working on delivering a cost-reduction plan for their conferencing services. The ideas I was building into the proposal were about reducing their travel costs and training people on how to use conferencing. I tailored everything to their roles, and didn't just use a standard approach, which would have been less meaningful for the customer.

My customer contact passed on the video to one of his colleagues, who then contacted me to start working with them on an additional training and communication project as well. Using technology to make content engaging and easy to share can lead to new opportunities and sales revenue, so give it a try.

For shorter sales cycles, it is about innovating to close deals or business more quickly and using the technologies you think will work best to achieve this. A retail business owner we know often uses text updates to communicate when she's having a sale, appointment confirmations, and latest news. She gets great feedback about this and it prompts existing customers to come into her store. Others have used Twitter for the same purpose to great effect.

In our opinion, the best tools for speeding up and controlling the sales cycle are conferencing and collaboration technologies. Your goal is to keep clients committed, keep in touch with them regularly, and pull in other people to help with the sale or the decision-making process from both sides, if needed. What could be better than the capability to instantly discuss, present ideas, see each other, and share content, all simultaneously and with as many people as needed without having to incur the time and cost to travel to a meeting place? It's called "conferencing and collaboration" for a reason: collaborating is about working together and this technology facilitates exactly that. Remember, the more you get your prospects to commit their time and resources during the sales journey, the better place you will be in. We believe conferencing and collaboration tools are the best technologies to support this. We discuss this in more detail later in this chapter.

As a minimum, you should try to have a regular, weekly catch-up meeting with your customer. This should be a meeting that you and the customer have committed to and put on your calendars. You can test the customer's openness to trying different technologies when you set this up week by week. You should also bring as much new and relevant information as you can to these meetings. Using social media is a great way to do this.

A few ideas to use depending on your customer:

Good for Techies: "Would you like to use a desktop HD video next week? I've just started using Ten Hands and you should give it a try; it's a great video tool and very easy to use."

Good for Innovators: "I use video recordings to give my clients a 2-minute summary of my proposal and then follow up by meeting with them for 20 minutes to discuss conferencing tools. This means you get two updates a week, keeping you at the cutting edge, but with very little time needed."

Good for Making the Customer Feel Valued: "If we have a weekly conference call, I can have my manager/head of department/customer service/project manager [insert title here] join as appropriate at different points of this journey so you can meet everyone without taking up too much of your time with face-to-face meetings, as I know you are busy."

For sales cycle management, the key thing is to make sure you put into place regular meetings, preferably weekly, with the client's firm commitment to attend. No matter how good the relationship with your contact, you need to keep his interest and commitment going.

Set up private, dedicated LinkedIn or Facebook groups for your customers so they feel they are receiving special attention and use social media to communicate with you and each other.

Technologies like Camtasia.com, Jing, and other screen capture technologies allow you to make quick presentations or demonstrations while capturing video. Several of our customers use this technology to send the demo to people who couldn't attend so they experience the demonstration as close as possible to being there in person. There is also a great technology called VYou that allows you to exchange video messages with each other. These are both very unique and captivating ways to engage customers and prospects, if they are receptive.

Reach Out to Specialists

Virtual meeting technologies make bringing in partners, experts, specialists, and colleagues from other functions around your business when you need them a breeze—regardless of whether they are based in the same building or on the other side of the planet. This is a great way to impress customers and add that all-important speed and quality of response. Always make the best impression possible!

You can also use specialists and additional resources tactically if you believe this could help speed the process or if you are worried you are not in as good a position to win the business as you previously believed.

For example: "Hi Jon, I have secured time with our head of service for a call to present options for your requirements. Can you make a call on Tuesday at 2:00 p.m. or Wednesday at 4:00 p.m.?"

■ **Note** Video technology allows you to bring in specialists and experts to a sales call easily. Doing so can help you close the sale.

Include additional people to drive attendance to your calls; change the dynamic of the conversation; and add new perspectives, expertise, and inputs throughout the sales process.

The same principle works with people you need to include from the customer's side, as the next section shows.

Add Decision-makers Quickly and Simply

I (Martin) was once delivering a pitch to sell conferencing services to a training company. I was using a Web conferencing tool to deliver my sales pitch and the presentation was going extremely well. I had just asked who else was involved in the decision-making process and my contact on the call, the IT director, advised the decision-makers were himself and the finance director, who was not on the call at that time. I asked if the finance director was available, so we could speed things up and he could hear directly from both of us. This is a classic example of getting "two birds with one stone."

The IT director said, "Let me send our finance director an instant message . . . Yes, he can give us ten minutes. I'll send him the dial-in details for this conference call."

I replied, "Don't worry, if you give me his number, I can dial out to him instantly using the conferencing service."

So now I also have the finance director's direct phone number, a commitment from the customer (to get his colleague involved), and a great practical demonstration of the exact technology I was selling to them.

I dialed the finance director, who joined the call and completely changed the focus of the conversation from the technology to the cold, hard numbers. I immediately altered my presentation to show a screen share of our website, which provided a graphic of average savings on travel costs. I didn't mention this graphic specifically; we talked for 5 or so minutes and then he mentioned the screen himself, so I switched to a presentation on our travel reduction approach—something that had caught his interest. I've said it so many times before, but here it is again: Adapt to your audience!

Because of the flexibility of this type of technology, we made the best use of everyone's time by getting all parties involved in the decision into the same meeting at once, instead of holding multiple meetings spread out over a longer period of time. We won the business and they multiplied their spend by five times what they had previously spent with the competition. Having all the right people participating in the decision from the start also meant that we had laid a great foundation for building more business in the future, as all of the key players were involved from the outset.

The key here is to think of technology as a way to help time-conscious people. It is much easier for your customers to agree to attend a 20-minute meeting without having to leave their desks than any other meeting type.

■ **Note** A 20-minute meeting via videoconference is the easiest kind of meeting for customers to agree to.

Use Technology That Gives the Customer Control

It is for these same reasons that you should use technology that allows customers to control their environment and interact with you. Remember, your objective is to get them to commit to interaction. Interaction is a sign of continued interest—it's that goal of commitment that you want to maintain—and any meeting should be as collaborative as possible. The more collaboratively you can work with your contacts, the more invested and committed they will be throughout the sales process. Web conferencing or any whiteboard technology is fantastic for this; it allows you to pass control back and forth, allowing either you or the client to highlight and add text or content to anything you are discussing. You can even allow her to control applications on your computer so she can amend presentations or share any other software you want to with her (and without her needing to have the same software installed).

It is a fantastic way to allow clients to make decisions and changes in real-time. I often find these meetings quite refreshing and I think clients do as well; *no one* likes being talked at or being talked through a boring, robotic presentation. Collaborating in this way is extremely engaging and encourages creativity and new ideas and solutions. You can have the world's greatest product but still struggle if you sell it poorly. Mix it up; I've never understood why so many people use only one piece of software in a presentation. PowerPoint and slide presentations are useful, but they are best not used in isolation.

Remember: The More Customers Commit, the More Business You Will Win

We've alluded to the relationship between your customer's commitment and the likelihood of gaining the sale several times throughout this chapter, and it should be at the forefront of your thinking. It's worth restating: the more customers commit, the more business you will win.

By commitment, we mean:

- Time they spend with you

- The people they involve

- The interaction they bring

- The actions they take during and between steps of the sales process

- The commitment they make for regular updates

- The money they commit for a trial run

- The agreement they make for a trial run or deadline-based event

Gaining commitment can be anything from checking in with the buyer for feedback and comments or asking for his views, opinions, and insight. Commitment can ultimately be the signing of an order, but it goes deeper than that. For example, why give a one-way sales pitch in which you are talking at your buyers? By building commitments (such as those listed) throughout the process, you could ultimately co-present your pitch with your main client stakeholder or a customer champion of the project. All at once you are strengthening that person's dedication to the process and acting like a business partner doing a consultative sell.

Note Gaining commitment from your sales prospects depends on your efforts to understand them and their unique problems and challenges.

This is an incredibly strong position to be in. Ask yourself, is a customer more likely to buy from someone who has little engagement during the sales process and is presenting his pitch by talking *at* them, or from someone who has engaged with his stakeholders, listened carefully, and is now co-presenting alongside her own colleagues with an in-depth understanding of their needs?

Sell to a User Base

If you sell to a user base (e.g., a mass audience or a large group of users), then the use of technology should be considered in exactly the way we have described but with one main difference. Think about the following:

Users are people—individuals—each with their own needs.

The word "user" takes out of the thought process the idea that each user is a person with his or her own individual needs and requirements. It makes us think instead "en masse," of something to treat as a large, homogeneous entity; it desensitizes us to the individuals at the other end.

Question: At the end of the day, what is a user in this context?

Answer:

- Either a customer or a potential customer

- Someone to be valued

- A person who has his or her own criteria of what good service means

- Someone you may never know personally, but who can make or break the deal

It is with this in mind that I believe you need a philosophy that starts with sales about how you want your user base to be treated. You need to consider what would impress you (put yourself into their shoes!), how you can personalize the sales approach, and what technology would best enable you to do this.

A mailing system such as MailChimp has great advantages for personalizing the sale, and you can also think about the call to action in the message so it matches what you want to achieve (sales, leads, conversations, phone numbers).

Example: Phinkit Alpha Team

When we had Phinkit.com in its early test version we put together an Alpha team (i.e., a test team) of 162 people (not users!).

Our aim was to see how they used the site, uncover any remaining bugs, and gain valuable early feedback.

I (Martin) have a passion for lifecycle messaging. Remember, this is tailored messaging that is delivered to customers at specific points or after certain events during their customer journey. It is based on a detailed understanding of customer behavior and how customers interact with your product or service. Lifecycle messaging can be incredibly effective when it's well executed, so my secondary aim was to evaluate what would work best for messaging. We sent out weekly development progress updates in the form of a short e-mail with two links that were calls to action (i.e., links to solicit an action from the customer) on the e-mail so we could measure responses based on different message types.

We then divided the Phinkit Alpha team into two groups based on job roles: those in customer-facing people roles such as sales or customer support, and those in non–customer-facing roles such as IT or finance. We used the same message as before, changing only a few elements and links to content based on their job roles.

The links pointed to different posts and content on the Phinkit site, based on the tailoring to the Alpha team members' job roles. By understanding the profiles of our team members and splitting the team into meaningful groups and tailoring the messaging to their job roles, we more than doubled the number of hits to the site from the week before!

In hindsight, this does not seem like any great surprise, but it is still a valuable lesson: If you make the messaging more specific to the needs of the individual, you will get better results, because the content will be of more value to them. I wasn't doing anything truly groundbreaking but I was applying some sensible logic and using the technology I had at my disposal to execute it.

If you sell or prospect en masse to a user group, then don't just work for the sake of it. It is very easy to just want to tick the box to get something done because you are very busy; putting in a bit more time and careful thought can deliver so much more for you.

Remember, users are people!

Treat Every Prospect as Unique

Whether you are selling to a wide user group or directly to individuals, it is important to always treat every prospect and interaction you have as unique. We are covering lots of different skills, thoughts, and reference points for selling. The next step is to make sure you do not fall into bad habits. It's easy to bring in something new like a piece of technology or new presentation software and then rely solely on using that instead of considering each customer's needs and adapting your use of technology to him or her.

The key is always to adapt to each and every prospect—remember they are each unique, with specific needs and circumstances—and carry out the sale in what you consider to be the best way to get them through the process to agree to a close using technology they are comfortable with or will respond best to.

■ **Note** You can make this easier by having a set of standard messages, proposals, and videos that cover the most common scenarios, and then modifying them to the specifics of your customer or prospect. You don't have to reinvent the wheel or create everything from scratch each time.

What Is Technology? A Definition

A reminder about what technology is: Quite simply, for sales, it is a tool to deliver what your prospects or customers want, faster and with better quality, not what you think is cool. And even if it is amazingly cool, you still need to apply it to what the customer cares about, which is never the technology itself, but rather what technology can help them gain or avoid. The last part is the most important. Like many things, it is the right balance and coordination of things that makes something great. Use the technology customers want to use. Deliver the content they want to see the way they want to see it.

And this, in sum, is the whole point of the book. Now go out and sell more!

Tips and Tactics

Sundry Items to Be Aware Of

While this book was being written, we took note of myriad valuable ideas that were relevant but didn't have an exact fit into any particular chapter.

This appendix captures many of these for you to use as you need. As stated in the introduction, we are not endorsing any particular vendor, company, or service (unless noted). We will also update this at www.ipgtraining.com.

Technology Is a Tool, Not the Answer

Technology will become your best friend if used properly, or it will turn against you and become a foe, a real time waster, if you think it replaces excellent selling skills and can do the sales job for you. It helps you on your destination, but it is not the vehicle. Put another way, a carpenter is a better carpenter by knowing how to use the best tools available. Or a person who can fly a jet plane might be the best pilot possible, he isn't the jet he is flying.

Have Your Own Website

Not having your own website is tantamount to having a faucet without a sink or a storefront that is always closed. The water will run everywhere, and so will your sales and marketing efforts. Everything we talk about regarding lead generation, social media, marketing, etc., is intended to bring people to specific pages on your website so you can capture data (which you can use in your customer relationship management [CRM] and further lead generation), provide relevant information, and improve your rankings in organic search. There are many companies that offer incredibly inexpensive websites (and hosting). Some are even free. If you are reluctant to have your own website, make sure your LinkedIn or Facebook pages are full of useful information and testimonials about you. People want to, or will want to know who they are buying from and if they can't find information about you then they are suspect.

Have Your Own YouTube Channel

If you have videos, then setting up a channel to host them is simple. If you have videos and don't, you are missing out on free promotion, search engine optimization (SEO) gain, and showing others you are open to change. Sometimes it is about showing yourself to the world, even for validation. The first thing we do when someone sells to us is check if they have a website. The second? See how it looks, see if they have videos, and assess how modern they are. It tells me all I need to know in 60 seconds.

Remember: Technology Is Sexy

Most people are impressed when they see someone using technology effectively, and, depending upon their industry and personality, they are equally impressed with early adopters. When salespeople walked into an office with the first few iPads, prospects were impressed. It was very cool and the early adopters presented an image of people who breathe technology. The Macbook Air, the iPhone, any tablet, and big screen smart phones are all worth the investments. (Plus, they are lightweight and you can watch movies on them!) But don't go overboard—Bluetooth headphones tend to be annoying if you are with someone (not in a sales environment) because the person doesn't know if you are speaking to her or someone else.

Run Contests

You can run contests or use gaming to bring attention to your offers. IPG has run contests to get information or reach out to new customers. Winners are awarded free training time with Jonathan or a donation to a choice of charities.

You can also run contests for your current accounts to learn from them and keep them loyal. Companies like Hotels.com and JetBlue run contests that ask participants to complete customer satisfaction surveys to qualify for a prize.

Everyone wants to win something for free, so contests are great if the prize is something people want and entering is worth giving a few minutes to.

Create Instant Appointments

In setting appointments to investigate some new technologies, we ran into timetrade.com, an automatic calendaring capability that allows you to set up meetings immediately if somebody expresses an interest in your offer. There are many other technologies and services you can use that take care of the mundane or repetitive issues so you can sell more. You may already know of some. .

Use Speech Recognition Software

Speech recognition has become much more ubiquitous, accurate, and usable in many applications. This technology will capture your voice and translate into characters that you can use in different applications such as Microsoft Word. This way you avoid wasting time by retyping everything.

Jonathan uses Dragon Naturally Speaking by Nuance to dictate short and long passages and capture important thoughts or observations. He then uses them in his teaching or in his proposals.

Take Lots of Pictures and Videos

Since you always have a camera with you via your smartphone, you can capture great moments to use in PowerPoints, proposals, blogs, etc. This goes a long way toward personalizing presentations and is much more impressive than using stock images or graphics, as most people do. You can also include video if your camera allows, or if you carry around a video camera. Jonathan uses the Flip Camera that Cisco recently wrote off. He captures conversations that can be repurposed for training, or included in proposals and marketing.

Martin's phone has an HD camera. He also uses a studio, a videocamera, a tablet, screen capture, and webconferencing. You never know what footage is useful. Start by profiling yourself and team, and do mini interviews. Let people see beyond the product.

Search "Best . . ."

Type in Best [whatever] into your favorite search engine to get the best blogs or websites for a subject. You will get a lot of ads but you will also a lot of information. For example, Jonathan wanted to find the sales blogs that my customers and prospects follow, so he typed in "best sales blogs" and found the top 40 blogs that people use. Many were competitors so now he can follow them, learn from them, and keep my eye on them.

Turn Off Your Technology

Experiment with turning technology off for a while so you can focus on what you need to get done. For example, I (Jonathan) will turn off my e-mail and phone when I am doing one of my S.M.A.R.T. (specific – measurable – aligned/agreed upon – realistic – timed) priorities. I also turn it off just to give my whole system a rest. This gives me a perspective and appreciation of what technology can and cannot do for me and makes me a better salesperson.

Know How to Use Social Media

If you don't you will become a dinosaur and your business will become extinct. Here are some examples among many of how to use social media properly:

- 13 Brands Using LinkedIn Company Page Features the Right Way – Hubspot.com

- How to Build a Facebook Timeline for Brands — It's All About Revenue: The Revenue Marketing Blog – Eloqua.com

- Lead Nurturing for After the Sales Cycle — It's All About Revenue: The Revenue Marketing Blog – Eloqua.com

- You need to limit social media to specific times in a day and to specific subjects that are most relevant to your business objectives. Otherwise, *you will get nothing done.*

Employ Location-Based Routing

Location-based routing gives you the ability to adjust who calls you and can get to you based on what you are doing. This is a very productive tool because you can screen callers. For example, if you are going to a meeting you can take in texts but not calls. If you are running a promo, you can take calls only from interested prospects. If you are playing or watching basketball, you can take calls only from your friends.

Survey Your Customers

Surveys are a great tool to get input from your customers, prospects, and social networks on things you are doing or want to do. You can use them to see how satisfied people are with your services. When I (Jonathan) first heard about NetPromoter Score I was curious what my clients would say about me so I sent a survey to my LinkedIn users. Figure A-1 shows what they said (which made us very happy).

	Response Percent
1. Would you recommend Jon London and IPG to your friends or business partners for sales training? 🍥 Create Chart	
Definitely	87.5%
Very likely	12.5%
Likely	0.0%
Not Sure	0.0%
No	0.0%
Not Applicable	0.0%

Figure A-1. A sample testimonial.

You can also use surveys to see which programs or services people like best, get ideas on which services to create, use as a post-sale survey to see how they feel about your offer, and get in touch with old customers or customers who have gone with another vendor.

Register Many Domain Names

Domain names are very affordable and can be bought and sold easily. The domain sex.com just sold for $14 million. We have several domain names that reflect and capture ideas we have or business we are considering. For example, IPG owns jonlondon.com, davidvsgoliathselling.com, sales-advisor.com, and many others. These names are all ideas of services and products we will be selling so we want to "own" the domain name. We suggest you lock up any names relevant to yourself and your business.

Get Anywhere Anytime Connectivity

Salespeople need mobility to connect to any person, service, software or data you need, regardless of where you are. One of Jonathan's favorite memories was watching the New York Yankees play in the World Series from a hotel lobby in Copenhagen at 3:00 a.m. while he was also listening to a webconference that he had recorded. Get your own mobile hotspot or use your smartphone to do the same. You never want to be disconnected unless you decide you want to be.

Getting to People with Technology

How else can you reach people with nontraditional technology? Here's what we use in prospecting: e-vites, birthday cards, VYou.com, invites to webinars, and video e-mails. Adobe Photoshop or similar products allow you to create unique marketing materials, brochures, fliers, cards, among other things, that can help you stand out in a good way. We also use Camtasia.com to record myself doing a demo or overlaying my image into a PowerPoint. They work well if you are saying something relevant and intelligent.

Use Outlook Fully

Most businesspeople have Microsoft Outlook on one of their computers. It's a great tool for salespeople. You can:

- Send a calendar invitation to people who sometimes will accept even when you haven't had much, if any, contact with them. There is a high risk of the appointment being canceled, of course, but it's worth the effort.

- Schedule follow-up e-mails so they go out on a specific day and time.

- Automate the sending of e-mails at night or on the weekend as long as the computer is turned on and online.

- Please use your out of office message! It's frustrating if people do not know where they stand.

Virtual Assistants

Because technology allows information to be shared and makes communication much easier, an entire industry of virtual assistants—people who work for you in other countries—can do most if not all of your administrative work at a significantly reduced cost. The book *The 4-Hour Work Week* by Timothy Ferriss does an excellent job explaining how to take advantage of these services

Appoint a Technology Maven

Create a position in your company responsible for staying on top of all existing and emerging technologies that can help you sell. Jonathan sets alerts to send him technology updates automatically. He also has an informal group of people he collaborates with to share their best ideas and uses of technology. He has joined different groups on LinkedIn to keep him up to date with the technologies that matter most to him. These include Technology-Enabled Sales and Marketing (TeSM); Cloud Computing, SaaS, and Virtualization; and WHU Web-Hosting Experts Group.

Send Visual Literature or Information about Your Company

Create your own videos and URLs instead of, or in addition to, traditional literature. I (Jonathan) have created videos of subjects that people can review or I can use to prospect with. If you have a Macbook Pro, you can use Photo Booth or iMovie to create videos or images.

Another amazing technology is Brainshark.com. It is free for certain services and lets you create interesting audio/video slides using PowerPoint and your phone. It has been around quite a while and has evolved from an expensive service to an SaaS cloud service.

Use SaaS

The beautiful thing about much of this technology is its availability as SaaS (software as a service) so you can use it with an individual license.

In addition, many providers offer their services for free in order to create a base of users and attract advertisers. Table A-1 provides some examples of items available at no charge.

Table A-1. Software Services Available Free of Charge

Item	Service
CRM	Freecrm, Zohocrm, Civicrm, Salesforce.com Free, With social CRM solutions such as Nimble or Reachable, assigned territories will be giving way to social proximity, in which leads are assigned to salespeople who have the best social connection with the prospect.
Lists/Database	Jigsaw, sohoost.com, LinkedIn, Facebook
Lead management software	www.capterra.com/lead-management-software (too many to mention)
Collaboration tools	15 Free from PC World www.pcworld.com/businesscenter/article/200835/15_free_online_collaboration_tools_for_business.html
Audio conferencing	Freecaudioonferencing.com, freeconference.com, freeconferenceusa.com
Videoconferencing	Skype, Google, others
Word processing, spreadsheets	Google Docs, Openoffice
Screen capture	Camstudio.com, camtasia.com
Animation (from http://download.cnet.com/mac/animation-software)	Stykz, Poser/DAZ Studio 3D, Singleframer, Lego Digital Designer, Barcode, Animoto
Radio	Internet-radio.com, blogtalkradio.com
Apps	Thousands from iTunes or Android
Presentation (Google search of free slide software presentation)	31,700,000 including iMeet, slideshare.com (trial), smilebox.com, openoffice.org's Impress, brainshark.com
Cloud services	Free (type the term into any search engine)
Photo or image editing	Free (type these words into your search engine to see what comes up)

Some technology does cost, but it is affordable (Table A-2).

Table A-2. Technology Available for Purchase

Other Technology	Current Price
Smart Phone	$99 or less
iPad	$399 (less if buy an older version or a non-Apple device)
Bluetooth Headset for Driving	$29
4G Mobile Hot Spot	$29–$59/month
Any technology	Type in whatever technology you want to use into a search engine to see if it is available in a free version.

Be a Virtual Warrior

Truth is, many people don't need an office. There are so many places that you can work from because they give you access to the Internet, including Starbuck's, Panera, a customer's office, hotels, and even public spaces in cities that provide free wi-fi. Martin and Jonathan have pulled off the side of a road to find a nice hotel lobby to do their work with great success. If you are an owner, manager or boss and you insist on having your people in the office, you should reconsider.

Because some of these places are noisy, you should invest in a noise reduction headset (Bose or others) so that when you talk on the phone, the sound is good. Jonathan joined the Terrace Club (www.terraceclub.com), which is an organization that provides excellent meeting facilities for virtual warriors. The accommodations are very nice and the service and food are excellent so you can also meet customers and prospects there and make a good impression.

Use the Phone

Too many people use e-mail in situations in which they should be speaking directly to people. Two vivid examples are negotiating and dealing with money. Jonathan received an e-mail from the assistant of a vendor/owner he does business with. The vendor believed he was owed money. After asking for an invoice supporting the request, he received another e-mail stating it was verbal agreement. Jonathan wanted to maintain a good relationship so he called his direct contact to discuss, and they resolved it quickly.

Negotiation is too emotional a subject to deal with via e-mail. Not only should you pick up the phone, but you should actually meet in person or have some video presence if that's not possible.

Create Your Own Sales Process

Use Table A-3 to align the measurements, skills, knowledge, resources, technology, and tools you need for your own success. You can also go to www.ipgtraining.com/forms to download the actual form.

Table A-3. Sample sales process aligning skills, resources, and technology

Sample Sales Process								
	1- Territory Identification	2- Gain Access to Power/ Prospecting	3- Discover, Qualify and Influence	4- Confirm Fit and Decide to Engage	5- Propose, Present and/or Demonstrate	6- Work	7- Negotiate	8- Close
Objective of Sales Step								
Metrics								
Skills								
Probability to Close								
Sales Tools								
Generic & industry								
Technology								

Create Playbooks

You can do this for yourself or there are companies that can capture the best practices for you throughout all stages of the sales process and help you create sales playbooks. Figure A-2 shows just some of what Qvidian playbooks have to offer. Other companies, such as iDashboards and XSalerator can help you analyze the effectiveness of your sales approach.

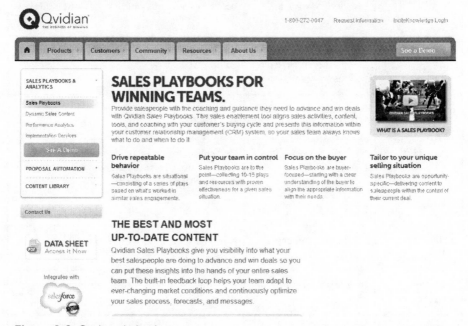

Figure A-2. Qvidian playbooks.

A Sample 12-Hour Sales Day

Table A-4 shows how one of our days recently went. Use the structure of the table to track your own time—you'll be amazed at how easy it is to waste time. (Note: the amount for each item will vary based on your reality.) If you can do all of this less time, fantastic!

Table A-4. Sample 1-Day Schedule

Time	Item	Notes
7:00–8:00 a.m.	Take client or prospect out to breakfast. Work business in Europe or Asia if appropriate via video.	Best time to entertain since people aren't busy and it is less expensive. If no breakfast or international responsibilities, check e-mails and take care of administrative details. Work with your virtual assistant if you have one.
8:00–8:45	Review social media, Google alerts, LinkedIn, RSS feeds; check e-mail.	You can do this daily or weekly depending on volume of activity.
8:45– 9:30	Prospect.	Use social media, phone, lead generation software or e-mail.
9:30–12:00 p.m.	Meet with prospects or clients.	Use collaboration technology when appropriate. Use smartphone while on road to make calls or check e-mail.
12:00–1:00	Have lunch and check e-mail.	If you have to; otherwise take client or prospects out.
1:00–4:45	Meet with prospects or clients.	If no meetings, prospect or work on strategic deals. Check e-mail at some point.
4:45–6:00	Prospect.	If you have done your prospecting and have enough meetings, work, on other priorities, generate proposals, work on presentations, etc. Attend internal meetings.
6:00–7:00	Finish to-dos	Use technology as much as you can to eliminate unnecessary busy-work and to complete mundane tasks. Enter info into CRM.

Use E-mail Productively

E-mail is undoubtedly one of the best tools for today's salesperson. The problem is that it has become so important and predominant that it becomes disruptive, controls people's lives (work and personal) and attention, and quite often prevents them from being more productive than they are.

According to an *Inc.* news article from March 2, 2011:[1]

> *Workers in small and medium-sized businesses spend half the work day on "necessary, yet unproductive tasks, including routine communications and filtering incoming information and correspondence," says a report from telephony company Fonality and research firm Webtorials. (No word, though, on how much of that e-mail is personal.)*

A report by the Radicati Group projects a steady growth rate in the number of business e-mails being sent and received per day (Table A-5). This does not include personal e-mails:

Table A-5. Business e-mails sent/received per user/day[2]

Average number of emails	2011	2012	2013	2014	2015
Sent	33	35	37	39	41
Received	72	75	78	81	84
Average emails per user/day	105	110	115	120	125

Depending on your industry and position, this could be more or less. E-mail is used as the primary way for people to communicate with each other to

---

[1] Courtney Rubin, "Study: Employees Are Unproductive Half the Day," Inc., March 2, 2011, www.inc.com/news/articles/201103/workers-spend-half-day-being-unproductive.html.

[2] Sara Radicati, "Email Statistics Report, 2011-2015," The Radicati Group, Inc., May 2011, www.radicati.com/wp/wp-content/uploads/2011/05/Email-Statistics-Report-2011-2015-Executive-Summary.pdf.

request information, get updates, and keep people aware of things they are doing (either directly or with a cc to others). Much e-mail is really a CYA (cover your ass) action. You send a message to more people than necessary so you feel you are protected politically. It is also a big time waster because the people receiving these also feel they need to read them and often respond for the same political reasons.

Organizations have become habituated to expecting immediate responses to e-mails, especially from a boss to a subordinate. In turn, there is pressure to respond to these e-mails ASAP or the boss could get angry. This type of environment is incredibly disruptive and makes it difficult to be proactive and strategic—the workplace becomes an "interrupt driven" environment. Salespeople are always on their computers or smartphones reacting to e-mails and don't feel comfortable being away from e-mail for any length of time. Please note that people are also spending time with instant messages and personal e-mail.

A Google search for "manage e-mail more effectively" showed 29,500 hits. Here are some ideas on how to better handle your e-mail:

- Create some internal rules in your company regarding what needs to be responded to immediately and what does not.

- Define when a "cc" is necessary or not so people don't waste time reading or responding to these e-mails.

- Turn your e-mail off when you are working on your priorities.

- Instead of checking e-mail all the time, create specific times in your calendar when you will (every hour for 10 minutes or beginning of day, lunchtime, and end of day).

- Delegate and assign accountability to others for certain tasks so you don't have to everything.

- Have your e-mail signature tell customers whom to call for different services.

- Use the filters on your e-mail system to highlight the most critical messages.

- Handle e-mail like people used to handle paper. Have a folder to read/do later/delegate.

- Stop cc'ing everybody yourself so you don't have to respond to their cc's.

- Be diligent and disciplined about whatever system you use so you are controlling it.

- If you are a manager, stop sending panic emergency e-mails for account or forecast updates. Have a regularly scheduled time to do so with your team.

- Ignore your e-mail when you are executing your priorities.

My (Jonathan's) last year at PictureTel was very strenuous because of the numbers we were expected to generate in a very competitive environment. I took a 10-day vacation before the fourth quarter to make sure I was at my best. I left voicemail and e-mail notifications that I was not going to answer or respond to any message and whom to reach out to otherwise. When I got back from my vacation my voicemail box was full (100 voicemails) and I think I had more than 500 e-mails (that would be 1,500 today). I didn't want to deal with this so I erased everything, and, to this day, I don't know of one negative repercussion of doing so. I realized I was creating my own "e-mail jail" and stopped cc'ing everyone and checking e-mail all the time. It was the best and biggest productivity boost and has served me well throughout my career.

What about Facebook, LinkedIn, Twitter, and other social media? You should spend no time on these during work if they have nothing to do with your job. Otherwise, use them as part of your prospecting and business branding efforts. Activate these as priorities so you use them at specific times with a specific purpose.

Employ Electronic Signatures

We use this capability for many of the documents we send for our business. The most common uses include sales contracts, vendor agreements, non-disclosure agreements, legal documents, and more. Life is now too short to wait around for the postal service to deliver important legal documents to your door.

Sell in Your Signature

Use call-to-action URLs and links in your signature. If you have video testimonials, write a short narrative and put in the link. These work better than anything. If you don't have any, then record some!

A Great Quote to Improve Your Use of Technology

> *"Technology is only as good as what you use it for, think about the customer first, then what is best to sell with or for them to use."*

—Jonathan London, Author, Lover of sales and technology

Index

A

Anywhere anytime connectivity, 310

B

Banner advertising, 210

B2B sales process, 36–37

Bing, 210

Blinkx, 210

Blogs, 308

Bluetooth headphones, 306

Brand confusion
 combined sales and marketing,
  266
 FTSE 50 organization sales
  training
  customer messaging, 265
  e-mail communication, 264
  marketing brand guidelines,
   266
  objectives, 264

Broadband networks, 186

Business Friend Forever (BFF), 174

C

Call-to-action URLs, 322

Cisco's TelePresence video
 conferencing, 108

Cloud computing, 186, 312

Constant Contact, 146

Consultative selling
 consultative method, 22
 definition, 22
 non-consultative method, 22
 professional goals and
  concomitant personal
  satisfaction, 26–27
 questionnaire, 23–25
 you and your offering, 27–28

Cost per thousand (CPM), 210

CRM. See Customer relationship
 management (CRM)

Customer lifecycle auto-emails, 285–
 286

Customer relationship management
 (CRM), 118, 191–192, 306
 database (see Salesforce.com)
 publishing software, 120–122

Customer service department
 communication controls and
  outcomes, 274
 conferencing solution
  implementation, 278
 commoditized view, 280

Customerservice depart, conferencing solution implementation (*cont.*)
    direct phone numbers and job roles, 281
    people and user difference, 281
    phoning time, end-users, 281
    price, 279
    provider changing risk, 279
    purchase decision, 279, 280
  customer experience, 277
  follow-up-calls
    conferencing, 274–275
    Customer Service call stats, 275–276
    sports analogy, 276
    web-hosting solution, 276
  issues drop-box, 273

Customer survey, 309–310

D

Data mining, 197–199
DiSC style, 97–98
  characteristics, 31
  example, 34–35
  matching prospect's style, 32
  pace, tone, and focus, 32–33
  risk and decisiveness, 33–34
  tailoring, 36
Domain names, 310

E

Electronic signatures, 321
E-mail, 207, 211, 314, 319–321
Essential skills
  competition, 44–45
  goal setting, 41–43
  master the sales process, 36–38
  network expansion, 43–44
  time management for salespeople, 39–41
  training, 38–39

F

Facebook, 195, 210, 309
  active users, 165–166
  business
    building audience, 170
    fans and newsfeeds, 170
    page setup, 168
    photography, 171
    shop window, 169
    Twitter account, 169
    Wildfire applications, 170
  business-to-business sales, 166–167
  design and organization, 168–169
  work ID and personal profiles, 168
Failsafe selling, 254

G

Google, 195–197, 210
  Alerts, 204, 217, 233, 235
  PPC, 210
  search, 188–190, 236
Government Securities Act (GSA), 201

H

Hubspot, 146, 207

I, J

Instant appointments, 307
Instant messaging (IM), 223
Interactive Advertising Bureau (IAB), 9
iPads, 306
IPG, 307
IPG's gaining access, power system, 57
  cold calling, 60–61
  follow up guidelines, 68–70

meeting contact prospects, 59
multipronged attack initiation, 59
objections handling and
    anticipation, 67–68
past gatekeepers, 63
phone call and e-mail access, 67–
    68
strategic territory plan, 58
voice mail messages, 62–63
iPhone, 306

K

Knowledge-management system, 252

L

LinkedIn, 210, 217, 309, *See also* Social
    media
    geographic criteria, 195
    group, 195
    online media, 197
    secondary connection, 197
    VPs, 195, 196, 197
Location-based routing, 309

M

Macbook Air, 306
Macbook Pro, 312
Marketo and MailChimp, 146
Memex, 175–176
Microsoft Outlook, 311
Microsoft PowerPoint
    cut words, 229–230
    four bullets usage, 230
    pictures and images usage, 229
    pictures instead of words, 230–
        231
    proposal writing software, 231–
        232

N

NetPromoter Score, 309
Non-conferencing video
    communications
    Freemium
        Skype, 128
        Ten Hands, 128
    Paid Options
        iMeet, 129
        Vidyo, 129

O

Old selling
    aphorisms, 28–30
    DiSC model (*see* DiSC style)
    pacing, 30–31
Own Website, 306
Own YouTube channel, 306

P

Pay per click (PPC), 210
PEER1 Hosting
    blogs, 218
    Google Alerts, 217
    news releases, 217, 218
Phinkit, 174
    Business Friend Forever, 174
    Memex, 175–176
Pictures and videos, 308
Pipeline management, 213
Private networks, 186
Prospect and gain access
    automation, 213–214
    awareness events, 203
    branding, 199
    cold call, 205
    contacting people
        blogs, 207–210
        e-mail, 207
        Hubspot, 207

Prospect and gain access, contacting people (*cont.*)
    Internet radio, 206
    online advertising, 210–211
    SEO, 206
  craft effective messages, 211
  Google Alerts, 204
  iLantern.com, 205
  LinkedIn group, 204
  moment of truth, 212
  multipronged attack, 201–202
  objections anticipation and
    handling, 212–213
  OneSource, 205
  overview, 200
  past gatekeepers, 212
  strategic territory plan, 200–201
  targeted marketing, 200

Q

Quicktime, 211
Qvidian playbooks, 317

R

Request for Proposal (RFP) response,
  284
Run contests, 307

S

Sales and marketing
  differences, 268, 272–273
  high and low-value approach, 267
  standard marketing collateral, 267
  strength recognization, 268–272
Sales-assisting technology, 106
  cloud, 146–147
  collaboration
    Adobe Connect, 126
    Cisco WebEx, 126
    features, 125
    Go To Meeting, 126
    pros and cons, 127

  conferencing, 122, 123
    benefits, 122
    failsafe selling, 124
  database and CRM (see
    Salesforce.com)
  e-mail
    benefits, 115
    establish creadibility, 115
    IPG training, 116
    and marketing campaigns,
      145–146
    No Scroll rule, 115
    out-of-office message, 114
    risks, 114
    speed/quality of response, 113
    TSI squared, 117
  internet, 109
    competitors, 110
    Google Alerts, 109
    LinkedIn, 111
    reasons to call, 112
    target market, 111
  multimedia content, 133
    HD video phones, 134
    Kwiksta, 133
    Microsoft Live Meeting, 133
  networking groups, 139–141
  non-conferencing video
    communications
    Freemium, 128
    Paid Options, 128
  presentation, 141
    Dos and Don'ts, 145
    PowerPoint, 142
    rules, 143–144
    Slide Rocket, 142
    SlideShare, 143
  Screencasting, 134
    Camtasia, 134
    Screencast.com, 135
    ScreenFlow, 134
  SEO, 137
    landscape, 138
    white hat vs. black hat, 137
  social media, 136–137

tablets and smartphones, 138–139
unified communications, 129–130
video conference, 127
video streaming, 130–132
visual media, 132–133
Sales day, 317–318
Sales Force Automation (SFA), 191–192
Salesforce.com, 119
   Hoover's business database, 119
   LexisNexis, 120
   OneSource, 120
Sales fundamentals, 282
   customer touch points, 285
      access to higher authority, 286
      customer lifecycle auto-emails, 285–286
      DiSC style, 287
      high D (Dominance) score, 287
   sales content, 283–284
   sales tools, 282–283
Sales management
   challenges, 261
   collaboration and best practice sharing, 249
   call and video recording, 251
   knowledge-management system, 252
   monthly team meeting, 250
   once-a-year event, 251
   own decision making, 250
   Polycom, 250
   themes, 249
   creativity
      flawed ideas, 260
      positive and flexible attitude, 260
      reward creative effort, 260
      top-down and bottom-up process, 260
   failsafe selling, 254
   inspirational approaches, 243–244

leadership, 242
meeting room preparation, 259
passing the buck management, 243
small-to medium-enterprises, 256–258
speed of response, 258
technology
   face-to-face meetings, 246
   management and sales benefits, 245
   videoconferencing, 247
   virtual meeting technology, 248, 249
   Web conferencing, 246–247
time-consuming recruitment process, 252–253
virtual team
   all hands and feet calls, 256
   recorded content, 254–255
   regular one-on-one meetings, 254
   share best practice, 255
   weekly team meeting, 254
   working from home, 254
Sales process, 289
   aligning skills, resources, and technology, 316
   baseline capabilities
      CRM, 191–192
      data, search engine, 188–191
      mobility, 186–187
   commitment, 300–301
   contact prospect and gain access, 57
      disadvantages, 56
      importance of, 56
      offering value, 56
      power system (see IPG's gaining access, power system)
      receptivity stages, 55
      sales cycle, 55
   decide to engage, confirm fit
      closing deal, 224

Sales process, decide to engage, confirm fit (*cont.*)
  CRM, 224
  decision-making criteria, 221
  Excel spreadsheet, 222
  ideal opportunity, 219
  overview, 220
  sales cycle, 224
  sales opportunity, 223
  S.C.O.O.P., 220
  team building, 222
decision-making process, 298–299
demo stage, 82, 87–89
interaction, 300
just enough technology, 292
match technology, 293–295
meeting with prospect, 71
  blogs, 218
  chatting, 214
  desktop video capabilities, 214
  follow-up steps and actions, 77
  Google Alerts, 217
  importance, 70–72
  LinkedIn, 217
  LivePerson, 214
  news releases, 217, 218
  overview, 215
  salespersons quality, 72
  S.PRI.N.G. dialogue, 72–76, 214
  Web/video conferencing, 215–216
negotiation and close, 235–237
negotiation strategies, 92–93
  DiSC analysis, 97–98
  Give/Get tactics, 97
  IPG's negotiation planner, 102–103
  resistance in, 99–101
  types, 95
  variables, 93–94
Phinkit Alpha team, 302–303
planning, 290, 291
playbooks creation, 317

presentation, 82
  good presentation skills, 83–84
  logistics planner, 84–85
  organizer, 85–86
  stage, 82
  technology, 83
profile territory and assignment, 50
  analysis and partner recruitment, 50–52
  BT conferencing, 53
  business opportunities, 192
  channel management, 53
  csv file, 194
  data mining and analytics, 197–199
  football analogy, 52
  Google and LinkedIn, 195–197
  OneSource's iSell portal, 194
  open territory, 51
  overview, 193
  remote surveillance, 53
proposal stage, 82
prospect and gain access (see Prospect and gain access)
social media sales worksheet, 294
solution presentation, proposal, and demonstration
  HDTV/projector, 226
  Microsoft PowerPoint (see Microsoft PowerPoint)
  overview, 225
  video conferencing (see Video conferencing)
  vivid screen, 226
  Web conferencing, 226–227
speed and control, sales cycle, 295–297
speed and quality, 291
team and sales development, 78
  criteria for, 79
  IPG's S.C.O.O.P., 80–81
  prospecting strategies, 80
  subject matter expert, 80

teams and partners, 79
technology, definition, 304
treat as unique, 304
user base, 302
virtual meeting technologies, 298
vs. business to consumer, 48
work strategy, 233–235
S.C.O.O.P.. See Strategic–
comprehensive–online–
optimized–process (S.C.O.O.P.)
Search engine optimization (SEO),
137, 206, 210, 306
landscape, 138
white hat vs. black hat, 137
Skiing, 28
Small- to medium-enterprises (SMEs),
256–258
Smartphone, 308
Social media, 309
blogs, 178–179
broadcasting, 181–182
corporate strategies, 179–181
Facebook (see Facebook)
goals, 154
LinkedIn
contact's connections, 159–
160
credibility, 160–161
definition, 159
groups and webinars, 162
sales approaches, 161
sales fundamentals, 160
niche- and target-specific groups,
177–178
objectives, 155
personal issues, 152–153
Phinkit, 174
Business Friend Forever, 174
Memex, 175–176
Pinterest, 173
pros and cons, 152
Twitter, 172–173
vs. brand
brand characteristics, 157

e-mail, 156–157
Phinkit, 157
YouTube, 163–165
Software as a service (SaaS), 312–314
Solution selling. See Consultative
selling
Speech recognition software, 307
Strategic–comprehensive–online–
optimized–process (S.C.O.O.P.),
80–81, 223

T

Technology, definition, 304
Technology-Enabled Sales and
Marketing (TeSM), 312
Technology Maven, 312
Technology, sales process, 1
B2B environment, 17
benefits, 13
buyers, 2
Facebook, thumbs up, 3
information and analytical
tools, 3
movie reviews, 3
unbiased information, 3
competition and constant change,
7
conferencing services, 12–13
defects, 1
Google Alerts, 16
human behavior, 18
initial prospecting step, 14
internet, 11
marketing, 9–10
negatives, 14
Polycom.com, 12
sales person, 4, 8
company's blogs creation, 15
information sharing, 16
products and services
knowledge, 16
skills, 11
subject matter expert, 15

Technology, sales process (*cont.*)
    sales structure, 6
    subject matter expert, 4
    time frame, 10
    trusted advisor, 4
    Vidyo.com, 11
    and web
        managed hosting, 5
        offshore services, 6
    wheel, 2
Telemarketing, 60–61
Time–Energy–Emotion–Ego–Money
    (TE^{3}M), 91
Twitter, 172–173

U
Ustream, 210

V
Video conferencing
    Skype, 228
    Vidyo, 228

vs. Web conferencing, 227
Vidyo, 228, 232
Vimeo, 210
Virtual assistants, 311
Virtualization, 312
Virtual warrior, 314
Visual Literature, 312
Voicemail, 211
VYou, 211

W, X
Webinars, 162, 216
WHU Web-Hosting Experts Group,
    312

Y, Z
Yahoo, 210
YouTube, 210, *See also* Social media

CPSIA information can be obtained at www.ICGtesting.com
Printed in the USA
LVOW121544160812

294644LV00001B/1/P

9 781430 239338